Combatting Unemployment

IZA Prize in Labor Economics Series

Since 2002, the Institute for the Study of Labor (IZA) has awarded the annual IZA Prize in Labor Economics for outstanding contributions to policy-relevant labor market research and methodological progress in this sub-discipline of economic science. The IZA Prize is the only international science prize awarded exclusively to labor economists. This special focus acknowledges the global significance of high-quality basic research in labor economics and sound policy advice based on these research findings. As issues of employment and unemployment are among the most urgent challenges of our time, labor economists have an important task and responsibility. The IZA Prize in Labor Economics is today considered one of the most prestigious international awards in the field. It aims to stimulate further research on topics that have enormous implications for our future. All prize-winners contribute a volume to the IZA Prize in Labor Economics Series published by Oxford University Press, which has been established to provide an overview of the laureates' most significant findings.

The IZA Prize in Labor Economics has become an integral part of the institute's manifold activities to promote progress in labor market research. Based on nominations submitted by the IZA Research Fellows, a high-ranking IZA Prize Committee selects the prize-winner. In conjunction with the Award Ceremony the IZA Prize Conference brings together a number of renowned experts to discuss topical labor market issues.

It is not by coincidence that the IZA Prize in Labor Economics Series is published by Oxford University Press. This well-reputed publishing house has shown a great interest in the project from the very beginning as this exclusive series perfectly complements their range of publications. We gratefully acknowledge their excellent cooperation.

K. F. Zimmermann (signature)

Klaus F. Zimmermann, IZA Director

Winners of the IZA Prize in Labor Economics

2010	Francine D. Blau (Cornell University)
2009	Richard A. Easterlin (University of Southern California)
2008	Richard Layard (London School of Economics)
	Stephen J. Nickell (Nuffield College)
2007	Richard B. Freeman (Harvard University)
2006	David Card (University of California, Berkeley)
	Alan B. Krueger (Princeton University)
2005	Dale T. Mortensen (Northwestern University)
	Christopher A. Pissarides (London School of Economics)
2004	Edward P. Lazear (Stanford University)
2003	Orley C. Ashenfelter (Princeton University)
2002	Jacob Mincer (Columbia University)

Richard Layard-Stephen J. Nickell
2008 IZA Prize Laureates

Combatting Unemployment

Richard Layard and Stephen J. Nickell

Edited by
Werner Eichhorst
Klaus F. Zimmermann

OXFORD
UNIVERSITY PRESS

OXFORD

UNIVERSITY PRESS

Great Clarendon Street, Oxford OX2 6DP

Oxford University Press is a department of the University of Oxford.
It furthers the University's objective of excellence in research, scholarship,
and education by publishing worldwide in

Oxford New York

Auckland Cape Town Dar es Salaam Hong Kong Karachi
Kuala Lumpur Madrid Melbourne Mexico City Nairobi
New Delhi Shanghai Taipei Toronto

With offices in

Argentina Austria Brazil Chile Czech Republic France Greece
Guatemala Hungary Italy Japan Poland Portugal Singapore
South Korea Switzerland Thailand Turkey Ukraine Vietnam
Oxford is a registered trade mark of Oxford University Press
in the UK and in certain other countries

Published in the United States
by Oxford University Press Inc., New York

British Library Cataloguing in Publication Data

Data available

Library of Congress Cataloging in Publication Data

Data available

Typeset by the IZA
Printed in Great Britain
on acid-free paper by
MPG Books Group, Bodmin and King's Lynn

ISBN 978–0–19–960978–9

1 3 5 7 9 10 8 6 4 2

Award Statement
of the IZA Prize Committee

The IZA Prize in Labor Economics 2008 goes to the outstanding European labor economists Richard Layard and Stephen Nickell for their path-breaking work on the relationship between labor market institutions and unemployment. Their research provided a theoretical and empirical framework for the analysis of equilibrium unemployment and the impact of labor market institutions on economic performance. Shaping the views of scholars and policymakers on how to address unemployment, the contributions of Layard and Nickell have served to illuminate the policy discourse in Europe and increased academics' understanding of the nature and causes of involuntary joblessness.

Their 1991 book "Unemployment: Macroeconomic Performance and the Labour Market" (co-authored with Richard Jackman) and their 1999 chapter "Labor Market Institutions and Economic Performance" in the Handbook of Labor Economics have become modern classics in labor economics. Layard and Nickell's approach incorporates stocks as well as flows into and out of unemployment in a way that previous models had neglected. Their work thus provides a unified framework for studying the sources of unemployment and the determinants of unemployment dynamics. In particular, it highlights the importance of understanding the impact of labor market institutions on labor market performance. For instance, Layard and Nickell have shown that stricter employment protection regulations do not generally increase the level of unemployment, but increase the persistence of unemployment by reducing short-term unemployment at the cost of raising long-term unemployment. The prizewinners have also pointed out that generous unemployment benefits need not be detrimental if they are granted only for a limited time and are accompanied by adequate instruments that require (and assist) unemployed individuals who are able to work to actively search for a new job. Moreover, Layard and Nickell have shed light on the interaction between wage setting institutions and unemployment. For example, they showed that higher union coverage tends to increase unemployment, but these negative effects of collective wage bargaining can be offset if unions and employers coordinate their wage bargaining activities effectively.

A recurrent theme in Nickell's research is the role of labor market institutions and the interplay between unemployment, wages, and investment, the latter being the focus of his early work. In each area he has developed the relevant theory and demonstrated its empirical relevance by using the theory to inform structural econometric models. Nickell pioneered the microeconometric analysis of unemployment duration and the way in which the behavior of the unemployed affects wage formation. His 1979 Econometrica article, "Estimating the Probability of Leaving Unemployment," broke new ground for the microeconometric analysis of unemployment duration and unemployment benefits. His seminal 1981 Econometrica paper, "Biases in Dynamic Models with Fixed Effects," inspired a whole new econometric and labor economics literature on the estimation of panel data models. In his 1990 Economic Journal article on "Insider Forces and Wage Determination" (with Sushil Wadhwani) he showed that the actions of those who already have secure employment have significant impact on the determination of wages, but that persistent long-term unemployment cannot be solely attributed to such insiders.

Nickell has also made formidable contributions to the literatures on labor supply, firms' investment decisions, and productivity. All his work uses first-class technique and painstaking data collection. His 1996 Journal of Political Economy article entitled "Competition and Corporate Performance" was one of the first articles that provided systematic evidence on the impact of competition on productivity. Nickell has shown that market power tends to reduce productivity, whereas competition has a positive influence on firms' productivity by increasing total factor productivity growth.

Apart from his fundamental work on the determinants of unemployment, Richard Layard has also studied such diverse topics as education, happiness, and income inequality. For instance, in his 1974 Journal of Political Economy article on "The Screening Hypothesis and the Returns to Education" (with George Psacharopoulos), he challenged the view that education primarily serves as a signaling device for pre-existing ability differentials by supporting the human capital interpretation of educational investments having direct productivity-enhancing effects. In addition to his academic contributions, Layard has always set a high value on translating scientific results into political practice. In his early career he was Senior Research Officer for the Robbins Committee on Higher Education. He was founder-director of the Centre for Economic Performance (CEP) at the London School of Economics, one of Europe's leading research groups covering all areas of economic policy. Lord Layard actively participated in the policy debate and worked as an economic advisor for several government institutions, such as the British Department for Education and Skills, HM Treasury, and the Russian Government.

Layard is an early advocate of a welfare system based on the philosophy of welfare-to-work. In this respect, he advised the British Labour government from 1997 to 2001 on policies to fight youth and long-term unemployment. He pursued a welfare reform based on a system of conditionality: benefit payments to the unemployed are provided in return for their active participation, e.g. in training activities or voluntary sector work. This idea has heavily influenced the "New Deal" programs implemented by the Labour government since the late 1990s.

Layard's recent research focus is on the economics of subjective well-being. He aims to achieve a unified understanding of the insights of economics, psychology, neuroscience, and philosophy. Specifically, Layard has analyzed the influence of social comparison as well as income aspiration processes. He pointed out that both have profound implications for optimal taxation of labor income and consumption. Layard has argued that – since individuals' well-being strongly depends on their relative income compared to peers like neighbors or colleagues – people could be stuck in a "hedonic treadmill:" in order to increase their relative income and status, many people tend to work "too much" and ultimately impair their life satisfaction.

Lord Richard Layard is currently Emeritus Professor of Economics at the London School of Economics and Director of the "Wellbeing Research Programme" at the CEP. He is a Fellow of the Econometric Society. Since 2000, he has been a Labour life peer in the House of Lords. Stephen Nickell is currently the Warden of Nuffield College, University of Oxford. He has served as Editor of the Review of Economic Studies and the Oxford Bulletin of Economics and Statistics. Nickell is a Past President of the Royal Economic Society and a Fellow of the Econometric Society. In 2007 he was appointed Commander of the Most Excellent Order of the British Empire.

The IZA Prize in Labor Economics 2008 honors the work of two scholars whose contributions have impressively demonstrated the practical relevance of labor market research for today's policymakers.

George A. Akerlof	University of California, Berkeley
Richard Portes	Centre for Economic Policy Research (CEPR)
Dennis J. Snower	Kiel Institute for the World Economy
Jan Svejnar	University of Michigan
Klaus F. Zimmermann	IZA; University of Bonn

Contents

Contents

Contents

A New Understanding of Labor Market Institutions – Layard and Nickell on Labor Economics and Policy Making

Werner Eichhorst and Klaus F. Zimmermann

Richard Layard and Stephen Nickell, the 2008 laureates of the IZA Prize in Labor Economics, have re-shaped the way we analyze and understand the role of labor market institutions and their impact on labor market outcomes – employment and unemployment structures and dynamics – fundamentally over the last 20 to 25 years. This volume brings together their major contributions on the functioning of labor market institutions and their effects in terms of employment performance. In particular, the work of both scientists have shaped the discussion on unemployment, institutional influence, and suitable policies to overcome persistent mass unemployment in the 1990s.

Layard and Nickell's perspective on the labor market focuses both on stocks as well as on flows into and out of unemployment in an integrated way that older economic models of the labor market had failed to achieve. The core mechanism they are interested in is wage and price setting – which, in turn, is influenced by labor market institutions such as employment protection, collective bargaining, taxes, active labor market policies, and, last but not least, unemployment benefits. As a major academic achievement, their work has given us a unified and easily accessible framework for explaining unemployment levels and persistence. Many subsequent academic studies and policy-oriented papers were explicitly or implicitly influenced by this

1

model. Layard and Nickell emphasize in particular the importance of understanding the different channels of impact of labor market institutions on labor market performance, while avoiding oversimplified statements or false stereotypes with respect to the impact of "rigid" or "flexible" institutional arrangements.

This particular strength of the analytical framework is the reason why their approach to labor market institutions has stood the test of time very well and continued to be a major orientation both for researchers and policy makers over the last two decades. And it will most probably continue to do so in the foreseeable future as the framework of Layard and Nickell still is a major reference in institutional explanations of employment and unemployment dynamics (see Blanchard 2007). For example, they could show that stricter employment protection regulation does not necessarily increase the overall level of unemployment, but that strong dismissal protection for regular contracts tends to increase the persistence of unemployment by reducing short-term unemployment at the cost of raising long-term unemployment which is particularly hard to overcome due to the loss of human capital and motivation.

Richard Layard and Stephen Nickell have also pointed out that generous unemployment benefits are not necessarily harmful to achieving low unemployment if they are granted only for a limited time and if they are accompanied by adequate instruments that require and assist unemployed individuals who are able to work to actively search for a new job. Therefore, according to Layard and Nickell, active labor market policies and "activation schemes" based on rights and duties of beneficiaries are indispensable complementary measures in a system with elaborate unemployment benefits. This insight has since become a major guiding principle in reforming labor market policies in Europe and the U.S.

Moreover, Layard and Nickell have analyzed the interaction between wage setting institutions and unemployment in a novel fashion. For example, they showed that higher union coverage tends to increase unemployment, but these negative effects of collective wage bargaining can be neutralized if unions and employers coordinate their wage bargaining activities effectively, i.e. in a typical corporatist setting with strong and centralized employers' associations and trade union confederations.

Hence, the work of Layard and Nickell shows us that labor market institutions are complex arrangements which can only be assessed properly if the interactions between different elements are taken into account. Furthermore, the actual impact of formal institutions on employment performance crucially depends on the practical implementation of formal institutional provisions, e.g. the treatment of the unemployed in a system with generous unemployment benefits or the bargaining strategies of unions. Layard and Nickell point out that labor market institutions not only work in one direction, but can have diverging effects in different contexts as they interact with each other. Under certain conditions – such as effective active labor market policies and activation as well as sufficient flexibility in coordinated wage bargaining – a reliable social security safety net can be compatible with good employment performance and low structural unemployment. As a consequence, societies have some leeway in choosing between different institutional arrangements that may bring about similar levels of employment, but the distributional effects will be different.

This way of understanding labor market institutions has been of tremendous influence on both the academic research, stimulated in particular by the 1991 volume, and on policy advice at the international and the national level. The ideas of Richard Layard and Stephen Nickell have, in many respects, been mirrored by the OECD Jobs Study and the subsequent formulation of the Jobs Strategy (OECD 1994) which, in turn, became one of the most influential bodies of employment policy-oriented recommendations over the 1990s. It is fair to say that, even today, this basic line of argument inspired by the research of Layard and Nickell continues to structure many policy debates on the design of labor market institutions.

In a productive response to the work by Layard and Nickell as well as to the OECD Jobs Strategy of the early 1990s, the European Employment Strategy as well as the EU's Lisbon Strategy took up these ideas and called for further reforms combining social policy objectives, fostering labor supply and employment promotion in a European context, in particular by addressing potential work disincentives of unemployment protection systems via activation provisions. Policy changes in the spirit of Layard and Nickell have been implemented in many countries – and there is evidence that this has helped improve employment performance (Bassanini and Duval 2006).

Recent research, therefore, confirms the general correctness of Layard and Nickell's theoretical framework and empirical work as well as their policy conclusions. Last, but not least, the work of Layard and Nickell also inspired IZA when it came to designing its research areas. Not only are current IZA Research Areas such as the "Evaluation of Labor Market Programs" or "Labor Market Institutions" close to their work and benefit from their seminal contributions to the literature, but the early structure of IZA research right after its foundation in 1998 also referred to Layard and Nickell's long-standing research interests such as "Mobility and Flexibility of Labor" or "Welfare State and Labor Market".

Hence, it is fair to say that the welfare-to-work approach now pursued in many countries draws on the laureates' finding that unemployment benefits have to be complemented with effective work tests and other active labor market policy schemes, therefore "replacing" purely passive benefit schemes that had been used to buffer unemployment and reduce labor supply in many European countries during the 1970s and the 1980s.

First and foremost, the work of Richard Layard and Stephen Nickell has had direct influence on the activation policies implemented in the United Kingdom in the 1990s and onward, most notably New Labour's different "New Deals" implemented after the change of government in 1997 in order to prevent inflow into long-term unemployment and reduce the stock of people on benefits. Similar developments have taken place in other EU member states such as Denmark, Switzerland, or the Netherlands since the mid-1990s, or in Germany in the context of the "Hartz reforms" between 2002 and 2005. Analytical work by leading labor economists such as Layard and Nickell, amplified and condensed through the work of the OECD and the EU, has certainly influenced the design of these reforms.

Hence it is no surprise that over the last decade we have seen a broad convergence of national policies aimed at increasing rather than reducing labor supply by stronger work requirements in unemployment insurance, social assistance, and disability benefits and more tailor-made job search assistance and training (Eichhorst and Konle-Seidl 2008). In particular the expansion of the activation principle to disabled or incapacitated working-age people is now the frontier for the creation of more inclusive labor market and social policies in many European countries, in particular in the UK or the Netherlands. Accommodating for structural change of the economy by reducing labor supply is clearly a thing of the past – and Layard and Nickell have contributed to the fact that the aim of raising employment for all rather than keeping unemployment low has become a main priority in policy-making in Europe.

The concept of "workfare," which was developed by IZA for Germany as a core element of a sustainable strategy to integrate the long-term unemployed and low-skilled people into the labor market, also relies heavily on the idea developed by Richard Layard and Stephen Nickell that combining rights and duties in unemployment benefit helps mitigate work disincentives that may stem from generous benefit levels granted for a longer period of time. The IZA "workfare" concept makes this link explicit and calls for benefit recipients to be available for job offers, training, or public employment opportunities in order to maintain their benefit entitlement. This helps shorten unemployment duration and bring people into gainful employment, even at low wages that would be unattractive otherwise, without having to lower benefit levels as such (Bonin, Schneider 2006). The basic idea is now embodied in existing German legislation, but the actual implementation is certainly less comprehensive – and in particular the actual treatment of the unemployed makes a difference as Layard and Nickell have shown.

The work of Layard and Nickell helped us at IZA in formulating policy advice to the German government during the critical phase of labor market reforms in the first half of this decade, i.e. in the context of the "Hartz reforms" and the "Agenda 2010." To foster program evaluation, IZA had developed an entire research area and produced an influential book on this topic (Schmidt et al. 2001). IZA has since then played an important role in helping to establish a program evaluation tradition in German research and policy making, which had a long-lasting effect on labor market reforms undertaken in the Schröder Federal Government after 2005. Beyond intensive policy advice to policy makers such as Chancellor Gerhard Schröder, Economics and Labor Minister Wolfgang Clement, and the Head of the Nuremberg Employment Agency Florian Gerster, IZA was also publicly and influentially advocating for the reforms through popular books (Zimmermann 2003, 2006) and a public campaign for reforms. As a consequence, there is now some substantial evidence on the effectiveness of labor policy measures in Germany drawing on the findings of a growing research community (Eichhorst and Zimmermann, 2007).

This volume brings together a selection of core texts of Richard Layard and Stephen Nickell that deal with labor market institutions and their impact on employment performance. Many of their contributions to theoretical and empirical labor market research, some of the most prominent ones compiled in this volume, have already become real modern classics that continue to be major references in ongoing comparative labor market research. This holds particularly for their 1991 book "Unemployment: Macroeconomic Performance and the Labour Market" (co-authored with Richard Jackman) and their 1999 chapter "Labor Market Institutions and Economic Performance" in the Handbook of Labor Economics edited by Orley Ashenfelter and David Card, both of whom are IZA Prize Laureates, too. The six articles in this volume cover twenty years of research on closely related aspects of the wider analytical framework – and they are still highly relevant for today's readers. The articles united in the volume are still among the most cited contributions to the topic as recent citation data shows, and, of course, both authors rank among the top labor economists in Europe.

We edited these articles with great caution, in order to keep the evolutionary character of their work visible so that the reader can trace the development of Layard and Nickell's thoughts on labor market institutions over time, the way they developed, refined, applied, and expanded their analytical tools over the last two and a half decades. Only marginal adjustments were made to improve the legibility of the volume. The volume, therefore, provides a unique compilation of a selection of highly influential and intimately linked articles that altogether fundamentally shaped our perception of the labor market.

Both Richard Layard and Stephen Nickell have always cooperated intensively with other researchers. Hence, some of the texts in this volume were co-authored with other scholars, namely Charles Bean and Richard Jackman.

Following the 2008/2009 financial and economic crisis it is of utmost importance to analyze the labor market implications both in the short and in the medium run and draw the right conclusions that do not repeat some of the early policy mistakes that were made in the 1970s and 1980s. We are convinced that the unified general framework of labor market adjustment developed by Richard Layard and Stephen Nickell can help us understand the situation we are in and devise appropriate policy responses. In particular, the policy-oriented conclusions that can be derived from the contributions in this volume point to the need to avoid extended periods of benefit receipt since this tends to be associated with severe difficulties in finding a new job due to loss of motivation and skills obsolescence.

So, even in a deep recession like the current one, European labor market policies should not fall back into a social policy approach to unemployment but maintain the principle of activation combined with skills-oriented active labor market policies and effective job placement rather than falling back into policies that try to cushion job losses by generous passive benefit systems. This will help avoid a new wave of mass and long-term unemployment. Richard Layard and Stephen Nickell were motivated to develop their analytical framework by the severe unemployment crisis in the UK in the early 1980s – and a substantial part of the employment gains observed since then can be explained by appropriate policy changes. If we do not draw the right lessons from policy experiences gained since then, we will run into bigger troubles in Europe's labor markets. This is why we think this volume comes at the right moment.

1

The Labor Market

The work of Richard Layard and Stephen Nickell on institutional explanations of unemployment goes back more than 20 years. This can be shown by sections 1 to 4 of an early article which was originally published in an edited volume from 1987. Richard Layard and Stephen Nickell start with the puzzling observation that there was high wage pressure in the UK in the early 1980s, even when unemployment was high. This triggered the development of the basic idea on the influence of wage setting and unemployment duration on unemployment levels – a concept that was further developed in subsequent articles. In particular, their main argument is that rather than the level of unemployment, the duration is of high importance when it comes to explaining wage bargaining outcomes. In fact, the long-term unemployed are found to have only a minor impact on wages and, in the long run, the inflation-reducing effects of extra unemployment decline rapidly as unemployment rises. On the one hand, if a large share of the unemployed have been out of work for a long time, the employers may consider them undesirable as workers; and on the other hand, the workers themselves may have largely given up searching. Therefore, the long-term unemployed are much less effective a labor supply than the short-term unemployed. Hence, the distribution of unemployment duration matters in explaining wage pressure and union behavior in a decentralized bargaining regime, whereas the effects of alternative explanations such as employment protection, mismatch, or changes in benefit generosity are more ambiguous. However, the administration of unemployment benefits, more specifically the implementation of work tests, matters in preventing long-term unemployment and can therefore mitigate wage pressure.

The original version of this chapter was published as: Layard, R., Nickell, S. (1987), The Labour Market, in: Dornbusch, R., Layard, R. (Eds.), The Performance of the British Economy, Oxford: Oxford University Press, 131-179. By permission of Oxford University Press.

"The biggest single cause of our high unemployment is the failure of our jobs market, the weak link in our economy."
White Paper of March 1985,
Employment, The Challenge for the Nation (pp. 12-13)

Most people are dissatisfied with Britain's economic performance over the last 15 years, and many blame the institutions of the labor market. It is a natural argument, since our most obvious economic failure is the rise of unemployment.

But can one argue that unemployment has nearly trebled since 1979 because our labor market institutions have got so much worse? Clearly not. Up to 1979 our institutional arrangements did become a bit more rigid, but since then they have become a bit less so. So the rigidity argument cannot be of the form, "Unemployment has risen because rigidity has risen." It must be of the form, "Unemployment has risen because the system has been subjected to deflationary shocks, and a rigid labor market has been unable to absorb them."

First, we shall look at the labor market as an aggregate, and try to explain why unemployment has ratcheted upward in the way shown in Figure 1.1 below. The central mystery is why, at present levels of unemployment, wage inflation is not falling. One approach is to focus on the impact of long-term unemployment on attachment to the labor force. According to this account, a sharp deflationary shock increases the number of long-term unemployed, many of whom effectively withdraw from the labor market. A rival, although related, interpretation focuses on the role of the unions. If unions are concerned mainly with "insiders" and there is a contraction of employment, the unions become concerned with a smaller proportion of the labor force.

To discriminate between these two approaches, we shall deploy one of the basic facts about the labor market: that unemployment has risen hugely while vacancies are now as high as they were in 1977-8. The fact that vacancies exist in that (limited) abundance argues in favor of the explanation in terms of workers' incentives to take work and firms' incentives to fill vacancies, as against explanations that focus solely on the role of unions in holding down the number of jobs, once this number has fallen.

A quite different explanation of unemployment focuses on structural issues and the rigidities in the structure of relative wages (rather

9

than of the general wage level). We show how inflexible relative wages are in this country – whether by industry, region, age, or sex. This makes unemployment higher than it would otherwise be. But there is no evidence that these problems have worsened in a way that could explain the *rise* in unemployment.

1.1. Aggregate Unemployment

1.1.1. Some Basic Facts

We shall begin with some basic facts. Unemployment has quadrupled since 1970 (see Figure 1.1). The most relevant series we have is for male unemployment, since measured female unemployment depends so much on women's varying entitlements to benefits. Male unemployment (on the official pre-1982 definition)[1] has increased from 4 to 17 percent – mainly though two huge steps, one in 1974-6 and the second in 1979-82. On the OECD's standardized definitions, male unemployment is now nearly twice as high in Britain as in France, Germany, Italy, or the United States (OECD 1985).[2] And male employment is now lower here than it was in 1911.

Figure 1.1

Male Unemployment Rate, 1955-1985
(pre-1982 Definition of Unemployment)

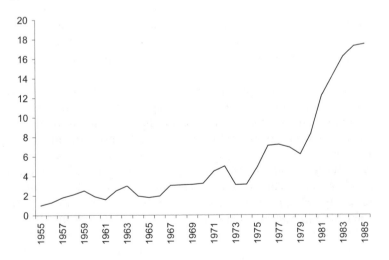

The increase in unemployment has come about almost entirely through an increase in the duration of unemployment. As can be seen from Figure 1.2, the inflow into unemployment in recent years has been rather less than it was in the late 1960s, though about a fifth above its level in the late 1970s. There has been a huge build-up of long-term unemployed – that is, of those unemployed for over a year (Figure 1.3). In fact, since 1981 short-term unemployment has actually fallen a bit, while long-term unemployment has soared.

Unemployment of this kind must be both inefficient and inequitable. It must be inefficient since it cannot reflect any necessary search or redeployment of labor and in fact causes huge depreciation of the stock of human capital. It must be inequitable since it reflects the concentration of the total man-weeks of unemployment in a very small proportion of the population. The number of men who become unemployed is roughly 2.5 million a year – only 16 percent of the male workforce. But the stock of unemployed men is nearly 2.5 million. So those who do become unemployed can expect on average to remain so for roughly a year.

Figure 1.2

Male Unemployment Inflows and Outflows
(pre-1982 Definition of Unemployment)

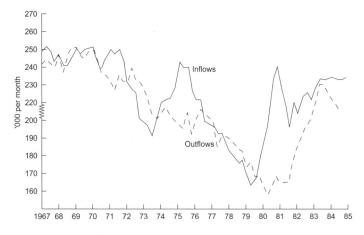

The rise in unemployment has not been matched by a commensurate fall in vacancies. Vacancies are indeed low (about two-thirds of their average level in the 1960s), but they are at about the same level as in the economic troughs of 1958, 1963, and 1971-2 and above their level in 1976 (see Figure 1.4). The outward shift of the u/v curve is thus a basic puzzle which we have to explain.

Figure 1.3

Male Unemployment by Duration, 1970-1985
(pre-1982 Definition of Unemployment)

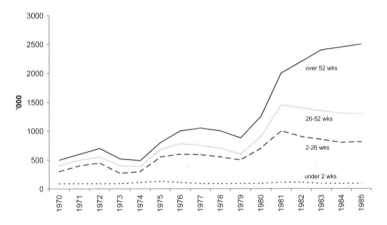

Figure 1.4

Vacancies and Male Unemployment, 1957-1985

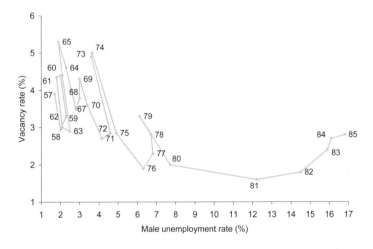

While unemployment has risen, the labor force has not stood still. Indeed, it has risen continuously since 1971 (except in 1983), though much more slowly than in the United States and Japan. The increase is entirely due to the rising number of women in the labor force. This reflects partly the size of the adult population, but also the increasing participation rate of women. By contrast, the participation rate of men has fallen, mainly owing to earlier retirement.

Figure 1.5

Rate of Growth of Hourly Earnings of Male Manual Workers, 1960-1985

The mechanism by which labor supply affects employment is through its effects on wages. At some level of unemployment, wage inflation will be stable – increasing at lower unemployment and falling at higher unemployment. Figure 1.5 therefore shows the history of wage inflation, while Figure 1.6 shows changes in wage inflation against the level of vacancies. There is clearly some relationship.

Figure 1.6

The Change Rate of Growth of Hourly Earnings (Male Manual) and the Vacancy Rate (x5), 1963-1985

1.1.2. A Labor Market Model

To explain the movement of unemployment, we shall present a simple model. This draws on earlier work (Layard and Nickell 1986a), but simplifies it and extends it to focus on the apparent ratchet effect in the level of unemployment. In the long run, unemployment is determined so that there is equality between

1. the "feasible" real wage, implied by the pricing behavior of firms, and
2. the "target" real wage, implied by the wage-setting behavior of wage-bargainers.

This is illustrated at point A in Figure 1.7.

Let us go behind the curves, starting with the price-setting relationship determining the "feasible" real wage. We shall define prices (p) as the price of value added; i.e., at the level of the firm, final prices adjusted for changes in materials' prices, and at the level of the whole economy, for changes in the price of imports. Firms set their value added prices as a mark-up on hourly labor cost (w). But this mark-up will tend to rise if output is higher. Since output is related to employment via the production function, it follows that the real wage falls as employment rises, as in Figure 1.7. The mark-up falls if inflation is greater than expected

$(p > p^e)$, both because prices will not be adjusted enough upward for the higher wages, and because firms will underestimate competitors' prices and keep their prices low to retain business.

Figure 1.7

The Consequences of a Positive Demand Shock

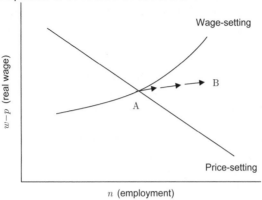

Wages in turn are set as a mark-up on expected prices. The mark-up increases as employment rises and is also affected by a whole host of wage pressure variables (z), to which we return later. If inflation is greater than expected the mark-up will fall, since, when prices turn out to be higher than expected, the real wage achieved will be lower than the real wage bargained for.

In the longer run, the growth of the capital stock will lead to productivity improvements, which, on the one hand, will lead firms to reduce their mark-up of prices on wages and, on the other hand, will lead firms and workers to bargain for a higher mark-up of wages on prices.[3] Thus, in static, log-linear form we have the following model:

(1) Price Setting: $p - w = \alpha_0 + \alpha_1 (p - p^e) + \alpha_2 (n - l)$

$$+ \alpha_3 (k - l), \ (\alpha_1 < 0, \ \alpha_2 \geq 0, \ \alpha_3 < 0),$$

(2) Wage Setting: $w - p = \beta_0 + \beta_1 (p - p^e) + \beta_2 (n - 1)$

$$+ \beta_3 (k - l) + z, \ (\beta_1 < 0, \ \beta_2 > 0, \ \beta_3 > 0),$$

15

where w = hourly labor cost (including employers' labor taxes)
  p = value added price
  k = capital stock
  l = labor force
  n = employment (note the unemployment rate $u = 1 - n$)
  z = "wage pressure" (the influence of mismatch, employment protection, replacement ratio, union power, incomes policy, relative import prices, and employers' labor taxes)

There are many points worth noting about this framework. First, it is very general. For example, if $\alpha_1 = 0$ and $\alpha_2 = -\alpha_3$, then (1) becomes the standard labor demand equation for a competitive industry. Similarly, a restricted version of (2) yields a competitive labor supply equation. On the other hand, if $\alpha_2 = 0$ we have the pure mark-up or normal cost pricing model, where prices are unaffected by demand in the short run. Second, to complete a model of a closed economy, we may add the following equations:

(3)   Production function: $y - k = f(n - k)$

(4)   Aggregate demand: $y = y^d(x)$

  where y = value added output
    x = exogenous determinants of real demand

So, given the resources of the economy as specified by k and l, the model will, in the short run, yield w, p, n, y for any given level of demand (x), price expectations (p^e), and wage pressure (z). In the longer term, when price surprises are ruled out ($p = p^e$), the model reveals, for given z, the level of y, n, $w - p$, and y^d consistent with no surprises. If no surprises is synonymous with stable inflation, these levels correspond to the NAIRU (non-accelerating inflation rate of unemployment).

The great advantage of writing the model as we have done is that (1) and (2) alone will yield the no-surprise (or NAIRU) values of employment and the real wage, and are thus eminently suitable for analyzing long-term unemployment trends.[4]

In order to see how the model operates, we consider, first, the consequences of an aggregate demand shock starting from a position of equilibrium ($p = p^e$). An increase in real demand raises employment, and this tends to raise prices relative to wages in the price equation, and wages relative to prices in the wage equation. The only way in which these tendencies can be made consistent is via the positive price surprise brought about by a rise in inflation. This tends to offset the consequences of the rise in the level of activity on both sides of the market, leading us to a point such as B, which is below the wage line and above the price line. (Note that the effect of a positive price surprise is to raise the price-determined real wage.) So we have the standard result that a positive demand shock will raise employment, raise inflation, but have an indeterminate impact on the real wage. However, we can be more precise on this latter point in certain special cases. If the product market is competitive, then $\alpha_1 = 0$ and $\alpha_2 = -\alpha_3$ in equation (1), as we have already noted. Thus B must lie on the price line, which slopes downward. The real wage must, therefore, fall. On the other hand, under strict normal cost pricing, $\alpha_2 = 0$ and the price line is horizontal. Under these circumstances the real wage must rise, since B must be above the horizontal price line.

Turning to the consequences of a supply shock, in Figure 1.8 we illustrate the outcome of a rise in wage pressure, z (a negative supply shock). If real demand remains fixed, then we move to a point such as B, with a fall in employment and positive price surprises generated by rising inflation. The real wage has risen, and we have the combination of inflation and "classical" unemployment typical of such a shock. If the rise in wage pressure is permanent, real demand must fall if inflation is to be stabilized. This may happen either autonomously (via real balance effects, for example) or as a result of a conscious policy shift. In consequence, we move to a new equilibrium at C, with lower "equilibrium" employment and a real wage that will be higher to the extent that prices are influenced by demand. In the extreme case of normal cost pricing, the price line is horizontal and the real wage will revert back to its original level. The additional unemployment will then apparently be entirely "Keynesian," although it has, in fact, been brought about by the rise in wage pressure.

It is clear from this analysis that the wage pressure variables are the key to the long-run analysis of unemployment. It is also clear that focusing on the real-wage outcome will not be very useful in trying to understand what is happening. The real wage that finally emerges has as much to do with the pricing policy of firms as with labor market activity.

Figure 1.8

The Consequences of a Rise in Wage Pressure

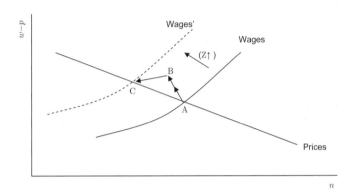

Our next step is to attach some numbers to the fundamental model. Our equations are based on Nickell (1987). The dynamic versions of each equation are (annual data 1956-83):[5]

(1')   Prices: $p - w = \alpha_0 - 0.61\Delta^2 w - 0.51\Delta^2 w_{-1} - 0.253u +$

$$0.075\Delta u - 0.338\Delta^2 u - 1.07\,(k - l).$$

(2')   Wages: $w - p = \beta_0 - 0.36\Delta^2 p - 0.104\log u + 0.532u -$

$$1.174\Delta u - 0.356\Delta^2 u + 1.07\,(k - l) + z.$$

A number of points are worth noting. The price surprise terms are presented by $\Delta^2 w$ in the price equation and $\Delta^2 p$ in the wage equation. One of the key properties of the wage equation is the dependence of wages on $\log u$ as well as u. This has profound implications and we shall return to this point at a later stage. At the moment it suffices to say that a percentage point rise in unemployment has a lesser impact on wages, the higher is its initial level. A final point concerns the role of the productivity variable $(k - l)$. The model imposes the restriction that increases in the stock of capital have no impact on unemployment *in the long run*. This is perfectly consistent with the data and implies that the long-run coefficient on $k - l$ is the same (in absolute value) in both price and wage equations. Were this not the case, the implication would be that firms and workers would be trying to extract, on a permanent basis, more or less than 100 percent of the growth in trend productivity. Since this would imply either *permanently* rising or *permanently* falling unemployment at stable inflation, we decided to rule out this possibility – it seems inconsistent with the apparent consequences of two centuries of economic growth.

To understand the long-run determinants of unemployment, we can write equations (1') and (2') in their long-run form, expanding the wage equation around an unemployment rate of $\bar{u}$. This gives

(1'')   Prices: $p - w = \alpha_0 - 0.253u - 1.07\ (k - l)$.

(2'')   *Wages*: $w - p = \beta'_0 - \left(\frac{0.104}{\bar{u}} - 0.532\right) u + 1.07\ (k - l) + z$.

The long-run level of unemployment is given by adding these equations to obtain

(5) $u = \left(0.253 + \frac{0.104}{\bar{u}} - 0.523\right)^{-1} (z + \alpha_0 + \beta'_0)$.

Thus, wage pressure (z) is crucial to our explanation of unemployment.[6] The next step, therefore, is to look at the movement of the wage pressure index (see Figure 1.9). We shall discuss its constituent parts later. As can be seen, it moves broadly in line with unemployment up to 1980, and any divergences are identified with increasing or decreasing inflation, as appropriate. However, since 1980 the index has risen little, with the years 1980-5 having wage pressure only 4 points higher than the 1974-80 average. The long-run NAIRU (for male unemployment) is now around 12 percent; yet actual unemployment is much higher than this, with the 1981-5 average being nearly 10 points above the level for 1974-80. Thus, the index does not seem to explain how the high unemployment of the 1980s could be accompanied by such relatively small reductions in wage inflation.

Figure 1.9
Wage Pressure Index, 1954-1985

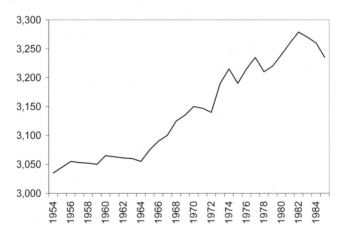

The answer to the apparent paradox lies in the fact that the short-term NAIRU is not the same as the long-term NAIRU. This arises from the dynamics of the system and especially of the wage equation (2'). As the wage pressure equation makes clear, wage pressure is less not only when unemployment is higher but also when unemployment is rising. By the same token, wage pressure at a given level of unemployment is higher when unemployment is falling. Thus, suppose the wage equation is, for simplicity,

$$(6) \qquad w - p = \beta_0 - \beta_2 \log u - \beta_3 (u - u_{-1}),$$

As compared with the long-run wage relationship

$$w - p = \beta_0 - \beta_2 \log u.$$

In Figure 1.10 we show the long-run NAIRU at point A as usual. But suppose last year's employment was at n_{-1}. The short-run wage pressure equation (6) is given by the dotted line and the short-run NAIRU is at B. This is the essence of our present difficulties. We have got to a very high level of unemployment, and reducing unemployment is always liable to produce increasing inflation.

What accounts for the long-lasting effect of past unemployment in the wage equation? The evidence suggests that it results from the effect of high unemployment on the numbers of the long-term unemployed. But in order to give all theories a run for their money, we need first to consider from basic principles how the unemployment situation might be expected to influence the degree of wage pressure.

Figure 1.10
Short-run NAIRU (at B) and Long-run NAIRU (at A)

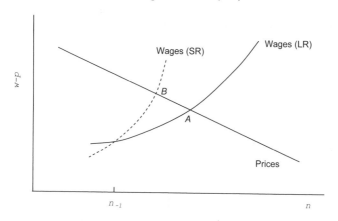

1.1.3. Unemployment and Wage Pressure

Two parties are involved in wage determination: firms and unions. Their relative importance differs in different parts of the economy.[7] Let us begin with firms. Firms, if they were free to choose wages, would set them at a level that would enable them to recruit, retain, and motivate workers. For recruitment purposes, they would choose lower wages, the more plentiful the supply of workers that they faced. Similar factors would affect the ability of firms to restrain quitting and to motivate workers, for workers are easier to retain and motivate, the more job market competition they would face if they themselves became unemployed.[8]

Thus, a key variable is the number of acceptable unemployed workers who are out there "beating at the gates." Since few unemployed workers (30 percent) get re-employed in the industry of their previous job, we would expect that it was general (rather than industry-specific) unemployment that affected wage behavior in each industry. And this turns out to be the case.

But the level of unemployment on its own does not adequately measure the number of acceptable workers beating at the gates. The composition of unemployment also matters. If a high proportion of the unemployed have been out of work for a long time, the employers may consider them undesirable as workers; equally, the workers themselves may be discouraged, and may have largely given up searching. Thus, long-term unemployment represents a less effective labor supply than short-term unemployment. So employers will be influenced both by the level of unemployment and by the proportion of the unemployed who are long-term unemployed (R). As we have seen this proportion has doubled since 1979, and we shall find that this is a major factor explaining the current degree of wage pressure.

But what about the union response to unemployment? Unions too will care about the numbers of workers "beating at the gates." For if wages are pushed too high, some union members will lose their jobs and end up in competition with other unemployed job-seekers.[9] So if general unemployment is high, and predominantly short-term, individual unions will be less inclined to push on wages and so risk unemployment for their members.

But unions will be concerned not only with the bleakness of the world outside, but also with the likelihood that their members will be ejected into it. So another key variable will be "fear" – the fear of job loss. The extent of job loss will of course depend on the wages that each union selects. But this will in turn depend on how unfavorable a demand curve the union faces. The union may evaluate its demand curve largely in terms of, say, last year's job loss.[10] This could be proxied by last year's rate of inflow into unemployment (I) or by the change in unemployment.

One extreme view is in fact that wage behavior depends *only* on the change in unemployment, and not at all on the level (Blanchard and Summers 1986).[11] This has been offered as an explanation of why wage inflation fell so much between 1980-1 and 1982-3, and so little since. The chief line of reasoning is that the unions care only about their members and set the wage so as to maintain the chances of their continued employment (see also Lindbeck and Snower 1984). If unemployment has been low and stable for some time, wage claims will be no higher than if unemployment has been high and stable for some time. For the unions are concerned only with ensuring the continued employment of those employed in the previous period, and this does not require a lower wage when unemployment is high. But when employment is falling, unions do moderate their behavior in order to try to prevent employment falling further.

There are many obvious problems with this "insider-outsider" line of argument. First, it provides no explanation of the fact that, over longish periods, the size of the labor force has a clear effect on the level of employment. This must involve some responsiveness of wages to the labor force, as well as to employment.[12] Second, given the huge level of annual turnover in enterprises, it is hard to understand why employment has not been steadily falling if wage-setting only takes account of surviving workers. Third, the theory fails to explain why it is general unemployment rather than industry-specific unemployment (or employment) that most clearly affects the wages in an industry.

But even so, it is important to investigate systematically the effect of flow variables like unemployment flows and the change in employment, as compared with the level of unemployment and the composition of unemployment by duration. This is done in Nickell (1986), and we shall summarize the results. The most successful equation is one that includes only the log of unemployment and the proportion of the unemployed out of work for over a year (R):[13]

$$(7) \qquad w - p = \beta_0'' - 0.36\Delta^2 p - 0.104\log u + 0.212R + 1.07\,(k - l) + z.$$
$$\qquad\qquad\qquad\qquad (7.8) \qquad\qquad (3.7)$$

IV estimates 1956-83, s.e. = 0.0114.

When this equation was expanded to include the inflow of unemployment, we obtained a t-statistic of only 1.3 and the significance of the duration term increased. When the equation was expanded to include lagged employment terms, the coefficients were

$(2.2.) \qquad\qquad\qquad\qquad n_{-1} : 0.46$

$(2.1.) \qquad\qquad\qquad\qquad n_{-2} : -0.52$

and the t-statistics on $\log u$ and R remained 5.7 and 4.1, respectively. However, this version of the equation fits very badly over the 1980s.

So our conclusion is that the story based on the effects of long-duration unemployment is the most persuasive.

Before pursuing the implications of this, we should refer to one other issue: the impact of region-specific unemployment rates. It is often suggested that, since wage bargaining is undertaken nationally in so many sectors (e.g. the public sector) and companies (e.g. ICI and the four main motor car manufacturers), wages may be most strongly influenced by the tightness of the labor market in the most buoyant region – that is, the South-East. So we added to our standard equation a variable measuring the South-East's unemployment rate relative to the national average, expecting it to reduce wage pressure. It did so – but its t-statistic was only 0.7. This is not surprising, given that this variable has recently had a high value, and yet there has been little apparent reduction of wage pressure.

We are therefore ready to investigate how the duration of unemployment affects the dynamics of wage behavior. The first step is to see how the proportion of unemployed out of work for over a year (R) is affected by the history of unemployment. The relevant equation is

$$(7')\qquad R = 0.054 + 0.61R_{-1} - 2.41u + 5.58u_{-1} - 2.18u_{-2}$$

$$(2.1)\quad\ (3.7)\qquad(5.6)\qquad(6.5)\qquad(2.4)$$

OLS estimation 1956-83, s.e. = 0.023, $\overline{R}^2 = 0.84$.

This equation makes very good sense. As unemployment rises, the long-term unemployed proportion falls initially, since historically increases in unemployment come about because the inflow rises. In the long run, however, the long-term proportion tends to rise with unemployment. If we now solve out for R and substitute into (7), we obtain, after some manipulation, equation $(2')$, which is how we obtained that equation in the first place (see Nickell 1986, equation (26)).

Interestingly, $(2')$ is similar to what is obtained from the following directly estimated dynamic wage equation:

$$(2''')\qquad w - p = \beta_0 - 0.113\log u + 0.452u - 0.803\Delta u + 1.07\,(k - l) + z$$

$$(5.2)\qquad\quad(1.03)\qquad(1.9)$$

IV estimation 1956-83, s.e. = 0.0125, D.W. = 1.81.

This was our most successful dynamic wage equation (except for one that depended heavily on unemployment lagged three years). But the important point is that (2") gives no behavioral insight into how the dynamics arise, whereas our two equations involving long-term unemployment, (7) and (7'), do just that.

We can now see how our model helps us to understand the movement of inflation. From (2') we can see that in the long run, if unemployment gets high enough (above 19 percent), further unemployment fails to reduce wage pressure, because the proportion of long-term unemployed becomes so high (see Figure 1.11).

But what happens to the rate of change of nominal wages? As equations (1') and (2') make clear, the rate of change of inflation is directly related to the difference between the target real wage and the feasible real wage (each measured in the absence of nominal inertia, i.e., with $\Delta^2 w = \Delta^2 p = 0$). To see this, we add (1') to (2') after first expanding (2') around $\bar{u}$, setting $\Delta^2 w = \Delta^2 w_{-1} = \Delta^2 p$, and omitting $\Delta^2 u$. This gives us

$$\Delta^2 w = -0.68 \left\{ \left(\frac{0.104}{\bar{u}} - 0.279 \right) u + 1.10 \Delta u - z - \alpha_0 - \beta_0' \right\}$$

where the term in brackets is the gap between feasible and target wage. Using (5), this can be rewritten

(8) $$\Delta^2 w = -0.68 \left\{ \left(\frac{0.104}{\bar{u}} - 0.279 \right) (u - u^*) + 1.10 \Delta u \right\}.$$

Thus, as unemployment grows, the effect of higher unemployment on cutting inflation is reduced. This is exactly what we should expect by looking at Figure 1.11 and bearing in mind that the change in inflation is proportional to the distance between the two lines. This distance reaches its minimum when unemployment is 37 percent, and if unemployment goes higher than this it starts to lose its power to reduce inflation.

Figure 1.11

How Unemployment Changes the Rate of Inflation
(using long-run wage price equations)

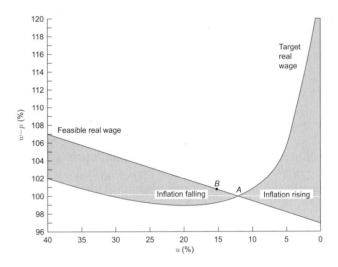

For beyond that point higher unemployment raises the target real wage more than it raises the feasible real wage. This observation is highly speculative since it lies way beyond the sample range, but it does raise the specter that, if wage pressure became fierce enough, there might be no unemployment rate that could stabilize inflation.

More relevant to our present range of experience, the diagram shows clearly how the benefits of additional unemployment vary with the existing level of unemployment. If unemployment is low, more unemployment will have a marked effect on the change in inflation. But if unemployment is already high, the counter inflation gains from further unemployment are very limited. Thus the following table shows the (negative) effect on the change of inflation of 1 extra point of unemployment, starting from different levels of unemployment.

$\bar{u}$	Effect of one extra percentage point of unemployment on $(-\Delta^2 w)$
0.07	0.82%
0.12	0.39%
0.17	0.22%

(The values correspond to 0.68 $(0.104/\bar{u} - 0.279)$.) This indicates, for example, that a 1 point rise in unemployment from a base line of 7 percent (i.e., 1979 male unemployment) will cause inflation to slow down at four times the speed of the slow-down induced by a similar rise in unemployment from a base-line of 17 percent (i.e., 1985 male unemployment). However, this is a long-run effect. The Δu term in (8) reveals, for example, that, if we start from the current base-line of 17 percent male unemployment and assume that this is 5 points above the long-run natural rate (our estimate is around 12 percent), then any attempt to reduce unemployment down to this level at a rate of more than 2 percentage points per year will actually generate increasing inflation from the start. Even if unemployment is reduced at 1 percentage point per year, inflation will start to rise well before the natural rate is attained. This arises because of the way in which the duration structure of unemployment changes when unemployment declines. Falls in unemployment lead initially to a sharp reduction in the short-term unemployed. This withdrawal of a considerable proportion of the most active and desirable workers from the unemployed pool generates an increase in wage pressure which eases off only when the duration structure returns to normal and the major reduction in unemployment has come from the long-term end of the spectrum.

To summarize, therefore, once we take account of the fact that the long-term unemployed have only a minor impact on wages, we find that, in the long run, the inflation-reducing effects of extra unemployment decline rapidly as unemployment rises. For the same reason, the impact of changes in wage pressure on unemployment increases as the general level of unemployment goes up.

1.2. Influences on Wage Pressure

Having established the overall framework, we now need to look at the various wage pressure factors (z), which determine the long-run NAIRU. How far does each help us to explain the long rise in unemployment, and how does the duration of unemployment (as a more endogenous influence) fit into the story? The wage pressure factors we shall investigate are (in order): the duration of unemployment, employment protection, mismatch, benefits, unions, incomes policy, taxes, and import prices.

1.2.1. The Duration of Unemployment and the u/v Curve

To think about the first four of these influences, we need to go behind the simplified model we have been using so far, and look at the flow of people through unemployment. This gives us a relationship between the unemployment rate (u), the vacancy rate (v), and a number of shift variables (x) : $f(u, v, x) = 0$. We can also conceive of the structural wage equation lying behind (2) as including vacancies (as well as unemployment) as a determinant of wages. The wage equation (2) we have used so far is therefore a semi-reduced form in which vacancies have been substituted out, using $f(u, v, x) = 0$. It therefore includes all the variables (x) that affect the relationship of vacancies and unemployment. However, to check on our interpretation of the role of these variables in equation (2), we must look directly at the structural u/v relationship. Where does it come from, and what factors affect it?

The u/v curve reflects the process by which unemployed workers are matched to vacancies to generate a flow of hirings (or job-matches). One would expect that the number of hirings would depend positively on the number of vacancies that firms are willing to fill per period, and also on the number of unemployed people looking for work per period. It will be reduced by any mismatch (mm) between unemployment and vacancies. The intensity with which firms want to fill vacancies will vary according to how they view the quality of the unemployed and on such things as employment protection legislation and the like. So the vacancies that are relevant per period are some proportion (g) that firms wish to fill. Similarly, workers may vary in their intensity of search, depending on their past experience and on the level of unemployment benefits and the like. So the unemployed that are relevant per period are some proportion (c). This gives us our matching equation:

$$(9) \qquad\qquad A = f(gV, cV, mm)$$
$$\qquad\qquad\qquad\quad +\quad +\quad -$$

where A is the numbers leaving unemployment per period and U and V are the numbers of vacancies and unemployed.

We can now see clearly how the proportion of long-term unemployed (R) has its effect. For both g and c will decrease as the proportion R rises. Hence (for given flows) the u/v curve shifts out as the proportion of long-term unemployed goes up. This is exactly what Budd, Levine, and Smith (1985) have found.[14] The fact that long-term unemployment shows up in the structural u/v relationship adds greatly to our confidence that its effect in the semi-reduced form wage equation (7) is also valid.

To obtain the long-run u/v curve, we note that in a steady state the outflow from unemployment equals the inflow. This has been roughly true for the last few years and was also true in the late 1970s. In this case $A = S$, where S is the inflow to unemployment. This gives us

$$(10) \qquad \frac{U}{N} = \frac{S/N}{A/U}$$

where S/N is the inflow into unemployment as a proportion of the employed, and A/U is the proportion of the unemployed who leave unemployment. The unemployment rate (relative to employment) is simply the ratio of these two proportions.

Which of these two proportions accounts for the huge rise in unemployment? A glance at Figure 1.2 shows that the increased inflow rate into unemployment (S/N) would have increased unemployment by only a fifth. The main "cause" of increased unemployment has been the halving in the outflow rate (A/U).

It is easy to see how the pile-up of long-term unemployment could help to explain this fall in the outflow rate (A/U). For the outflow rate is always very much lower for those who have been unemployed longer. As Figure 1.12 shows, for people who have been unemployed over four years it is now 4 percent per quarter, compared with 41 percent per quarter for those who have recently lost their jobs. Thus, when long-term unemployment piles up, the overall outflow rate falls even if the duration-specific outflow rates remain constant. We can therefore examine the effect of the duration structure upon the outflow rate by constructing an index of the outflow rate as it would have been over time with the duration-specific outflow rates unchanging but with the duration structure of unemployment changing as it has. This is shown in Figure 1.13. The (fixed) duration-specific outflow rates are those for January 1984 (as shown in Figure 1.12).

Figure 1.12

Proportion of Unemloyed in January 1984 Leaving Unemployment in the Next Three Months

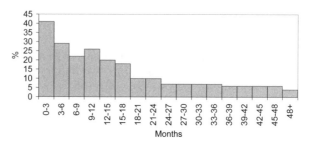

Months

As the index shows, the change in the duration structure of unemployment accounts for all of the fall in the overall outflow rate since early 1981. This is the period during which the proportion of long-term unemployed has continuously risen while (as Table 1.1 shows) the duration-specific outflow rates have changed little. Before 1981 there was no increase in the proportion of long-term unemployed, and the fall in the outflow rate was due entirely to the sharp fall in the duration-specific outflow rates (Table 1.2).

So what happened in the 1980s was this. The proportions of people leaving unemployment at each duration fell, but they fell by nothing like one-half (Table 1.2). This, however, led to an increase in the proportion of the unemployed who were long-term unemployed. Because the outflow rates are lower for the long-term unemployed than for those with shorter durations, an equiproportionate fall in all outflow rates leads to a more than proportionate fall in the average outflow rate.[15] If there were now a major economic recovery, the inflow into unemployment would fall sharply and so would short-term unemployment. But it is most unlikely that long-term unemployment would fall at all rapidly, unless specific measures were taken to encourage employers to hire the long-term unemployed.

Table 1.1

Outflow from Unemployment, 1976-1985

| | % of unemployed in Jan. leaving in the next 3 mos, by duration (mos.) in January | | | |
	0-3	3-6	6-9	9+
1976	56.2	38.9	31.8	18.1
1977	56.0	41.4	35.1	20.1
1978	54.9	41.8	37.5	21.5
1979	56.6	41.0	35.0	16.6
1980	52.0	36.7	30.0	17.3
1981	36.7	29.4	26.1	13.9
1982	40.4	31.4	23.9	15.3
1983	39.2	28.1	21.5	13.8
1984	41.1	29.7	22.2	13.6
1985	41.8	28.6	22.7	12.1

Table 1.2

Outflow from Unemployment, 1981-1985

| | % of unemployment in Jan. leaving in next 3 mos, by duration (mos) in Jan. | | | | | | | | | |
	0-3	3-6	6-9	9-12	12-15	15-18	18-24	24-36	36-48	48+
1981	36,7	29,4	26,1	19,3	17,4	—	—	—	—	—
1982	40,4	31,4	23,9	21,8	18,7	24,4	18,9	—	—	—
1983	39,2	28,1	21,5	20,2	17,9	23,8	10,8	8,7	—	—
1984	41,1	29,7	22,2	25,3	21,4	18,7	10,4	7,8	6,0	4,3
1985	41,8	28,6	22,7	23,7	21,1	—	—	8,1	6,4	5,1

Reverting to the u/v curve (9), Pissarides (1986) has shown that it exhibits constant returns to scale. We can therefore divide both sides by unemployment to get

$$\frac{A}{U} = f\left(g\frac{V}{U}, \ c, \ mm\right)$$

which can be substituted into (10) to get the long-run u/v curve. Clearly, a complete model would need an equation to explain the inflow rate (S/N). This was attempted in Nickell (1982) but is not reported here. An important factor affecting flows both into and out of unemployment is employment protection, our next factor affecting the u/v relationship.

Figure 1.13

Outflow Rate from Unemployment (per Three Mos.), Males, 1976-1984

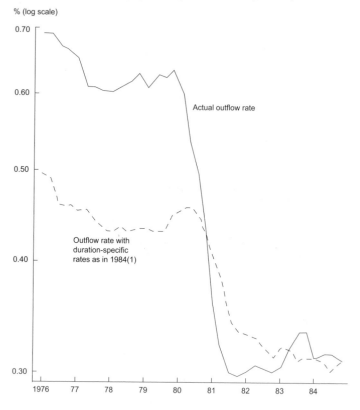

1.2.2. Employment Protection

If the cost of firing workers increases, employers will become more leary about hiring. Thus the proportion (g) of vacancies they are willing to fill per period will fall. Of course, at the same time the number of firings will fall also. Since in equilibrium firings equal hirings (a), in equilibrium a also falls. What happens to the u/v curve (and thus to equilibrium unemployment) depends on which of these effects dominates.

Let us begin with the facts about employment protection laws and then give evidence on their net effect. There have been three main changes. The Redundancy Payments Act 1965 introduced statutory payments when a worker is made redundant, a part of which is a direct cost to the employer. The Industrial Relations Act 1971 established legal rights against unfair dismissal (now covering all workers employed for over two years by the same employer). The Employment Protection Act 1975 extended the periods of notice required before termination.

Employment protection has been studied in some detail in Nickell (1979, 1982), with mixed results. The net impact on unemployment is unclear. As we have said, if it becomes more difficult or expensive for firms to reduce employment, this will reduce flows into unemployment. So employment protection must be a cause of the downward trend in inflow during the 1970s. But, by making employers more choosy in hiring, it will also reduce the outflow from unemployment. Both these effects were detected in Nickell (1982), but the net impact was in the direction of a reduction in unemployment. This result is, however, very tentative, since the variable used to capture the legislation (numbers of Industrial Tribunal cases) is clearly rather weak. Survey evidence is also ambiguous (see Jackman, Layard and Pissarides 1984). A survey by the CBI asked employers how (1) abolition or reduction of redundancy entitlements and (2) abolition or reduction of unfair dismissal rights would affect the number of their employees. The replies were

	Definitely increase employment	Possibly increase employment
Redundancy entitlements	5%	14%
Unfair dismissal rights	3%	7%

Thus, reverting to the u/v curve, it seems quite likely that employment protection has had little effect, reducing equilibrium a and g by roughly offsetting magnitudes.

1.2.3. Mismatch

Another variable affecting the location of the u/v curve is the mismatch (mm) between unemployment and vacancies. Other things equal, unemployment will tend to rise if the unemployed became less well matched to the vacancies available. We can therefore ask: Are structural factors an important part of the explanation for the rise in unemployment? This is a tough question. The first issue is which structural dimension matters most? Probably the most serious is the regional dimension. Hardly any of the unemployed find work in a different region from the one they worked in before. By contrast, two-thirds of men who became unemployed in autumn 1978 and found work within four months found it in a different industry (24 categories) or occupation (18 categories) from their previous job.

The next issue is how to measure mismatch. The most obvious concept of a good match is one where the ratio of unemployment to vacancies is the same in each region.[16] The incidence of structural unemployment could then be measured by the proportion of the unemployed who would have to be in a different region if perfect matching were secured. This is given by

$$mm = \frac{1}{2} \sum |u_i - v_i|$$

where u_i is the proportion of the unemployed in region i and v_i is the proportion of vacancies. This index is charted in Figure 1.14.[17] It shows that the degree of regional mismatch has been reduced.

Figure 1.14a

Mismatch Indices, 1964-1985

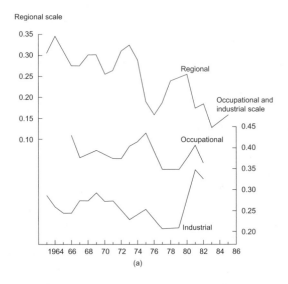

(a)

Figure 1.14b

Index of Change in the Industrial Composition of Employment, 1964-1983

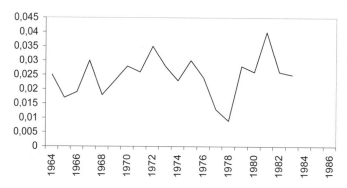

This may seem surprising, for many people feel that the amount of structural unemployment has risen. However, both statements are true. When we measure regional mismatch we are trying to find an index that could have *caused* an increase in unemployment. When we measure the amount of structural unemployment, we measure the *number* of unemployed people who would have to shift regions in order to restore proportionality between unemployment and vacancies. This is given by

$$SU = mm(uL).$$

In recent years structural unemployment has risen because of the increase in unemployment, but not because of an increase in mismatch. Mismatch has fallen, because the proportional rise in unemployment rates has been less in the high-unemployment regions. Structural unemployment has risen, because the *absolute* rise in unemployment rates has been greater in the high-unemployment regions.[18] But to see that regional imbalance is not a *cause* of the shift of the aggregate u/v curve, we have only to note that the proportional increase in unemployment at given vacancies is on average higher *within* each region than it is for the national aggregate.[19]

Turning to other dimensions of mismatch, we find in Figure 1.14 no obvious trend in occupational mismatch (similarly calculated). As regards industrial mismatch, however, this was high in 1981 and 1982. This measure depends classifying the unemployed by the industry of their last job, and unfortunately this analysis of the unemployed has now been discontinued, so we cannot tell how mismatch has been progressing recently in that dimension.

But it is important to form some view. Presumably, mismatch is increased by larger changes in the industrial structure of employment. Industrial structure did change quite sharply in 1981 and 1982, but this turbulence has now declined. To indicate this we show, in Figure 1.14, one half of the sum of the absolute changes in employment shares in each of 24 sectors.[20] There has been no major upward trend in this measure of turbulence since the early 1970s. In the econometric work reported earlier we used a simplified version of this index – namely, the absolute change in the share of unemployment falling within the "production industries." This suggested that since the 1960s increases in mismatch have raised wage pressure by 1 percentage point, implying a rise in unemployment of a little over 1 point.[21]

Our general conclusion is that increases in mismatch are not an important reason for the outward shift of the u/v curve. We also doubt whether employment protection is that important. So what could account for that part of the outward shift not explained by long-term unemployment?

1.2.4. Benefits

The obvious explanation is some aspect of the benefit system. Let us examine first the level of benefits. If, when productivity rises, benefits rise as much as wages, we should probably expect unemployment to remain unchanged. But if the replacement ratio (of benefits to net income in work) changed, we should expect unemployment to change. But the replacement ratio has changed little since the mid-1960s, though it has fluctuated considerably, rising by about 30 percent between the late 1950s and the late 1960s.[22] So the replacement ratio cannot explain much of the increase in unemployment since 1970.

A more important factor may be the administration of benefits, and the application of the work test. There is good evidence that this was applied less strictly from the later 1960s onward, even before the economic troubles of the 1970s (Layard 1986). Then during the 1970s the job centers became physically separated from the benefit offices, making it even more difficult to ensure that claimants were encouraged to seek work. Since 1982 claimants have not even been required to register at job centers. Casual impression also suggests that there have been profound changes in social attitudes to living on the dole – the most obvious of these being the attitudes of students. Thus, by a process of elimination, and on grounds of inherent plausibility, there is good reason to suppose that an important reason for the shift of the u/v curve has been changes in the intensity with which the unemployed seek work at given vacancies.

Jackman and Williams (1985) have used individual cross-section data to study the intensity of job search, as measured by the number of job applications; for men who became unemployed in autumn 1978 and were still unemployed four months later, the median number of applications was one per month. (The figure in the United States seems to be four times as high.) Application rates are lower for those made redundant than for those who quit. Since the unemployed now include a lower than usual proportion who quit, this might help to explain the outward shift of the u/v curve.

Jackman and Williams also find that application rates are affected by benefits. The effect of benefits on application rates is directly in line with the findings of Narendranathan, Nickell, and Stern (1985), who estimate the effect of benefits on job-finding using the same sample. The respective elasticities with respect to benefits were -0.25 and -0.40.[23] These elasticities are not high. They reflect the amount by which benefits displace the wage line in Figure 1.2 to the left. The total effect on unemployment should be slightly less than this. However, when we include the replacement ratio in our time-series wage equation, we estimate the total elasticity of unemployment with respect to benefits to be around 0.7 at the sample mean. Even this is not high. It implies that the 30 percent rise in the replacement ratio between the late 1950s and the late 1960s increased unemployment by only about 20 percent – or half a percentage point.

Finally, while we are considering the role of benefits, we must refer to a more indirect mechanism through which they may exert their influence. If benefits are available without time limit and without an effective work test, it is not surprising that, when employment is reduced by a major adverse shock, long-term unemployment develops with all the bad implications we have already discussed. A sensible solution seems to be the one advocated by Beveridge, that, after some time limit, public support for those without regular jobs should be provided through payment for work done (or training received) on a public program.

1.2.5. Unions

We come now to a radically different way of viewing the labor market, in which unions play a crucial role. As we have already said, we do not believe that specifically union-oriented analysis throws much light on the rise in unemployment since 1979, since it cannot also explain the shift in the u/v curve (which is evidently closely related to the rise in unemployment).[24] However, the unions are an important feature of the scene, and we must attempt to clarify their impact.

We can begin with union membership. Almost half of all employees in employment are members (roughly 60 percent of manual workers and 40 percent of white-collar). The rates vary widely between sectors, as the following figures for 1979 show (Bain 1983):

Manufacturing	
Manual	80%
White collar	44%
All	70%
Construction	37%
Private services	17%
Public sector	82%

About one-fifth of all workers are in closed shops, meaning that to hold the job they have to join the union. But more important are the proportion of workers whose wages are determined by collective bargaining, whether or not they themselves are union members. Of full-time workers in 1978, the proportions "covered" by collective agreements were 71 percent of men and 68 percent of women (New Earnings Survey for 1978). Most of the collective bargaining that matters is now with single employers, and the majority of that is at the plant level. Thus, if we confine ourselves to private sector employees, and ask what is the most important level of pay bargaining affecting their wages, the answers from the 1980 Workplace Industrial Relations Survey were as follows (Bain 1983):

Single-employer bargains	
Plant level	30%
Firm level	18%
Multi-employer arrangements	
National or regional bargains	21%

Wages councils	5%
Management decisions	26%

For non-manual workers, management decision is more common, and national or regional bargains less common. Likewise, for smaller establishments, managerial decision is more common and firm-level bargaining less so. The general conclusion is that, although 80 percent of unionists are now in the largest 22 unions, the pattern of bargaining is highly decentralized.

What are its effects? First, unions appear to raise the wages of manual male trade unionists by about 11 percent above those of other similar workers. This estimate comes from Stewart (1983) and is based on individual data from the National Training Survey. According to Stewart (1985), trade unions have affected wages mainly where there is a closed shop, especially where a pre-entry closed shop (now outlawed) existed.

To get some feeling for how the union mark-up has changed over time, we have to use a different procedure, based on a cross-section of industries rather than individuals (Layard, Metcalf and Nickell 1978). The results of this, updated and scaled for consistency with Stewart, are shown in Figure 1.15. This shows that the mark-up has tended to rise over time. During the 1970s the rise was accompanied by a rise in trade union membership and, at least up to 1973, can be taken as associated with autonomous wage-push (the end of deference and all that).

Figure 1.15

Estimated Mark-up of Union over Non Union Wages, 1955-1985

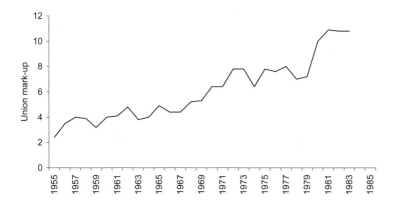

Since 1980 union membership has fallen somewhat, even among employees. One might therefore be inclined to explain the high mark-up in the 1980s by the disinflation of 1981-3, since deflation typically causes a rise in the union mark-up (Lewis 1963). On the other hand, Batstone (1984) reports that shop steward organization and activity has not declined significantly since 1980, and today's high mark-up may therefore in part reflect continued militancy.

If this is the effect of unions on wages, what is their effect on employment?[25] The effect is indirect. For unions do not normally bargain over the level of employment in their enterprises (Oswald and Turnbull 1985; Oswald 1987). Bargaining does take place when redundancies are proposed, but experience of the last five years shows that unions' ability to affect the scale of redundancy is limited. (They do of course frequently ensure that there is maximum use of voluntary redundancy, and that compulsory redundancy follows the principle of "last in first out.") Bargaining also takes place over manning levels, but this affects the ratio of employment to capital rather than the total level of employment. (Investment is not generally bargained over.) So bargains basically concern wages, and then employers determine employment subject to the wages that have been determined.

The outcome is unlikely to clear the market in the union sector. But what about the non-union sector? Will not this be market-clearing? Suppose it is. Then all unemployment will be voluntary. Jobs are always available in the non-union sector, and workers choose not to take them, either because they want a holiday, permanent or temporary (Minford 1985), or because it is more efficient to search for a union job while unemployed than while working in the non-union sector (Hall 1975).[26]

This model may be depicted as in Figure 1.16 (ignoring issues to do with search). A few points should be noted. First, the supply curve is rising as a function of the real wage in the competitive sector, given the level of real benefit. It is essential to recognize the diversity of human nature in this way, and misleading to say that wages in the competitive sector are determined at the level of benefit (plus or minus a fixed mark-up) – as though all workers were equally hard-working. According to our earlier estimate from Narendranathan, Nickell, and Stern (1985), the elasticity of this supply curve is in fact only 0.1 (when unemployment is 10 percent). The next point to note is that the demand for union labor depends on μW_c where μ is 1 plus the mark-up of the union over the non-union wage. Clearly, if μ rises, the aggregate labor demand curve DD moves to the left; competitive wages fall, and employment falls because fewer people are willing to work. This, in essence, is Minford's account of how unions destroy employment.

Figure 1.16

A Market-clearing Model of the Labor Market

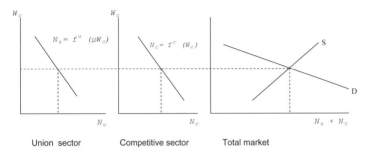

| Union sector | Competitive sector | Total market |

There is, however, one reason that makes it impossible to accept the model as a satisfactory stylization of the system. All the evidence suggests that even unskilled markets may fail to clear, and, even more important, that the degree to which they do clear varies sharply from period to period. This evidence comes from the answers of Confederation of British Industry employers to the question: Is your output likely to be limited in the next four months by shortages of (a) skilled labor, (b) other labor? The answers are graphed in Figure 1.17. They show how unhelpful is the assumption of continuous market-clearing. They also show that the less skilled occupations (which in Confederation of British Industry firms tend to be less unionized) have a particular excess supply of labor.[27]

Figure 1.17

Shortage of Skilled and Other Labor

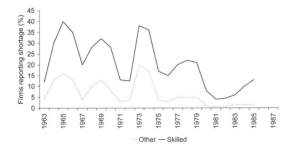

If the market-clearing framework helps little, how can one conceive of the effect of union power upon employment? We adopt a simple synthetic approach. In some cases wages are set by firms, and *their* efficiency wages may not be market-clearing. In other cases unions play a role in bargaining, and again their pushfulness will raise the degree of wage pressure. The final outcome is one where at prevailing wages more people are wanting work than there is work available. Most of them eventually get into work through the process of matching the unemployed to vacancies. Benefits slow down the speed of this matching and thus create wage pressure and reduce employment. Union power also creates wage pressure and reduces employment. In our estimates, the increase in the trade union mark-up since the 1960s has raised wage pressure by 3-4 percentage points and unemployment by 2-3 points.

1.2.6. Incomes Policy

A standard way to reduce wage pressure is through incomes policy. A glance at Figure 1.5 shows the powerful effect of the 1975-7 incomes policy on the rate of wage inflation. (In 1975-6 the £6 a week limit equaled 10 percent of average pay, and in 1976-7 the limit was 5 percent.) Wadhwani (1985) has traced these dynamic effects in a quarterly model. Our annual model has been less successful at picking them up.

Of course, after 1977 the policy began to break down,[28] making some rise in unemployment after 1979 quite likely. A major problem arose from the inability of unions to control their shop stewards. This made the TUC unwilling to endorse the policy formally after the first two years (even though it did not oppose it). Bruno and Sachs (1985) have suggested that countries responded best to the oil shock of 1973 if they had rather centralized wage bargaining, making possible "corporatist" solutions (as in Austria and Sweden). In more recent work with Bean, Layard, and Nickell (1986), we have further explored this and shown that, among 17 OECD countries, the *more* centralized countries have "target" real consumption wages that respond *more* strongly to unemployment and to falls in the "feasible" real consumption wage. In the scale of corporativeness Britain ranks twelfth – near the bottom. This means that it is peculiarly vulnerable to supply shocks.

1.2.7. Taxes and Import Prices

A supply shock is anything that reduces the feasible real consumption wage at given employment. If we write w^* as the log of the wage (so that $w = w^* + t_1$ where t_1 is employers' labor taxes), then the log real consumption wage is

$$w^* - t_2 - (\overline{p} + t_3) + \text{constant}$$

where t_2 is the personal tax rate, t_3 is the indirect tax rate, and $\overline{p}$ is the log final output price. The relation of the latter to the price of value added (p) is given by

$$\overline{p} = p + v(p_m - p)$$

where p_m is the log price of imports and v the share of imports in GDP. Thus the log real consumption wage is

$$w - p - t_1 - t_2 - t_3 - v(p_m - p) + \text{constant}.$$

If $w - p$ remains constant, then the real consumption wage falls whenever there is a rise in taxes or in relative import prices. Thus, if taxes or relative import prices rise, and workers try to maintain their real consumption wage, they will push up $w - p$ and unemployment will have to rise to restore equilibrium. It is only if rises in taxes or relative import prices are voluntarily absorbed by workers that they do not generate wage pressure.

We estimate that all taxes except t_1 are voluntarily absorbed in the long run, but that employers' labor taxes and rises in relative import prices do increase unemployment. Since the 1960s, we tentatively estimate that labor taxes raised wage pressure by 1.5 points, and unemployment by between 1 and 2 points. The rise in relative import prices in the early 1970s raised wage pressure by 3.5 points and unemployment by 2 points, but developments in the 1980s have been more favorable, and we await their further course with bated breath.

It has often been suggested that the falls in productivity growth in the 1970s caused problems because they were resisted in wage demands. But we found no evidence that falls in productivity growth generated wage pressure.

1.2.8. Conclusion

Thus, to understand unemployment we have to understand the wage pressure generated at a given level of unemployment. This is now very high owing to the high proportion of long-term unemployed. Looking back over the last 15 years, wage pressure has increased partly because of union militancy, partly because of taxes, and partly because of easier social security. Mismatch has contributed little to the increase in unemployment. Even so, it is a serious problem, and we would be much better off if we had a better match between the structure of labor demand and supply. We turn now to this subject.

1.3. Relative Wage Rigidity and the Structure of Employment

In the preceding section we focused on the aggregate labor market, analyzing its problems in terms of the inflexibility of the general level of real wages. In this section we look at the flexibility or otherwise of the relative wages of different groups, and ask how far this accounts for mismatch or other problems. There are at least five dimensions of matching that are important: industry, region, skill, age, and sex.

1.3.1. Industry

We shall begin with industrial structure; for, even though many workers are not closely attached to industries, it is changes in industrial structure that primarily affect the fortunes of the different regions. The basic change in industrial structure has been the huge decline in manufacturing employment (Figure 1.18). This has certainly led to a migration of workers out of manufacturing, but to little change in relative wages. These processes have been studied in detail by Pissarides (1978) and Pissarides and McMaster (1984). Movement of workers between industries was found to respond to sector-specific vacancies and to relative wages, with both playing a roughly equal role in the redeployment of labor. But the role of wages is not particularly functional, since wages do not respond to sector-specific vacancies as much as to aggregate vacancies in the economy as a whole.[29]

Figure 1.18

Manufacturing and Non-Manufacturing Employees in Employment, 1973-1986

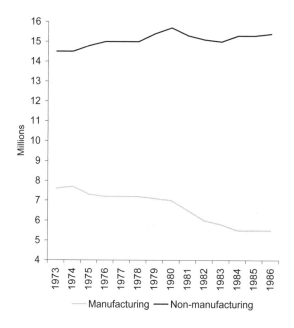

1.3.2. Region

Turning to the more serious problem of regional imbalance, workers do tend to leave the high-unemployment regions (in net terms). But the movement is much less than it would be if we had a more flexible housing market (see for example Hughes and McCormick 1981). Moreover, the wage structure plays a small role in the adjustment process. It is remarkable how similar wages are in the different regions despite the huge differences in unemployment. This reflects the fact that relative wages react very weakly to unemployment differences (Pissarides and McMaster 1984). In the upshot, if a region starts with 1 point of unemployment above the national average, it will experience 12 man-years of unemployment before all excess unemployment has been eliminated. Thus, to evaluate regional policy, one could compute the present value of a policy to create a lower productivity job in the region or permit the outmigration to occur toward higher-productivity regions.

1.3.3. Skill

One of the most basic facts about unemployment is that it is concentrated on manual workers, and nearly half of it on semi- and unskilled manual workers. In 1983 male unemployment rates were

Non-manual	5%
Skilled manual	12%
Semi- and unskilled manual	23%

Why is this?

There is no doubt that relative wages affect the relative demand for labor at different skill levels. Nissim (1984), working on certain engineering industries, estimated the Allen elasticity of substitution between skilled and semi-skilled workers at around 2.5 (s.e. = 0.3). This is crudely illustrated in Figure 1.19 (crudely because the Allen elasticity is not the same as a "direct" elasticity).

Figure 1.19

The Relative Demand for Non-skilled Workers, 1979 and 1985

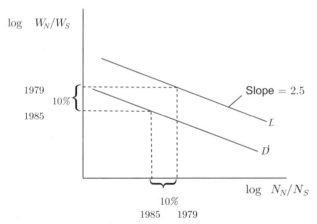

Given the effect of wages on demand, low-wage differentials seem an obvious explanation of the unemployment of the less-skilled. Such differentials might be due to union preferences for equality,[30] or to employers' concepts of efficiency wages – or even of fair wages. Wages councils do not appear to be a major explanation, since only about 1.5 million workers are covered by them alone and not also by collective bargaining.

One cannot estimate how flexible skill differentials are with respect to relative unemployment rates, since there is no adequate time-series of unemployment rates by skill. However, the evidence of the Family Expenditure Survey suggests that unemployment rates for the less skilled have risen roughly in proportion to unemployment rates for the skilled (Micklewright 1984). In other words, the proportional fall in employment has been twice as great for the less-skilled as for the skilled manual workers. At the same time, differentials have widened for men to an extraordinary degree. Thus relative unskilled wages (say at the bottom decile) have fallen since 1979 by roughly 10 percent relative to the mean. This is illustrated in Figure 1.19.

If both relative employment and relative wages have fallen, relative demand must have fallen substantially. With an elasticity of substitution of 2.5, relative demand must have fallen by around a third. This is a huge change. It must reflect partly increasing mechanization and partly the reduction of relative overmanning. But it brings into sharp focus the problems now facing the less skilled.

In such a situation there are two possible solutions. One is to improve the relative employment of the less skilled by subsidies to employers of less skilled labor (Layard 1985). This can reduce the NAIRU by matching demand more closely to supply. The other is to train the less skilled and thus reduce the NAIRU by matching supply more closely to demand. In any normal optimization exercise, a bit of both would be indicated.

This brings us to the subject of training. If unemployment is due partly to rigid relative wages, the social returns to training are huge and greatly exceed the private returns (Johnson and Layard 1986). For suppose that at the NAIRU skilled labor was fully employed and unskilled was not. The social return to training an unskilled person to be skilled would be the marginal product of skilled labor (rather more if skilled labor and less-skilled are complementary so that more skilled labor raises the demand for the less-skilled). But what are the private returns to training – to the firm and the worker combined? They are the skilled wage minus the unskilled wage (after adjusting both for the probability of employment). When there is involuntary unemployment of the less skilled, there is thus a huge externality in the returns to training.

This provides a strong argument for state subsidization. Other arguments stem from imperfect capital markets (higher cost of capital for workers than firms), biased information, and so on. For these reasons, the Industrial Training Act 1964 set up a levy-grant system whereby firms paid a small percentage of payroll into a fund but were rebated if they spent an equivalent amount on training. As time went by, the system lost its marginal effect as the percentage of payroll was so low relative to the amount that firms were paying anyway. Yet despite this, firms were paying remarkably little. In consequence, the general view is that British workmen are less well trained than those in other European countries (Prais 1981). The government now organizes a two-year Youth Training Scheme which is open to all children who leave school at 16. But the second year of this has been introduced only this year, and it remains to be seen how effective it will be. Under present arrangements it will still be perfectly possible (which it is not in Germany) for someone to go straight into employment at 16 and to receive no training at all.[31] And even if the Youth Training Scheme does well, there will remain major shortcomings at the level of technician training and school education.[32]

1.3.4. Age

There are two dimensions of supply which the individual is powerless to affect: age and sex. Over time, youth unemployment has risen hugely relative to adult unemployment. This is due partly to relative wages, partly to relative population movements, and partly to general economic conditions. For the period 1959-85, the following regression explained relative male youth unemployment quite well:[33]

$$\log \frac{u_Y}{u_A} = 2.31 + 3.4 \log \frac{W_Y}{W_A} + 0.42 \log \frac{POP_Y}{POP_A} - 0.20 \log v$$
$$\phantom{\log \frac{u_Y}{u_A} = 2.31 + } (7.0) \qquad\qquad (0.9) \qquad\qquad (2.1)$$

s.e. = 0.14, D.W. = 1.37 (t-statistics in brackets)

where W_Y/W_A is relative hourly earnings, POP_Y/POP_A is 15-19-year-olds relative to 15-60-year-olds, and v is the vacancy rate.

Up to the mid 1970s, relative wages were a potent force in explaining the rise. No one fully understands why relative wages rose so much, but the best explanation seems to be the desire of collective bargainers to pay adult rates at ever earlier ages (Layard 1982). Since the late 1970s relative youth wages have if anything fallen, presumably in response to relative unemployment. But at the same time the economic situation has worsened and relative population movements have been adverse to youth (up to now, but with an improvement hereafter). All in all, however, the performance of the British labor market in providing jobs for young people in recent years has been nothing but dismal.

1.3.5. Sex

When we come to sex differences in the workforce, we have to start with the huge increase in female participation. This is one of the most profound social changes of our time. After a small hiccough in the early l980s, it seems to be proceeding unabated. The increase is entirely on the part of currently married women, the participation rate of other women having been more or less constant for the last 30 years. Most of the increase has been of part-time work.

What has caused the rush of women to the labor market? The natural first step is to look at wage levels. Women's hourly wages were very stable relative to men's up to the early 1970s (at nearly 65 percent). The Equal Pay Act outlawed separate pay scales for men and women, and as a result women's earnings rose to around 75 percent of men's, where they have stayed ever since. How much of this difference reflects continuing discrimination is a difficult issue. Zabalza and Arrufat (1983) argue that at least two-thirds of it reflects differences in work experience and other measurable variables; Stewart and Greenhalgh (1984) seem to indicate something more like a half.

But how far do wage movements explain the rise in women's labor supply? Up to the mid-1970s the real wages of men and women rose at roughly the same rate. Rises in men's wages tend to decrease women's labor supply (through negative income and substitution effects); rises in women's wages tend to increase it (through a large positive substitution effect, offset by a small income effect). The key issue is the relative size of these two effects. As Joshi, Layard, and Owen (1985, p. 149) show, elasticities estimated from cross-section data suggest that general wage changes cannot explain by any means all of the increase in women's participation in the early 1970s. They are however quite successful at explaining the rise in women's participation *since* the early 1970s. It is, however, remarkable that these changes have persisted so strongly in the face of the adverse economic situation.

This brings us to the question of women's employment. One would suppose on the demand side that the externally imposed rise in relative wages would have reduced relative employment. The reverse has happened. Even if we confine ourselves to the private sector, the ratio of female person-hours to male has risen since the early 1970s (see Joshi, Layard and Owen 1985).

Two factors must account for this. The first is the shift in labor demand toward more female-intensive industries (especially services). This indeed accounts for a part of the increase. But a fixed weight demand index[34] accounts for only half of the rise in relative female employment since 1970.

What can account for the rest? Relative wage movements would have suggested a fall. Against this, the Sex Discrimination Act which also became operative in 1976 outlawed discrimination in employment on grounds of sex. This might have been interpreted to mean that employers should not reduce relative employment when relative wages were raised by the Equal Pay Act. But one would not have expected a rise in relative employment.

One explanation may be employment protection. This might lead firms to prefer part-time workers; but in fact, only those working less than 16 hours a week are exempt and two-thirds of part-time women work more than this. (Until 1975, all workers under 21 hours were exempt – or about two-thirds of part-time women workers.)

Given the buoyant employment position of women, one naturally asks whether there might not have been a growing mismatch in terms of sex between the pattern of jobs on offer and the pattern of labor supplied. To answer this, we first need evidence on the relative unemployment rates of men and women. Using survey-based estimates, we find that in the early 1970s female unemployment was about 50 percent higher than male, becoming similar in the late 1970s and about 20 percent lower than male in the 1980s (Table 1.3). This suggests that mismatch may have been lower in the late 1970s. However, to obtain a more exact measure, we need to estimate the share of vacancies that was "female-oriented." To do this, we take the vacancies in each two-digit industry and divide them between men and women in proportion to employment in that industry. We then construct the index $U_f/U - V_f/V$ and find some evidence that this was positive in the 1970s and negative in the 1980s (Table 1.3). However, the mismatch now in favor of women is not much greater than the mismatch in favor of men earlier.

Table 1.3

Mismatch in Job Opportunities by Sex

	Unemployment rates			Index
	Male	Female	Female-male	$\dfrac{U_f}{U} - \dfrac{V_f}{V}$
	(1)	(2)	(3)	(4)
1971	3.4	5.1	1.7	-1.0
1972	4.6	7.9	3.3	6.2
1973	3.4	5.5	2.1	9.7
1974	4.0	4.9	0.9	2.7
1975	4.9	5.0	0.1	-3.4
1976	6.5	8.5	2.0	6.9
1977	6.4	8.5	2.1	8.0
1978	6.8	8.6	1.8	-6.4
1979	6.9	7.4	0.5	1.7
1980	6.6	6.9	0.3	-1.4
1981	10.8	10.1	-0.7	-6.1
1982	12.7	10.0	-2.7	-7.4
1983	12.2	9.4	-2.8	-9.8
1984	12.8	11.4	-1.4	-6.4

1.3.6. Conclusion

In sum, the behavior of relative wages does not do much to even out the relative imbalances in the labor market generated by shocks to demand (as between industries, regions, or skills) or to supply (as with changes in the number of young people). There is however *some* flexibility in relative wages by skill, but this is not enough to prevent a large relative oversupply of the less-skilled.

2

Why Does Unemployment Persist?

Richard Layard and Charles Bean pursue the line of argument developed in the previous 1987 article with their 1989 paper on the question of unemployment persistence. Sections 1 and 2 of this article have been selected for this volume in order to show that the main movements of unemployment correspond to fluctuations in the short-run NAIRU around a stable long-term NAIRU. These supply-side fluctuations have two main origins: first, variations in the number of "labor market insiders" involved in wage setting, and second, variations in the effectiveness of the unemployed "outsiders" as potential job-seekers. The evidence of micro-level studies suggests that the latter factor is more important than the first one, and this helps to explain the widespread shift outwards in the u/v curve, too. To derive these arguments more rigorously, the article presents a parsimonious model of efficiency wages and another of collective bargaining.

2.1. Introduction and Summary

Macroeconomics was invented to explain the persistence of unemployment. In thinking about this issue there are three key facts to be accounted for. Fact 1 is persistence itself: if unemployment becomes unusually high, it does not quickly revert to its earlier level, and the same is true if it becomes abnormally low. This is true in all countries and is illustrated for Britain in Figure 2.1. As the figure shows, the history of unemployment consists of some minor wiggles plus occasional major changes of level. The main movements of unemployment do not correspond to business cycle fluctuations which correct themselves within a few years.[1]

This chapter represents sections 1 and 2 of Layard, R., Bean, C. (1989). Why Does Unemployment Persist?, in: Scandinavian Journal of Economics, 91(2), 371-388. By permission of Oxford University Press.

However, Fact 2 is that unemployment is in the long run untrended. In other words there is a long-run "natural" rate of unemployment to which the system tends eventually to return. To avoid the suggestion that this is beyond the power of man to affect we shall call this the long-run NAIRU (Non-Accelerating-Inflation Rate of Unemployment) – meaning the level of unemployment at which there is no upward or downward pressure on the inflation rate (or more precisely no "price surprises"). The fact that the unemployment rate is untrended is quite remarkable, given the large changes in labor force which have occurred in most countries, mainly for demographic reasons. In the long run employment follows the labor force, and any meaningful model of the economy must reflect this tendency.

Figure 2.1

Unemployment in the United Kingdom, 1900-1985

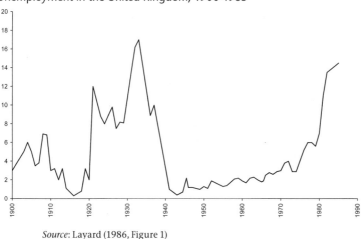

Source: Layard (1986, Figure 1)

Fact 3 is that unemployment is often far from the long-run NAIRU without any upward or downward pressure on inflation. In the late 1980s European inflation has been very stable despite high unemployment; it was also stable in the 1950s and 1960s despite low unemployment. This means that in any year the prevailing (or short-run) NAIRU can be far away from the long-run NAIRU. In fact very little of the variation in unemployment is associated with changes in inflation (or "price surprises"). It follows that most of the variation in unemployment reflects the evolution of the short-run NAIRU. Thus the short-run NAIRU has to become one of the central concepts in macroeconomics. The aim of this paper is to explain its evolution.

As we shall see, the initial impulse changing unemployment may come either from demand or supply shocks. But after such a shock, the continuing evolution of unemployment is most fruitfully thought of in terms of the evolution of the short-run NAIRU.[2]

This is a story of the supply side of the economy. One then asks: What causes such persistence in the economy's capacity to produce without increasing (or decreasing) inflation? One answer is in terms of the evolution of the physical capital stock (Malinvaud 1982). As Modigliani et al. (1987) argue this is not very plausible. The number of workers per machine, office, or restaurant can be varied on any shift; the number of shifts can be varied; and new capacity can be quite quickly installed. The history of investment also suggests that capacity responds quickly to its rate of utilization. Thus, as Blanchard (1988) also argues, the main supply constraint originates in the labor market itself.

2.1.1. How the NAIRU is Determined

To understand how this constraint operates, the first step is to develop the basic theory of the NAIRU. Unemployment is in equilibrium only when there is consistency between the intended mark-up of prices over wages and the intended mark-up of wages over prices (Blanchard 1986). The NAIRU brings peace in the battle of the mark-ups.

Beginning with prices, firms set these on the basis of marginal cost. Thus in general

$$(1) \qquad\qquad p - w^e = a_0 - a_1 u,$$

where p is the logarithm of the price of output (value-added), w^e is the logarithm of the expected wage, u is the unemployment rate, and a_0 captures the effects of technical progress, the capital/labor-force ratio, and the degree of monopoly power in product markets. If the elasticity of product demand is constant, unemployment must reduce the price level for given wages if it raises the marginal product of labor. However a_1 could be zero (normal-cost pricing) if the marginal product was constant or if the elasticity of demand rose sufficiently in a boom.

Thus firms are setting prices as a mark-up on expected wages. By contrast wage-setters set wages as a mark-up on expected prices, the mark-up being lower the more unemployment there is. Thus

$$(2) \qquad\qquad w - p^e = b_0 - b_1 u.$$

To close the model we can assume an aggregate demand equation of the form

$$(3) \qquad\qquad u = c_0 - c_1 (m - p),$$

where m is the logarithm of the money stock. In the very short run equations (1)–(3) determine unemployment, wages, and prices.

But if there are no nominal surprises ($p - p^e = w - w^e = 0$) then, by adding (1) and (2), unemployment is at the NAIRU given by

$$\text{NAIRU} = u^* = \frac{a_0 + b_0}{a_1 + b_1}.$$

This is illustrated in Figure 2.2. Aggregate real demand is purely passive.

If however there *are* price surprises, then actual unemployment is

$$(4) \qquad\qquad u = \frac{a_0 + b_0 - (p - p^e) - (w - w^e)}{a_1 + b_1}.$$

Low unemployment is associated with positive price surprises and vice versa. However equation (4) is not a Lucas supply curve. It is a relationship obtained from price- and wage-setting behavior – based in other words on the battle for distributive shares. If unemployment is too low, price-setters will be aiming at a profit mark-up incompatible with the real wage intended by wage-setters. The mechanism by which this inconsistency is resolved is the price and wage surprise (generally associated with changing inflation or changing prices, whichever variable is currently untrended).

Figure 2.2

The NAIRU (with $p - p^e = w - w^e = 0$)

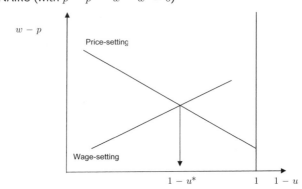

If by contrast there are no wage and price surprises, then unemployment is at just the right level to bring peace in the struggle for shares. The leap-frogging of prices over wages and vice versa has been eliminated. We have also eliminated the leap-frogging of wages over wages (not modeled here) by ensuring that each group settles for the same wage as all equivalent groups, rather than trying to improve its relativity.

In this model pricing behavior is relatively straightforward, and in equilibrium ensures that each group of labor is employed on the labor demand curve. But will each group also be employed on its labor supply curve? It could be so, in which case (2) can indeed be thought of as the labor supply curve. But job-queues exist widely and we shall therefore focus on those cases where more workers are willing to work at the prevailing wage than can find work.

This does not mean that we think all unemployment is involuntary. It may well be the case that everybody could get some job. In other words there is a "secondary" labor market which is market-clearing. But there is also a larger "primary" sector where job queues exist. Many of those who cannot get primary sector jobs are unwilling to take lower-paid and nastier jobs in the secondary sector. So unemployment results (Bulow and Summers 1986; Johnson and Layard 1986). And in practice movements in unemployment are mainly the result of movements in primary sector employment. Since most of the action takes place in this sector we shall henceforth ignore the role of the secondary sector.

2.1.2. What Stops the Wage Dropping and What Causes Persistence?

Two questions immediately arise: (i) What stops the wage dropping in the face of an excess supply of labor? (ii) What causes unemployment deviations to persist?

There are two main mechanisms which can cause wages to be above the supply price of labor. First, employers may voluntarily pay more – the case of efficiency wages. Second, they may be forced to pay more – the case of collective bargaining with unions.

But what causes persistence in each of these cases? Again there are two main mechanisms. First, there is the "insider" mechanism. If the number of employed people falls due to some shock, the wage pressure at given unemployment will rise as there are fewer workers worried about their jobs. This effect most naturally operates when there are unions who can organize the insiders. Second, there is an "outsider" mechanism. If the unemployed "outsiders" are demoralized or stigmatized by, for example, long spells of unemployment, the wage pressure at given unemployment will also rise – because the effective excess supply of labor is reduced. This "outsider" effect can operate whether wages are set by employers (efficiency wages) or by bargaining with unions.

In the rest of this overview we shall therefore review first the insider mechanism and then the outsider mechanism in a fairly schematic way. Then we shall explicitly derive the efficiency wage and the bargained wage, and show exactly how insider and outsider considerations operate within each.

2.1.3. Insider Power

We begin with the role of insider power in generating persistence. This has been stressed both by Lindbeck and Snower (1988) and Blanchard and Summers (1986). It is convenient to begin with Blanchard and Summers' most extreme version of the story, which (unlike some their later models) leads to total hysteresis – that is, employment follows a random walk with drift.

The idea is that insiders fix real wages to ensure their continued employment. If a shock reduces the number of insiders, next period's employment (with no further shocks) will be lower by the same amount. Thus the "natural" level of employment this period (N^*) is simply equal to last period's actual employment (N_{-1}). Allowing for turnover at rate s, employment would be expected to drift down, unless there were positive shocks or sufficient risk aversion for workers to select N^* much higher than $(1 - s)N_{-1}$.

The model outlined above is one of "pure hysteresis," with employment showing no tendency to converge on a given proportion of the labor force. Alternatively one could allow for an independent effect of outside unemployment, giving a model with "partial hysteresis." There would then be convergence to a long-run NAIRU but the short-run NAIRU would be much affected by recent levels of employment.

The most obvious source of insider power would come from trade union activity. This might help to explain the greater persistence of unemployment in recent years in Europe than in the U.S. (though in the 1930s, when unions everywhere were weak, the degree of persistence was the other way round).

Models of unemployment that focus on insider power leave much of the time-series variation of unemployment unexplained:[3]

(a) The *extreme* version of pure hysteresis is inconsistent with our original Fact 2: in the long run the *labor force* clearly affects the level of employment. Furthermore in wage equations for 19 OECD countries over the period 1952-82 the negative effect of the labor force upon wages on average exactly offsets the positive effect of employment suggesting that it is only unemployment that matters (Layard 1986). This explains *why* the labor force ultimately affects employment, one for one. Indeed Arrow (1974) has emphasized that a major triumph of economics as a social science is that it alone can explain this.

Thus the *extreme version* of insider power with pure hysteresis can be rejected. But does not the insider model still provide the main reason why the short-run NAIRU can diverge so long from the long-run NAIRU? Probably not. For there are two further facts which do not support the exclusive role of the insider mechanism in accounting for persistence.

(b) In microeconomic *panel data studies* of firms, it is possible to examine the independent effect upon wages of (i) lagged employment within the firm and (ii) the unemployment rate in the *outside* labor market. The evidence is that outside unemployment has a powerful effect and inside employment (lagged) a weak effect, if any (Nickell and Wadhwani 1988; Nickell and Kong 1988). This illustrates a general point about the future of macroeconomic research. There is little power in aggregate time series to discriminate between competing macroeconomic theories. There is, however, a wealth of disaggregated and microeconomic data which can also be brought to bear, both in distinguishing between models and in measuring the magnitude of parameters. Integration of this information should lead to a far better understanding of the mechanisms at work – so that the right policy conclusions can be drawn.

(c) There is a third key fact which is inconsistent with the insider model. This is the *huge movement of the unemployment-vacancy* (u/v) *curve* in most countries where unemployment has risen sharply. If the insider model were correct, a large rise in unemployment should have no effect on the location of the u/v curve but should simply lead to a collapse in the vacancy rate. Yet in Britain there is now the same vacancy rate as in 1959 while unemployment is five times as high (see Figure 2.3). Britain is perhaps an extreme case, but in most high-unemployment countries the u/v curve has shifted out (Johnson and Layard 1986).

Figure 2.3

Vacancies and Male Unemployment, 1957-1985

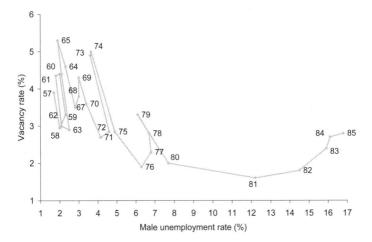

2.1.4. Outsider Ineffectiveness

To explain the shift of the u/v curve, one naturally turns to the characteristics of the unemployed. Have they become less well matched to the available vacancies (in terms of location, industry, or skill)? There is no clear evidence that mismatch (except perhaps by skill) has worsened (Jackman and Roper 1987). Perhaps they have become more choosy about which jobs they will accept? But there is little evidence that unemployment benefits have suddenly become more generous.

A key fact is that the unemployed have now been out of work for very much longer than in the past. There is also clear evidence that in all countries the rate at which unemployed people find work is at any instant much lower for long-term than for short-term unemployed. In Britain the rate is but one-tenth of its initial value for those who have been unemployed over 4 years. Psychological evidence indicates that this is largely due to the effect of prolonged unemployment, rather than heterogeneity among those who become unemployed (Warr and Jackson 1985). The time-series evidence on the movement of exit rates at different durations also supports this thesis (Jackman and Layard 1987).

If this is so, long-term unemployment reduces the "effectiveness" of unemployed people as job-seekers – lowering their motivation, morale, and skills and their quality as perceived by employers. Given this, it is easy to see how the u/v curve can shift out if the unemployed include a higher proportion of long-term unemployed. Econometric evidence supports the view that in many countries this has been an important mechanism shifting out the u/v curve (Budd, Levine, and Smith 1987; Franz 1987). For the same reason unemployment exerts less downward pressure on wages if a high proportion of the unemployed have been out of work for a long time (Layard and Nickell 1987, see Chapter 1).

We have here a clear mechanism generating persistence. An adverse shock reduces employment. This reduces the outflow from unemployment. In consequence, a higher proportion of the unemployed have experienced long spells without work. This means that wage pressure at given unemployment is lower than it would otherwise be. Since the duration structure of unemployment is itself a function of current and past levels of unemployment, there is a long-run NAIRU. But in the short-term the NAIRU will exceed this, due to the high proportion of long-term unemployed.

Our original model therefore has to be modified as follows. We still have the same price equation (1) as before, but the wage equation is now

$$(2') \qquad\qquad w - p^e = b_0 - b_1 \bar{c} u$$

where $\bar{c}$ is an index of the average "effectiveness" of the unemployed outsiders. This effectiveness depends negatively on the average duration of unemployment, which in turn is positively related to past levels of unemployment. Allowing first for only one lag, we can approximate "effective unemployment," $\bar{c}u$, by

(5) $$\bar{c}u = c_0 + c_1u - c_2u_{-1} \qquad (c_2 < c_1).$$

We can now investigate how the short-run NAIRU evolves in this system, once unemployment has been displaced from the long-run NAIRU. To do this we proceed as usual by setting $p - p^e = w - w^e = 0$, and then add equations (1) and (2'), after first substituting in (2') for $\bar{c}u$. This gives an unemployment equation of the form

$$0 = d_0 - d_1u + d_2u_{-1} \qquad (d_1 > d_2)$$

where $d_0 = a_0 + b_0 - c_0b_1$, $d_1 = a_1 + b_1c_1$ and $d_2 = b_1c_2$. This equation governs the evolution of the short-run NAIRU. Clearly the long-run NAIRU is given by:

Long-run NAIRU $= u^* = \dfrac{d_0}{d_1 - d_2}$.

But the short-run NAIRU is

Short-run NAIRU $= \dfrac{d_0 + d_2u_{-1}}{d_1} = \dfrac{(d_1 - d_2)u^* + d_2u_{-1}}{d_1}$.

Thus in this model the short-run NAIRU always lies between the long-run NAIRU and last period's unemployment. It is a weighted average of the two, with weights depending on the ratio of d_2 to d_1. As d_2 tends to d_1, we tend to the special case of pure hysteresis, with the short-run NAIRU equal to last period's unemployment. But in general we have a system in which (given no further price surprises) unemployment converges monotonically on the long-run NAIRU. Each period the change in unemployment is

$$u - u_{-1} = \frac{d_1 - d_2}{d_1}(u^* - u_{-1}),$$

so that a given fraction of the divergence is eliminated each period. This is the semi-comforting story that, if unemployment is high, it can always be reduced somewhat without inflationary pressure, but not by going directly to the long-run NAIRU.

However this story is rather too simple. For the evidence is that c depends on at least two lags of unemployment (Layard and Nickell 1987, see Chapter 1). Hence a more accurate representation of the NAIRU process is

$$(6) \qquad 0 = d_0 - d_1 u + d_2 u_{-1} + d_3 \Delta u_{-1} \qquad (d_1 > d_2),$$

where Δ denotes a first difference. This has the same long-run NAIRU. But after a one-off shock unemployment will now cycle before it converges on u^*. It can easily be the case that, if in one period unemployment is shocked upward from the long-run NAIRU, the short-run NAIRU in the next period is higher than this period's unemployment.[4] This may well have been the case in many European countries after the two oil shocks, which helps to explain why it took so much unemployment to get inflation down.

We have talked so far as if the mechanism of persistence is only due to the ineffectiveness of the outsiders. We do not believe that. We also think the insider mechanism matters. Thus the dynamics in equation (6) in practice reflects both outsider and insider mechanisms.

Clearly the parameters of the persistence process in equation (6) depend on labor market institutions. For example the degree of persistence will be higher when unemployment benefits last indefinitely (thus raising c_2). Similarly reducing the role of insiders by limiting union power or alternatively ensuring that the interests of outsiders are respected in the wage-setting process as in the fully corporatist economies of the Nordic countries reduces persistence.[5]

2.1.5. Some Concepts

Before going into greater detail we must clarify various matters of terminology. First, equilibrium. Our theory is one in which there is an equilibrium level of unemployment, the long-run NAIRU. This is not a market-clearing situation, nor indeed are most equilibria in natural or social sciences. It is a situation to which the system tends to return. There is also a short-run or temporary equilibrium, corresponding to the absence of price surprises.

Next, rationing. In product markets we shall assume monopolistic competition. Thus all firms are rationed, in the sense that they would like to sell more at the prevailing price. But they have fixed the price. By contrast workers without jobs are rationed because someone else has fixed the price (or rather the wage): at the prevailing wage no firm has an incentive to hire more workers. Whether we are in equilibrium or not, there is always rationing of this kind.

If we are in equilibrium, the level of employment is determined wholly by the supply side of the economy. Real aggregate demand has adjusted passively to the capacity of the economy to employ workers at constant inflation. Out of long-run equilibrium, there are two possible situations. In one, aggregate demand is extremely active, and forcing the economy to a level of unemployment different from the short-run NAIRU. In the other case aggregate demand is passive and merely lets the labor market evolve along the path of the short-run NAIRU.

We implicitly assume optimizing behavior by individual agents at all times. But this does not lead to market-clearing, due to transactions costs and other externalities and imperfections.

Finally, there is the relation of unemployment to real wages. If the real wage implied in price-setting is higher when unemployment is higher (as is assumed in Figure 2.2), then one *could* say that unemployment was high because real wages were too high to sustain employment. This is the line taken by Bruno and Sachs (1985). But this focus can be quite misleading. For, if there were "normal cost pricing," so that the price line were flat, the story would be quite wrong. Real wages could never be too high. By contrast if the price line had ever so small a slope, one could explain a huge amount of unemployment by a minute displacement of the real wage. The truth is that the whole approach gets us only a little way. For it does not tell us why wages are set as they are. For this we need to bring in the wage-setting line. It is the relationship between the two which *explains* unemployment.

2.2. Helpful Theories of Unemployment

Any fruitful theory of unemployment revolves around the battle of the mark-ups of prices over wages and vice versa. Unemployment has to be high enough to prevent the wage-price spiral *and* the wage-wage spiral. This is so whether wages are set by firms or by union bargaining.

2.2.1. Efficiency Wages

Let us begin with the case where firms set wages unilaterally. It has long been a commonplace of personnel management that wages should be set in a way that helps the firm to "recruit, retain, and motivate" staff. There is plenty of evidence that pay can have important effects on all these dimensions of performance. Wages have been shown to affect job queues (Holzer, Katz and Krueger 1988), quits (Pencavel 1972), absenteeism (Krueger and Summers 1988), and output (Wadhwani and Wall 1991).

Efficiency wage models trace out the implications of these facts for the behavior of rational firms, and thus for the equilibrium of the system. Different models concentrate on different mechanisms. For example Shapiro and Stiglitz (1984) show how firms will pay workers more than their supply price in order to have a credible threat when they wish to discipline the worker. Jackman, Layard and Pissarides (1984) show how monopsonistic competition in hiring and retention of labor will also lead to a wage that prevents market-clearing. In all these stories the essential point is that firms have an incentive to bid up wages against each other (the wage-wage spiral). Only if unemployment is high enough does this incentive vanish, because the pay-off to paying above the going rate is eliminated.

The basic message of all these stories can be seen from the following simple model in which the relative wage affects the worker's effort (e). Hence

$$e = e\left(\frac{W}{\overline{W}}, \overline{c}u\right) \qquad (e_1, e_2 > 0; \ e_{12} < 0),$$

where $\overline{W}$ is the average outside wage, and $\overline{c}u$ measures the competition for jobs outside the firm.

For simplicity we shall assume that output is given by eN, where N is employment in the firm. Profits are

$$\pi = R(eN) - WN = R(eN) - (W/e)eN$$

which is to be maximized with respect to W and N. This can be done sequentially by first choosing W to minimize (W/e):

$$e - (W/\overline{W})e_1 = 0.$$

In a symmetric general equilibrium $W = \overline{W}$. Hence the equilibrium unemployment rate is given by:

$$e_1(1, \overline{c}u) = e(1, \overline{c}u).$$

The lower is $\overline{c}$, the higher is u.

The source of unemployment in this model is that the wage performs two functions: it generates effort and it determines employment. Because firms use the wage to generate effort, it cannot also clear the market for employment. Thus critics of the theory ask why some other instrument could not be deployed to generate effort. Could not workers post bonds which they would lose if they are not efficient, or (if imperfect capital markets prevent that) could they not be underpaid while young and overpaid later, subject to good behavior? The answer is that in general such schemes can never adequately achieve the efficiency objective (Akerlof and Katz 1988).

But what positive evidence is there in support of these theories? Most businessmen recognize this account of their actions. If asked why they do not drop wages when people are queueing up for jobs, they give explanations of this kind (Akerlof and Yellen 1986, 1990). We have already quoted evidence on the way in which firms can benefit from raising wages. There is also evidence that wages persistently differ between industries in ways that cannot be explained by worker quality or by union strength. The obvious explanation is that wages affect output differently in different industries and are therefore higher where effort matters more – for example where capital-intensity is high (Krueger and Summers 1988).

In the model discussed in Section 2.1. persistence comes from the dependence of $\overline{c}$ on past levels of unemployment. But there may be another source of persistence in efficiency wage models (Johnson and Layard 1986). We have so far assumed that effort depends on the wage relative to the outside wage. But workers may also compare their wage with what they think is fair, based on past experience. Suppose the fair wage (W_f), defined in real terms, adjusts adaptively to past experience:

$$\Delta W_f = \phi(W - W_f)_{-1}.$$

And suppose individual output is given by

$$e = e\left(\frac{W}{W_f}, \bar{c}u\right)\lambda.$$

Then, in the steady state, equilibrium unemployment will be independent of productivity λ. But now suppose λ falls, due for example to an oil price shock. The fair wage W_f will not instantly adjust downward. Employers will therefore find it worthwhile paying a wage that is also out of line with productivity, and unemployment will rise. W will only converge on its long-run level as W_f converges on W at the new lower level.

Thus efficiency wage models can easily generate persistence if (i) outsider effectiveness depends on lagged unemployment, or (ii) the "fair wage" that people expect adjusts slowly to supply shocks. Nevertheless it is noticeable that persistence has been stronger in economies where firms have to bargain with unions than where they do not. (The exception is some Nordic economies and Austria, where bargaining is highly centralized and the external diseconomies of bargaining can be overcome.) This suggests that in most European countries a sensible story of the labor market also requires that we model collective bargaining and thus insider power.[6]

2.2.2. Union Bargaining

If firms know that wages affect individual effort, they will take this into account in bargaining. However for simplicity we shall at this stage drop the efficiency wage issue and consider the following simple model of collective bargaining based on Jackman, Layard and Nickell (1988). It is more consistent with reality than any other we have found, and does generate an insider effect provided certain key assumptions are satisfied.

Unions bargain over wages, knowing that employers will then determine employment on the basis of the bargained wage (Oswald 1987).[7] Individual union members want to maximize their expected income (non-linear utility adds no further insight). Union policy is decided by the median voter's preferences.

Does this imply any persistence mechanism involving insider power? In other words, does last period's employment affect current wage demands? The answer is that this only happens if two assumptions hold: (i) It is uncertain how much employment there will be for a given wage, and (ii) It is uncertain which individual workers will be employed in a given total employment.

Suppose first that, once the wage is determined, the volume of employment is known. Under normal circumstances workers know that the outcome of the wage bargain will be similar to what it was last year (relative to productivity). So employment will be similar. Hence with say 30 percent turnover, none of the existing workers is at risk. The local objective of the union will therefore be to maximize the wage.

Now suppose that the volume of employment is uncertain even after the wage is set, but workers know in what order they will be laid off. This order might most plausibly be in inverse order of seniority (Oswald 1987). In this case the median voter will be far from the firing line. He will be quite happy if the union presses locally for the highest wage it can get – knowing that the countervailing power of the firm will prevent anything substantially different from last year's wage (Blanchard and Layard 1988). Once again the union's local objective function is the wage, and the number of insiders plays no role.

However in reality the order in which workers will be laid off if wages rise is not certain. It is true that there is a general presumption in favor of last in - first out (LIFO), but this only operates within skill groups and (often) within individual plants or workshops. Firms will deliberately try to keep their workers uncertain about which shops or plants will be closed in the event of cut-backs – precisely in order to induce moderation in wage demands.[8] So we can assume for simplicity that, if employment turns out to be less than the number of insiders, lay-off is by random assignment.

In this case, the median voter's expected income is the same as everybody else's. So the union's objective function is this expected income, Ω^e, given by

$$\Omega^e = SW + (1 - S)A,$$

where S is the probability of individual survival in the firm and A is expected outside income.

How is the survival probability determined? Each worker (which includes the median voter) knows that, if wages are raised, this reduces expected total employment. Hence there is a higher chance that there will be some layoffs and thus that any individual will be laid off. Thus the individual probability of surviving in employment depends inversely on the wage. But it also depends inversely on the number of existing employees (N_{-1}), since for given employment the more insiders there are the less likely any one insider is to be employed. Hence an individual's chance of survival is

$$S = S(W, N_{-1}) \qquad (S_1, S_2 < 0).$$

And how is A determined? It measures the expected value of the outside opportunities for someone laid off. These depend on outside wages ($\overline{W}$), benefits (B), and on the chances of getting a job if searching with given effectiveness. If discount rates are small relative to turnover rates, this expected value (in flow terms) is approximately[9]

$$A = (1 - \overline{c}u)\overline{W} + \overline{c}uB.$$

We can now examine the outcome of the bargain. This is found by maximizing the Nash expression:

$$\max_{w}(\Omega^e - \overline{\Omega})^{\beta} \, (\pi^e - \overline{\pi}) = S^{\beta}(W - A)^{\beta} \, \pi^e(W),$$

where $\pi^e(W)$ is expected operating profit. We have assumed here that workers' fallback income during any dispute ($\overline{\Omega}$) equals A, that firms' fallback operating profit ($\overline{\pi}$) is zero, and that β is an index of the bargaining power of the union.[10] Differentiating logarithmically, the outcome of the wage bargain is given by

$$\frac{\beta S_1}{S} + \frac{\beta}{W - A} - \frac{N^e}{\pi^e} = 0,$$

where N^e is expected employment. Multiplying by W and rearranging gives the partial equilibrium wage equation

(7)
$$\frac{W - A}{W} = \frac{1}{\left(\dfrac{WN^e}{\beta\pi^e}\right) + \varepsilon_{SW}},$$

where ε_{SW} is (the absolute value of) the elasticity of the survival probability with respect to the wage.

We turn now to general equilibrium. The economy consists of many sectors in each of which the representative bargain has proceeded as described. In equilibrium, unemployment must prevent a wage-wage spiral, so that $W = \overline{W}$. Hence, substituting for A

$$(8) \qquad \overline{c}u(1 - B/W) = \frac{1}{\left(\frac{WN^e}{\beta\pi^e}\right) + \varepsilon_{SW}}.$$

In general ε_{SW} varies positively with N_{-1}/N^e.[11] For if the number of insiders is very low relative to expected employment, a change in expected employment has a small effect on the expected layoff rate. But, if there are many insiders, any change in expected employment will have a significant effect on layoffs. In fact using the simple Dixit-Stiglitz (1977) model of monopolistic competition with product demand elasticity η and constant marginal product of labor, ε_{SW} can be written as

$$\varepsilon_{SW} = \eta f[N_{-1}/N^e(W)] \qquad (f' > 0).$$

In addition $WN^e/\pi^e = \eta - 1$. Thus the wage equation is given by

$$cu(1 - B/W) = \frac{1}{(\eta - 1) / \beta + \eta f [N_{-1}/N^e(W)]}.$$

The real wage is increasing in real benefits and decreasing in unemployment. It is also higher the higher the bargaining power of the union and the lower the elasticity of product demand – monopoly in the product market being a potent source of monopoly power in the labor market. Since on reasonable assumptions $f(\cdot)$ is twice-differentiable, there is no asymmetry in wage behavior: it is not true that a small fall in unemployment reduces the wage much less than a small rise in unemployment raises it. Asymmetries of this kind are usually based on models, such as Lindbeck and Snower (1988), without firm-level or individual uncertainty, and thus inconsistent with *any* insider effects (as explained above). Moreover there is no convincing empirical evidence for the existence of asymmetries (see, e.g., Nickell and Wadhwani 1988).

If we now take the replacement ratio as given, we can examine the evolution of unemployment. Ignoring turnover, the long-run NAIRU is given by

$$\bar{c}u(1- B/W) = \frac{1}{(\eta - 1) / \beta + \eta f(1)}.$$

But the short-run NAIRU is given by

$$s\bar{c}u(1 - B/W) = \frac{1}{(\eta - 1) / \beta + \eta f\left(\frac{1 - u_{-1}}{1 - u}\right)}$$

assuming a constant labor force. This is an equation with persistence coming through insider power *and* outsider ineffectiveness (via $\bar{c}$). Linearizing and substituting for $\bar{c}u$ gives an equation of the form

$$0 = e_0 - e_1 u + e_2 u_{-1} + e_3 \Delta u_{-1} + e_4 B/W$$

as in Section 2.1.[12]

3

Combatting Unemployment: Is Flexibility Enough?

This more policy-oriented paper continues with the discussion and analysis of core institutional variables influencing labor market performance. What drives unemployment? On the one hand, Richard Layard, Stephen Nickell, and Richard Jackman show that wage setting coordination tends to be associated with lower unemployment rates when union coverage is high while skills mismatch and training deficits tend to increase unemployment. Treating the unemployed appropriately can help counter work disincentives stemming from long benefit duration often found in mature welfare states. Participation in well-designed active labor market policies can act as a superior "replacement" to purely passive income protection and therefore help lower unemployment. But there are also indications that problems of skill mismatch have exacerbated European unemployment. On the other hand, the article gives a very skeptical account of the effectiveness of policies that aim at reducing unemployment via lower working hours, i.e. by work-sharing or early retirement. Also, with respect to lower employment taxes it is not clear if this would bring about lower unemployment as specific effects of these taxes cannot be identified. Regarding more flexible employment protection, the authors point out that there is no clear evidence of whether stricter dismissal protection decreases the outflow rate from unemployment by more or less than it decreases the inflow rate. These institutional factors, which had been discussed intensely and sometimes perceived as panaceas in Europe, are found to have negligible effects if at all. One has to note that the authors add an explicit note of caution to a narrow concept of labor market flexibility. Lower unemployment benefits and weaker employment protection are,

The original version of this chapter was published as: Layard, R., Nickell, S., Jackman, R. (1996). Combatting Unemployment: Is Flexibility Enough?, in: OECD (Ed.), Macroeconomic Policies and Structural Reform, Paris, 19-49. By permission of Oxford University Press.

> *of course, good examples of more flexibility. Designing effective active labor market policy, coordinated wage bargaining, and skill training clearly go beyond the usual definition of labor market flexibility. The authors rather recommend focusing on the role of government in dealing with unemployment. Lower benefits of shorter duration would reduce unemployment, but these policies should be accompanied by more (not less) active labor market policy. Similarly governments should not dismantle bargaining structures. And they ought to ensure that most young people enter adult life with a basic level of competence. What is of highest importance in the European context is to keep unemployment at a low level by preventing entry to long-term unemployment (by replacing long-term benefits by active labor market policy), and by preventing young people ceasing their education until they have acquired basic literacy, numeracy, and vocational competencies.*

What is the route to lower unemployment? Is it through greater labor market flexibility, involving deregulation and decentralization? Or are there areas where more collective action, rather than less, is required? To examine this issue we have tried to see how differences of policy and institutions affect the unemployment levels in the different OECD countries. (We are concerned not with cyclical fluctuations but with the average levels of unemployment over a run of years.) The factors whose possible influence we examine are:

(i) how unemployed people are treated (benefit levels and active help with job-finding);

(ii) how wages are determined;

(iii) how skills are formed;

(iv) how far jobs are protected by redundancy legislation;

(v) how heavily employment is taxed; and

(vi) how far labor supply is reduced through reductions in hours of work and through early retirement.

Our conclusions are that the most important influences on unemployment come from the first three factors.

(i) The longer *unemployment benefits* are available the longer unemployment lasts. Similarly, higher levels of benefits generate higher unemployment with an elasticity of around one half. On the other hand *active help* in finding work can reduce unemployment. So more "flexibility" may need to be complemented by more intervention to provide active help.

(ii)   Union coverage and union power raise unemployment. But if *wage bargaining* is decentralized, wage bargainers have incentives to settle for more than the "going rate," and only higher unemployment can prevent them leapfrogging. Although decentralization makes it easier to vary *relative* wages, this advantage is more than offset by the extra upward pressure on the *general* level of wages. Thus, where union coverage is high, co-ordinated wage bargaining leads to lower unemployment.

(iii)   Conscious intervention to raise the *skill levels* of less able workers is an important component of any policy to combat unemployment. Pure wage flexibility may not be sufficient because it leads to growing inequality which in turn discourages labor supply from less able workers.

Thus in our first three areas it is clear what types of reform are needed. If well designed, such reforms might halve the level of unemployment in many countries.

But there are other proposed remedies some of which have been advocated either in the OECD Jobs Study or the Delors White Paper. These include: less employment protection, lower taxes on employment, and lower working hours. Our research does not suggest that lower employment taxes or lower hours would have any long term effects; while the effects of lower employment protection would be small.

(i)   *Lower employment protection* has two effects. It increases hiring and thus reduces long-term unemployment. But it also increases firing and thus increases short-term unemployment. The first (good) effect is almost offset by the second (bad) one. The gains from flexibility are small.

(ii)   *Employment taxes* do not appear to have any long-term effect on unemployment and are borne entirely by labor. There may be some short-term effects, but it is not clear that there would be any fall in inflationary pressure if taxes on polluting products were raised at the same time as taxes on employment were lowered.

(iii)   *Hours of work* appear to have no long-term effect upon unemployment. Equally, if *early retirement* is used in order to reduce labor supply, it is necessary to reduce employment pari passu unless inflationary pressure is to increase. While flexible hours and participation can reduce the fluctuations in unemployment over the cycle, they cannot affect its average level.

We can now proceed to the evidence for these assertions. We begin by looking at the pattern of unemployment differences between countries and estimate an equation which explains it, using all the factors we find significant. We then discuss each factor in turn, drawing on other evidence where relevant. We end with policy conclusions.

3.1. Country Differences

There are wide differences in unemployment rates across countries, but one feature of these differences has been little noticed: a large part of the variation is in long-term unemployment. This is shown in Table 3.1. It appears that countries can live with very different rates of long-term unemployment whereas some short-term unemployment seems inevitable. The reason for this "optional" nature of long-term unemployment appears to be that long-term unemployment has a much lower effect on wage pressure than does short-term unemployment (OECD 1993).

To explain unemployment it is therefore useful to explain separately not only the total of unemployment but also its two different parts (short-term and long-term). We shall explain unemployment rates in 1983-88 and 1989-94, using the following main explanatory variables:

Replacement rate (percent);
Benefit duration (years; indefinite = 4 years);
Active labor market policy per unemployed person as percent of output per worker (ALMP);
Union coverage (1 under 25 percent, 2 middle, 3 over 75 percent);
Co-ordination in wage bargaining (1 low, 2 middle, 3 high);
Employment protection (ranking: 1 low, 20 high);
Change in inflation (percentage points per annum).

Table 3.1

Unemployment Rates, Total, Long-term and Short-term

| | Percentage | | | | | |
| | 1983-1988 | | | 1989-94 | | |
	Total	Long-term	Short-term	Total	Long-term	Short-term
Belgium	11.3	8.0	3.3	8.1	5.1	2.9
Denmark	9.0	3.0	6.0	10.8	3.0	7.9
France	9.8	4.4	5.4	10.4	3.9	6.5
Germany	6.8	3.1	3.7	5.4	2.2	3.2
Ireland	16.1	9.2	6.9	14.8	9.4	5.4
Italy	6.9	3.8	3.1	8.2	5.3	2.9
Netherlands	10.5	5.5	5.0	7.0	3.5	3.5
Portugal	7.6	4.2	3.5	5.0	2.0	3.0
Spain	19.6	11.3	8.4	18.9	9.7	9.1
United Kingdom	10.9	5.1	5.8	8.9	3.4	5.5
Australia	8.4	2.4	5.9	9.0	2.7	6.2
New Zealand	4.9	0.6	4.3	8.9	2.3	6.6
Canada	9.9	0.9	9.0	9.8	0.9	8.9
United States	7.1	0.7	6.4	6.2	0.6	5.6
Japan	2.7	0.4	2.2	2.3	0.4	1.9
Austria	3.6	n.k.	n.k.	3.7	n.k.	n.k.
Finland	5.1	1.0	4.0	10.5	1.7	8.9
Norway	2.7	0.2	2.5	5.5	1.2	4.3
Sweden	2.6	0.3	2.3	4.4	0.4	4.0
Switzerland	0.8	0.1	0.7	2.3	0.5	1.8

Note: Long-term means over one year.
Source: Total: OECD standardized rates except for Italy (which is the US BLS measure).
Long-term: Total times share of long-term in total (as in OECD Employment Outlook, appendix).

The last variable is included because it is always possible to achieve a temporary fall in unemployment through allowing inflation to increase.[1] The value of the variables are in Table 3.2.

The explanatory regression was a pooled regression for the two sub-periods. (We checked that the two sets of coefficients in the two sub-periods were not as a set significantly different.) The results are in Table 3.3. In the equation for long-term unemployment we also include short-term unemployment as a regressor.

OECD countries do of course display quite severe persistence in unemployment, and our two six-year periods may not be long enough to eliminate these effects. However, terms measuring lagged unemployment were either insignificant or incorrectly signed, and have therefore not been included. The pooled regression was however estimated by the random-effects method which to some extent discounts the effects of persistent country specific factors.

Turning to our results, we can first explain the cross-country variation of *long-term* unemployment. All the variables reflecting the treat-

Table 3.2

Explanatory Variables[a]

	Replacement rate	Benefit duration	ALMP	Union Coverage	Union coordination	Employer coordination	Employment protection	Change in inflation
Belgium	60	4	10.0 14.6	3	2	2	17	-0.76 -0.52
Denmark	90	2.5	10.6 10.3	3	3	3	5	-0.86 -0.46
France	57	3.75 3	7.2 8.8	3	2	2	14	-1.38 -0.30
Germany	63	4	12.9 25.7	3	2	3	15	-0.34 -0.04
Ireland	50 37	4	9.2 9.1	3	1	1	12	-1.52 -0.54
Italy	2 20	0.5	10.1 10.3	3	2	1 2	20	-1.68 -0.52
Netherlands	70	4	4.0 6.9	3	2	2	9	-0.14 0.14
Portugal	60 65	0.5	5.9 18.8	3	2	2	18	-2.74 -1.28
Spain	80 70	3.5	3.2 4.7	3	2	1	19	-1.24 -0.60
United Kingdom	36 38	4	7.8 6.4	3 2	1	1	7	0.16 -1.02
Australia	39 36	4	4.1 3.2	3	2	1	4	0.02 -1.24
New Zealand	38 30	4	15.4 6.8	2	2 1	1	2	0.36 -1.22
Canada	60 59	0.5 1	6.3 5.9	2	1	1	3	-0.08 -0.84
United States	50	0.5	3.9 3.0	1	1	1	1	-0.04 -0.48
Japan	60	0.5	5.4 4.3	2	2	2	8	-0.20 -0.36
Austria	60 50	4	8.7 8.3	3	3	3	16	-0.46 0.06
Finland	75 63	4 2	18.4 16.4	3	3 2	3	10	-0.26 -0.72
Norway	65	1.5	9.5 14.7	3	3	3	11	-0.34 -1.12
Sweden	80	1.2	59.5 59.3	3	3	3	13	-0.75 -1.02
Switzerland	70	1	23.0 8.2	2	1	3	6	-0.12 -0.54

[a] When variable changes between the two sub-periods, the first number is for 1983-88 and the second for 1989-94

Source: Replacement rate and benefit duration: Mainly US Department of Health and Social Services, Social Security Programmes throughout the World, 1985 and 1993. See LNJ Annex 1.3 ALMP: OECD Employment Outlook, 1988 and 1995. For the first sub-period the data relate to 1987 and for the second to 1991. We include all active spending, except on the disabled. Union coverage – union co-ordination and employer co-ordination: See LNJ Annex 1.4 and OECD Employment Outlook 1994 pp 175-185. Employment Protection: OECD Jobs Study (1994) Part II Table 6.7 Col. 5 p. 74. Country ranking with 20 as the most strictly regulated. Inflation: OECD Economic Outlook.

ment of unemployed people come in with the predicted sign. The system of wage bargaining is also important. Employment protection *raises* long-term unemployment.

Table 3.3

Regressions to Explain Long Unemployment Rate

	20 OECD countries , 1983-88 and 1989-94, percentage					
	Total unemployment (1)		Long-term unemployment (2)		Short-term unemployment (3)	
Replacement rate (percentage)	0.011	(1.6)	0.004	(0.5)	0.009	(1.2)
Benefit duration (years)	0.09	(1.3)	0.16	(1.9)	0.04	(0.6)
ALMP	-0.008	(0.7)	-0.03	(2.0)	-0.0008	(0.07)
Union coverage (1-3)	0.66	(2.7)	0.56	(1.7)	0.54	(2.2)
Co-ordination (1-3)	-0.68	(3.2)	-0.29	(0.9)	-0.57	(2.4)
Employment protection (1-20)	-0.005	(0.2)	0.09	(2.7)	-0.04	(1.6)
Change in inflation (percentage points per annum	-0.17	(1.7)	-0.13	(1.1)	-0.15	(1.6)
Constant	-3.96	(7.3)	-3.28	(2.9)	-3.8	(7.0)
Dummy for 89-94	0.16	(1.9)	0.1	(0.9)	0.16	(2.1)
Log (short-term unemployment)	-		0.94	(4.0)		-
R^2	0.59		0.81		0.41	
s.e.	0.51		0.59		0.52	
N	40		38		38	

Dependent variables:
(1)   Total unemployed as percentage of labor force.
(2)   Long-term unemployed (over one year) as percentage of labor force.
(3)   Short-term unemployed (under one year) as percentage of labor force.
t-statistics in brackets. These are based on the method of "random effects".
Notes: ALMP is measured by current active labor market spending as percentage of GDP divided by current employment. To handle problems of endogeneity and measurement error this is instrumented by active labor market spending in 1987 as percentage of GDP divided by average unemployment of a unit change in an independent variable; where the unit is measured as in Table 3.2.

However when we turn to *short-term* unemployment, things change. Not surprisingly, benefit duration and active labor market policy (ALMP) are unimportant. And, as expected, employment protection *reduces* short-term unemployment, by reducing the inflow to unemployment.

Turning to the effects on total unemployment, employment protection has an insignificant effect. But unemployment does respond to how unemployed people are treated and to how wages are determined.

To understand why all these variables might affect unemployment, we need to see how they fit into an integrated framework. This is provided by the system of wage and price equations. Assuming no price surprises, we have

Wage equation

$$(1) \qquad \log W = -\gamma \log(cu) + Z + \log(Y/L),$$

price equation (simplified)

$$(2) \qquad \log W = \beta + \log(Y/L),$$

where W is the real cost per worker, u the unemployment rate, c the "effectiveness" of the unemployed, Z the impact of other wage pressure variables, and Y/L is output per head of labor force.

Thus the equilibrium unemployment rate is given by

$$(3) \qquad \log(cu) = \frac{Z - \beta}{\gamma}.$$

The key variables affecting unemployment are those which affect wage pressure (namely c and the Zs) plus the effect of unemployment in offsetting wage pressure (γ). We can now examine each of the possible causes of unemployment for their effect on wage pressure.

3.2. Policies to the Unemployed
3.2.1. Benefits

Benefits work through two mechanisms. First, they reduce the fear of unemployment and thus directly increase wage pressure from the unions (a simple Z factor). But second, and more important, they reduce the "effectiveness" of unemployed people (c) as fillers of vacancies. This encourages *employers* to raise wages. It also reduces the competition which newly unemployed workers will face in their search for jobs, which again encourages the *unions* to push for higher wages.

Since any reduction in effectiveness (c) leads to an equiproportional increase in unemployment, one can obtain an estimate of the effects of benefits (working through c) from micro cross-sectional studies which explain exit rates by benefits, holding vacancies constant. These estimates typically give an elasticity of exit rates with respect to the replacement ratio of around one half, with a wide range on either side (Narendranathan, Nickell and Stern 1985; Atkinson and Micklewright 1991).

A second key dimension of unemployment benefits is their potential duration. Long-term benefits increase long-term unemployment. There are two processes at work here. First benefits reduce exit rates in general. But the resulting long-term unemployment further reduces exit rates. For in those countries where long-term unemployment is common, the exit rates for the long-term unemployed are much lower than for the short-term unemployed – in other words they have lower c. At least in part this appears to reflect a state-dependence of exit rates on duration (Jackman and Layard 1991). Thus the incidence of long-term unemployment shifts out the u/v curve in many European countries (Budd, Levine and Smith 1988).

However when unemployment benefits run out quite quickly exit rates decline much less as duration lengthens. This is confirmed by Meyer and Katz (1990) and Carling et al. (1995) for the US and Sweden, where benefits run out after 6 and 14 months respectively. By contrast in Britain and Australia, where benefits are long-lived, there is much more state dependence (Jackman and Layard 1991; Fahrer and Pease 1993).

3.2.2. Active Labor Market Policies (ALMP)

If long-duration benefits have negative effects, one approach is simply to provide no help to unemployed people beyond some period. Given sufficient wage flexibility, this will increase employment. But the cost will be more unequal wages, and not all of long-term unemployment will be eliminated.

An alternative is to provide some help to all who do not get benefit, but to give it through activity rather than though benefits. This cuts off the flow of long-term unemployment at least for the period for which the active measures last, and gives all the unemployed at least a chance to prove themselves.

This latter alternative is the Swedish model: active labor market policy *replaces* benefits. It should be sharply distinguished from other systems of active labor market policy where the uptake of the help offered is voluntary, so that labor market activity is an *optional alternative* to benefits. While active labor market policies of the second kind do continue in many countries, there is an interesting shift toward the Swedish model in Switzerland, while Denmark which has always had a similar general approach to Sweden's has now shortened the "passive" period of benefit duration to two years (Schwanse 1995). In our regression equation, we find that dropping Sweden eliminates the effect of active labor market policy spending on long-term unemployment, consistent with the view that only Swedish-style ALMPs make a real difference.

The case for active labor market policy comes of course from social cost-benefit analysis. But it is also important to note that in terms of costs and benefits to the Ministry of Finance, *optional* ALMP is quite costly per unit reduction in unemployment, since those helped by the subsidy will include a disproportionate number of people who would have exited anyway (the problem of "deadweight"). Replacement ALMP can more nearly break-even, since all of those still unemployed are helped; there is thus a known maximum for the proportion of those helped who would have exited otherwise (the problem of "deadweight" is reduced, through avoiding creaming).

The other problem with active labor market policy is "substitution and displacement" – if an employer employs someone who would not have exited otherwise, this may disemploy someone else who would otherwise have been employed. In normal discussions this problem is greatly exaggerated. For the aim of ALMP is to help people who would otherwise have had low exit probabilities. By positive discrimination in their favor, vacancies go to them rather than to others who had better exit probabilities (were more employable). The effect is to increase the total stock of employable workers who are still unemployed. So vacancies get filled later and employment expands. By helping the hard to place, the total stock of employable labor expands. In response the total stock of jobs expands.

We can easily see this in the context of our model – equations (1) and (2). There is a certain required level of cu. Through the active labor market policy the average effectiveness of the unemployed (c) is increased. This decreases wage pressure at each level of unemployment (see Figure 3.1). In consequence there is an increase in the equilibrium employment rate. Assuming that when prices are set the mark-up of prices over wages is constant, as in Figure 3.1, unemployment falls by the same proportion that average effectiveness (c) rises.

But what about substitution and displacement? If for example action is taken to help the long-term unemployed, does this increase short-term unemployment? The logic of our model says No.

Suppose the short-term unemployed have effectiveness c_S and the long-term unemployed have effectiveness c_L. Equilibrium requires a given level of $(c_S u_S + c_L u_L)$ in order to restrain wage pressure. We now through ALMP improve c_L, while c_S remains unchanged. What happens? u_L falls and u_S remains unchanged. Why?

Figure 3.1
Effects of Active Labor Market Policies

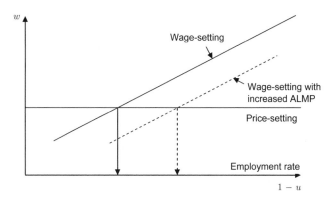

The stock of short-term unemployed depends on the total inflow into unemployment (S) and on the exit rate from short-term unemployment. This latter is equal to c times the exit rate for a person with effectiveness equal to unity, *i.e.*, it equals $c_S S / cuL$, where L is labor force. But cu is given. Thus if S/L and c_S remain unchanged, so does the exit rate from short-term unemployment and so does the stock of short-term unemployed.

The short-term unemployed get the same number of jobs per period because the long-term unemployed also get the same number of jobs per period. The only thing that has changed is that the *stock* of long-term unemployed has fallen since the exit rate from long-term unemployment has risen. Thus the long-term unemployed do not take jobs from the short-term unemployed.

There is no job-fund. Employment expands as the effective supply of labor expands. This should be obvious to anyone who contemplates the employment miracle which occurred when the Pilgrim Fathers landed at Cape Cod and found a sudden increase in the demand for labor on those inhospitable shores. But, as expressed so far, it is a medium-term argument. In the short-run there may be some constraints on the demand side. For example, if nominal demand is fixed, an increase in the effective supply of labor will generate *some* new jobs, due to lower inflation, but the increase in jobs will be less than the increase in labor supply. If, however, the government has an inflation target, then even in the short-run employment will increase in line with the effective supply of labor.

This result provides important insights but may need modifying to suit the details of particular schemes. In any case it says nothing about the effectiveness of particular schemes. This depends on how well they do indeed improve the effectiveness of the individuals who are exposed to them.

Clearly schemes are more effective when they are not optional (see above) but then they are also more difficult to study – since there is no control group. Thus most studies of ALMP relate to optional schemes and compare people who were and were not exposed to such schemes. The microeconomic studies have been well summarized in OECD (1993) and Fay (1995). The general findings are *I)* a good return to assistance with job-finding; *II)* a goodish return to subsidized self-employment; *III)* some return to targeted recruitment subsidies; *IV)* a weaker return to public sector job creation, and *V)* an often weak return to the training of unemployed people, in most cases heavy deadweight being the main factor reducing the return.

Our conclusion is that major expansions of ALMP can only be justified where the aim is to achieve universal coverage of some group (e.g. the long-term unemployed). This will greatly reduce deadweight, since in any disadvantaged group the overall outflow rates are generally low. It is also the only way to make any large dent in unemployment.

Going further, what is needed is in fact a change of regime. When people enter unemployment they need to understand that there will be no possibility of indefinite life on benefits. Instead it should be made clear that, after a period of say one year, public support will be provided only through participation on a program. But access to the program is guaranteed. This will have the twin effect of *a)* helping those who really need help, and *b)* driving off the public purse those who only want help in the form of cash.

This is the Swedish model, which played a central role in holding down Swedish unemployment to around 2 percent until the end of the 1980s.[2] The model has of course come under heavy pressure recently due to bad macroeconomic management: over-expansionary policy in the late 1980s followed by over-contraction. The Swedes have been right to continue with ALMP, since institutional/ cultural arrangements of this kind cannot easily be re-established once they have been abandoned (Layard 1995). But the experience makes it clear that ALMP is not primarily a counter-cyclical device – it needs to be a permanent feature of the economic and social system.[3]

3.3. Wage Bargaining

The next key factor affecting equilibrium unemployment is the system of wage determination. In systems where wages are settled in a decentralized way (either by employers' fiat or by bargaining) there is always a problem of leapfrogging. Even in the absence of bargaining, some employers may have an incentive to pay an "efficiency" wage above the supply price of labor, in order to motivate and retain staff. Indeed, unless unemployment is high enough, they will generally try to pay more than the going wage paid by other employers. Unions will also seek to raise their pay above that of other unions.

This problem of leapfrogging can be reduced when wages are centrally coordinated (namely by centralized positions adopted by the unions and the employers). A simple illustration will suffice; where unions can freely choose their pay so as to maximize the expected income of their members, if the choice is *decentralized*, the union chooses the firm-level wage (W_i) to maximize a function like $(W_i - A)N_i$, where N_i is firm-level employment, and A is expected income outside the firm. A is then given by $(1 - u)W^e + uB$, where W^e is the expected outside wage and B benefits. (The price level is taken as exogenous.) This leads to a wage given by

$$\frac{W_i - A}{W_i} = \left(\frac{\delta N_i}{\delta W_i}\frac{W_i}{N_i}\right)^{-1}.$$

So, for equilibrium (W_i equal to W^e), unemployment is given by

$$u = \left(\frac{\delta N_i}{\delta W_i}\frac{W_i}{N_i}\right)^{-1}\left(1 - \frac{B}{W}\right)^{-1}.$$

By contrast a *centralized* union would be setting the wage for everybody and would choose it to maximize NW, recognizing that workers disemployed by the wage settlement would have no alternative income opportunity (so that $A = 0$), unemployment benefits simply being a transfer from employed to unemployed union members. Unless an increase in employment required a more than proportionate fall in the real wage, the union would choose a wage consistent with full employment. A similar result can be obtained in a wage bargaining model. If by contrast employers set efficiency wages, there are also advantages from co-ordination to reduce leap-frogging, though employers would collectively choose non-zero unemployment as a worker-discipline device.

All this is on the assumption of homogenous labor. If labor is heterogenous, the arguments for decentralization become more powerful. Under coordinated bargaining it is quite difficult to achieve the shifts in relative wages that may be required in response to differential shifts of relative demands and supplies. Thus coordinated bargaining reduces unemployment by cutting out leapfrogging, but increases it by worsening structural imbalances. The overall outcome is an empirical issue.

The issue appears to be quite clearly resolved in Table 3.2. Coordination has a powerful influence in reducing unemployment. An uncoordinated economy will have, other things equal, an unemployment rate more than twice as high as an economy with highly co-ordinated wage-setting arrangements. Our results suggest, however, that a fully coordinated economy with high degree of union coverage will have approximately the same unemployment rate as an economy with low union coverage and no co-ordination.

In this context we should perhaps refer to the view of Calmfors and Driffill (1988) that, while full centralization has advantages, coordination at the industry level gives the worst of all worlds (due to the low demand elasticity for labor in one industry). The implication is that if full centralization is too difficult one should go for full decentralization. We believe this argument is misleading. On the empirical level the finding is not robust (Soskice 1990). Moreover it ignores the obvious point that, when comparing countries, it is not only the degree of centralization which rises but the degree of union coverage. The United States does not have decentralized bargaining; it has hardly any unions. Other things equal, higher coverage is bad for employment but this effect can be offset by sufficient co-ordination. This is precisely what our equation shows.

With regard to the impact of relative wage flexibility, we tried introducing the degree of wage dispersion as a further independent variable in the Table 3.3 regression. It turned out insignificant in relation to total unemployment ($t = 0.6$) and long-term unemployment ($t = -0.9$), but to have a significant positive effect ($t = 4.2$) in increasing short-term unemployment. These results suggest the complexity of the issues surrounding wage flexibility.

The truth is that coordination is a very subtle affair. But the more there is, it appears, the better. Equally the task of achieving it appears to have become more difficult, possibly reflecting the greater exposure to international competition in both product and factor markets in recent years.

3.4. Skills Imbalance[4]

One possible reason why unemployment is higher than in the 1970s is the steady fall in the demand for unskilled workers. If this is nor matched by an equal fall in supply, this can certainly cause an increase in unemployment.

To see this we can (for simplicity) divide the labor force into two categories, skilled and unskilled – denoted 1 and 2 respectively. We shall assume that output is produced by a Cobb-Douglas production function

$$Y = A N_i^{\alpha_1} \; N_2^{\alpha_2} \; K^{\alpha_3} \quad (\alpha_1 + \alpha_2 + \alpha_3 = 1).$$

Thus the demand for labor of type i is given by[5]

(4) $$Y = \ln W_i - \log \alpha_1 + \log(Y/L) - \log l_i + u_i,$$

where W is the cost per worker, L total labor force, and $l_i = L_i/L$. It follows that, if the unemployment rate of a group is to remain constant when α_i rises or falls, wages must adjust in line. Equally, when the labor force composition changes, wages must also adjust.

The problem is that wages do not normally adjust as they "should." Usually it takes extra unemployment to get wages down. There is much evidence to support the following equation

(5) $$\ln W_i = -\gamma \log u_i + z_i + \log(Y/L)$$

where z_i measures a return of wage pressure effects. From (1) and (2) we can see that the unemployment of a group is determined by

$$u_1 + \gamma \log u_i = \log l_i - \log \alpha_i + z_i.$$

If the relative demand for a group (α_i) falls faster than the relative supply of people in that group (l_i) then $(\log l_i - \log \alpha_i)$ falls, and the unemployment rate in that group rises. There is thus a ceaseless race between shifts in demand and shifts in supply.

The change in unemployment of group i is

$$du_i = \phi_i(d \log l_i - d \log \alpha_i),$$

where $\phi_i = u_i/(u_i + \gamma)$. We can interpret this in terms of Figure 3.2. The demand for type i labor (relative to its supply) shifts to the left by the same amount if the labor supply (l_i) increases by 1 percent or the labor demand (α_i) falls by 1 percent. Both of the shifts in supply and demand have the same effect. The effect on unemployment is greater the more rigid are wages. The lower is γ the more rigid are wages and the greater the rise in unemployment. Moreover the absolute rise in unemployment is greater the higher the existing level of unemployment (u_i) – due to the curved nature of the wage function.

In modern societies a race is in progress between the increase in the demand for skilled labor (measured by α_1) and the supply of skilled labor (measured by l_i). If the supply of skill fails to increase as fast as the demand, total unemployment will rise. To see this, note that the total change in unemployment is

$$du = d(u_1l_1 + u_2l_2) = u_1dl_1 - u_2dl_1 + l_1du_1 + (1 - l_1)du_2$$

$$= -(u_2 - u_1)dl_1 - (\phi_2 - \phi_1)dl_1 + (\theta_2 - \theta_1)d\alpha_1,$$

where $\theta_i = \phi_i l_i / \alpha_i$. The first of these terms is a pure composition effect – if the labor force becomes more concentrated in low-unemployment groups, unemployment will tend to fall. The second term reflects the problems which stem from wage rigidity. Since log wages depend on *log* unemployment, one extra point of unemployment reduces wages less for a group whose unemployment is high. Thus switching labor into the skilled group *reduces* overall unemployment – the downward force on skilled wages outweighs the upward force on unskilled wages $(\phi_2 - \phi_1 > 0)$. The third term shows the effect of technical progress raising the relative demand for skilled labor. Since $l_2 / \alpha_2 > 1$ and $l_1 / \alpha_1 < 1$, a rise in the demand for skilled labor (α_1) *raises* overall unemployment, by raising the demand for labor where the wage pressure responds sharply to extra demand and reducing demand where wages are unresponsive to demand.

Figure 3.2

Effect on an Upward Shift in the Relative Supply (l_j) and Demand of Labor (α_j)

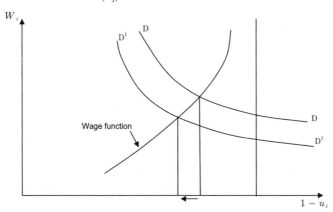

Note: For definitions see text.

3.4.1. Empirical Work

Empirical work using this kind of approach is still at a preliminary stage. However Nickell and Bell (1995, 1996) give results using a similar model, with a more general CES production function. They tentatively estimated that on average one fifth of the rise in unemployment from the late 1970s to the late 1980s in Germany, Holland, Spain, the United Kingdom, and Canada was due to structural shifts of demand relative to supply; Nickell (1995b) gives similar results.

3.5. Employment Protection

It is widely believed that labor market flexibility is good for the macro-economy and that employment protection legislation is an impediment to such flexibility. So it is argued that freedom of action for employers to dismiss workers on economic grounds is necessary for a smoothly functioning economy, though it is of course desirable to protect employees from arbitrary, unfair, or discriminating dismissals. However, it may be tricky in practice to protect employees from arbitrary dismissal while simultaneously allowing freedom of action for employers to dismiss on economic grounds.[6] Thus it may be felt necessary by benevolent legislators to circumscribe this freedom of action. The macroeconomic consequences of this are, however, of major importance – both on the process of short-run adjustment and on the long-run equilibrium level of unemployment.

3.5.1. Theoretical Background

Employment protection has a potential impact at a number of different points in the operation of the labor market. It obviously impedes employment adjustment by reducing both flows from employment, because of the legal hurdles, and flows into employment by making employers more cautious about hiring. It may also influence wage determination, for example by raising the power of insiders or by lengthening unemployment duration. Finally, because of the excessive caution of employers, it may impede the absorption of new entrants into the labor market thereby reducing participation rates and raising relative youth unemployment rates.

Consider the following model, where we ignore nominal inertia (wage/price stickiness), labor force growth, and trend productivity effects. Wage setting is given by

$$(7) \qquad \log W = -\gamma_1 u - \gamma_{11} \Delta u + z_w,$$

where z_w are wage pressure shocks. The demand for labor is given by

$$(8) \qquad n = \lambda n_{-1} - (1 - \lambda)\beta_1 \log W + (1 - \lambda)z_n$$

where $n = \log$ employment, $z_n =$ labor demand shifts (e.g., productivity shocks) and β_1 is the *long-run* labor demand elasticity. If we suppose the labor force to be fixed and normalized to unity, (8) can be written as

$$(9) \qquad u = \lambda u_{-1} + (1 - \lambda)\beta_1 \log W - (1 - \lambda)z_n.$$

Then, eliminating real wages from (7) and (9), we obtain

$$(10) \qquad u = \alpha_{11} u_{-1} + (1 - \alpha_{11})u^*,$$

where u^* is the equilibrium unemployment rate, given by

$$(11) \qquad u^* = \frac{\beta_1 z_w - z_n}{1 + \beta_1 \gamma_1},$$

and the speed of adjustment, $1 - \alpha_{11}$, is given by

$$(12) \qquad 1 - \alpha_{11} = \frac{\beta_1 \gamma_1 + 1}{\beta_1 \gamma_1 + \beta_1 \gamma_{11} + (1 - \lambda)^{-1}}.$$

From this analysis, we see that there are two important questions. First, how might employment protection influence the *speed of adjustment*, $1 - \alpha_{11}$? Second how might employment protection affect the *equilibrium unemployment rate*, u^*? The first of these is straightforward. We would expect employment protection to raise employment adjustment costs and this would increase λ. Furthermore, employment protection may tend to increase long-term unemployment by reducing the rate of flow from unemployment to employment, as employers become more cautious about hiring. This will typically generate hysteresis effects in wage determination and thereby raise γ_{11}. Increases in both λ and γ_{11} will tend to reduce the overall speed of adjustment, $1 - \alpha_{11}$.

Turning to the second question, namely the impact on equilibrium unemployment, it is important to recognize that, just because employment protection may tend to lengthen the duration of unemployment spells, this does not mean that it will necessarily raise equilibrium unemployment, u^*. For offsetting the duration effect is the reduction in flows. The flow into unemployment is obviously reduced by regulations designed to restrict dismissals. Since the unemployment rate is the product of the inflow rate and the mean duration, the overall effect of employment protection on u^* is indeterminate.

Looking at the formula for u^* in (11), there are a number of possibilities. First, employment protection may influence wage pressure, z_w, directly, for example, by raising the power of insiders. Second, employment protection can raise the impact of unemployment on wages, γ_1, by making the threat of unemployment more unpleasant (longer duration, harder to find alternative employment). On the other hand, of course, since employees are protected against dismissal to some extent, the threat of unemployment is less germane and this will *reduce* γ_1. So the overall effect on u^* is ambiguous.

Finally, we have not modeled participation in this exercise but we should consider the implications of employment protection for employment rates as well as unemployment rates when we come to our empirical investigation.

3.5.2. Evidence on Unemployment Dynamics

Our purpose is to explore the evidence on the relationship between employment protection, employment adjustment, and both the dynamics of labor demand (λ) and the extent of hysteresis in wage determination (γ_{11}).[7]

We first investigate the relationship between some empirical measures of λ, a measure of the rate of turnover of employees within companies (the percentage of employees with job tenures less than two years, PL2), and the OECD composite ranking of the tightness of employment protection (EP). The data are reported in Table 3.4. The first point to note is the very strong correlation between EP and PL2, the correlation coefficient between the two variables being 0.9. So the variation in the rate of turnover (as captured by the proportion of employees with less than two years tenure) is explained almost entirely by the strictness of the employment protection laws. The relationship between PL2 and our various measures of λ is set out in Table 3.5. In two out of the three cases, we see that PL2 is significantly related to the aggregate measure of labor demand sluggishness (λ). Overall, therefore, there is some evidence in favor of the hypothesis that the speed of adjustment in labor demand is negatively related to the strictness of employment protection legislation.

Turning next to wage determination, we are concerned here with the relationship between the degrees of hysteresis $(\gamma_{1\ 1})$ and employment protection, operating via long-term unemployment. The impact of long-term unemployment on the extent of hysteresis is confirmed explicitly in Layard, Nickell and Jackman (1991, Chapter 9, Table 9) and implicitly in OECD (1993, Chapter 3).[8] So we can simply focus on the impact of employment protection on long-term unemployment, in particular on the proportion of the unemployed who have a duration of more than one year. As well as employment protection, we should also expect the long-term proportion to be influenced by the duration of benefit availability (BD) and by expenditure on active labor market policies (ALMP), many of which are designed to prevent the build-up of long-term unemployment. In Table 3.4 we provide two measures of long-term unemployment. The first is simply the 1985-93 average proportion of unemployed with durations exceeding one year. The second attempts to standardize this proportion, when possible, by measuring it for each country when unemployment lies between 5 and 7 percent. The idea here is to focus on the extent of long-term unemployment at *given levels of aggregate unemployment.* Because the long-term proportion tends to be an increasing function of the overall unemployment rate in the long-run, anything which explains unemployment in general will tend to be correlated with the long-term proportion in a cross-section. The standardized measure will eliminate this problem.

The relevant regressions explaining the two measures of the long-term proportion are:

Table 3.4

Further Data Used for Analyzing Employment Protection

	λ (INJ)	λ (NS)	λ (BLN)	Percentage of employees with tenure <2 years (PL2)	LTU 85-93	LTU (standardized)	γ1	Employment rate 1990	Employment protection
Belgium	0.64	0.92	0.76	18	67	35.9	4.06	55.0	17
Denmark	0.48	–	0.26	27	29.4	36.2	1.74	75.7	5
France	0.74	0.90	0.72	22.2	40.8	30.3	4.35	57.9	14
West Germany	0.86	0.88	0.36	21	44.1	21.2	1.01	62.9	15
Ireland	0.85	0.86	0.71	22	54.6	31.8	1.82	50.2	12
Italy	0.81	0.74	0.65	13	66.2	35.8	12.94	52.6	20
Netherlands	0.85	0.91	0.90	26.9	50.4	27.1	2.28	59.2	9
Portugal								67.2	18
Spain	0.66	–	–	13.6	55.4	27.5	1.21	47.4	19
United Kingdom	0.70	0.88	0.37	31	40.9	24.5	0.98	70.4	7
Australia	0.35	0.49	0.43	36.8	29.3	21.1	0.73	68.6	4
New Zealand	0.84	–	–	–	–	14.7	3.23	66.1	2
Canada	0.92	0.91	0.17	33.7	8.8	3.5	2.38	70.5	3
United States	0.38	0.10	0	39.7	8.2	4.2	0.94	71.6	1
Japan	0.85	0.83	0.65	20	15.1	18.8	14.50	71.7	8
Austria	0.85	0.84	0.56	–	–	13.3	3.11	65.0	16
Finland	0.45	0.91	0.32	26.3	17.4	12.0	1.55	73.5	10
Norway	0.88	0	0.07	17	14.5	10.8	10.59	73.6	11
Sweden	0.60	0.78	0.16	–	7.9	6.8	12.16	81.7	13
Switzerland	0.81	0.83	0.12	29.3	18.9	17.0	7.33	79.5	6

Notes: λ = coefficient on lagged dependent variable in an employment equation. LNJ = Layard, Nickell and Jackman (1991, Chapter 9, Table A1, p. 450); NS = Newell and Symons (1985); BLN = Bean, Layard and Nickell (1986) both as reported in Alogoskoufis and Manning (1988, Table 6); in Layard, Nickell and Jackman (1991, Chapter 9, Table A3, pp. 454-466).

PL2 = percentage of manufacturing employees with tenure less than 2 years. It is based on Metcalf (1986), Table 4, and on OECD (1993), Table 4.1. Where information for a given country appears in both places, the average is reported. The figure for Spain is derived as follows: In OECD (1993), Table 4.1, it is reported that 31.6 percent of employees had tenure of less than 2 years. But much of this was a consequence of the introduction of fixed term workers in 1990. 23.8 percent of employees held fixed term ($\leq$3 year) contracts so, if we suppose that three quarters of these have a job tenure under 2 years, removing these leaves 13.6 percent as reported in the table.

EP = a measure whereby countries are ranked by the strictness of their employment protection legislation (i.e. 1 = least strict, etc.). These data are taken from OECD (1994), Table 6.7. col. 5.

LTU85-93 = percentage of unemployed with a duration of unemployment of more than 1 year. Where possible, this is measured for each country when the aggregate unemployment rate is between 5 and 7 percent (OECD, Employment Outlook, various issues, statistical annex).

LTU (standardized) = percentage of unemployed with a duration of unemployment of more than 1 year. Where possible, this is measured for each country when the aggregate unemployment rate is between 5 and 7 percent (OECD, Employment Outlook, various issues. The data refer to various dates in the 1980s).

Employment rate = employment as a proportion of the population of working age. OECD Jobs Study. Evidence and Explanations. Table 6.8.

$$LTU(\text{standardized}) = 21.5 + 0.24BD - 0.51ALMP87 + 0.55EP + 13.8IT.$$
$$(2.7) \qquad\qquad (3.2) \qquad\qquad (1.5) \qquad (2.8)$$

$$N = 19, \ R^2 = 0.55$$

(IT is a dummy for Italy, which is included because although Italy has only a short benefit duration, the level of benefit is negligible, so its duration is irrelevant.) The overall picture is that there is some evidence that stricter employment protection legislation raises long-term unemployment and thus enhances hysteresis in wage setting. When added to the results on labor demand, we feel that we have some fairly strong and coherent evidence that the strictness of employment protection legislation does influence labor market dynamics by raising unemployment persistence. Whether or not it influences the equilibrium level of unemployment is the issue we consider next.

Table 3.5

Slope Coefficients in a Regression of λ on PL2

Dependent variable	λ (LNJ)	λ (NS)	λ (BLN)
PL2	-0.011 (2.1)	-0.0081 (0.6)	-0.010 (2.4)
N	16.00	14.00	15.00
R^2	0.23	0.04	0.23

$$LTU \ 85-93 = 37.4 + 0.55BD - 0.33ALMP91 + 1.77EP + 30.6IT.$$
$$(3.4) \qquad (3.9) \qquad\qquad (3.3) \qquad (3.6)$$

$$N = 17, \ R^2 = 0.82$$

3.5.3. Evidence on Equilibrium Unemployment

As we noted earlier, employment protection can influence equilibrium unemployment by directly influencing wage pressure and/or by affecting the impact of unemployment on wages (γ_1). This latter parameter is crucial in translating wage pressure into unemployment (see equation (11)).

We begin by looking at the effect of employment protection on γ_1 and then move on to consider its overall impact on average unemployment. As we argue in Layard, Nickell and Jackman (1991), there are a number of other possible factors which can influence γ_1. These include the structure of the benefit system (replacement rates and benefit duration), and the extent of union and employer co-ordination in wage bargaining. In Table 3.4 we present estimates for γ_1 from Layard, Nickell and Jackman (Chapter 9, Table 7). The relevant regression to explain γ_1 is

$$\gamma_1 = 11.9 - 0.078RR - 2.12BD + 1.32(UNCD + EMCD) + 0.23EP.$$
$$\quad (0.9) \qquad (4.8) \qquad (2.3) \qquad\qquad\qquad (1.7)$$

$$N = 19, \; R^2 = 0.71$$

This indicates that if employment protection legislation is very strict, this tends to be associated with high values of γ_1. Of course, EP is not significant at conventional levels but it is most unlikely that there is, in reality, a strong effect in the opposite direction. So, from this channel the data indicate, if anything, employment protection reduces unemployment. But, since we know that employment protection can also increase wage pressure, we must also investigate its total impact on unemployment.

There is some weak evidence that employment protection tends overall to increase employment. But the t-statistics are never very significant. We ran a large number of further variations using alternative measures of union density and union coverage and also different measures of employment protection. In some eighteen regressions, we were able to obtain only two significant negative coefficients on EP. So there is no strong evidence that employment protection affects equilibrium unemployment. This is, of course, consistent with the fact that while we have good reason to expect employment protection legislation to reduce flows both into and out of unemployment, we have no strong reasons for believing either effect to dominate.

3.5.4. Conclusions

We would expect employment protection legislation to slow down the speed with which the labor market adjusts to shocks but to have only a minor impact on the long-run equilibrium. It may however affect the position of those entering or reentering the labor market because of the effective restrictions on hiring. In practice, there is considerable evidence that employment protection reduces adjustment speeds in the labor market. But it is hard to find any significant effects on equilibrium unemployment rates.

3.6. Taxes on Employment

Lowering payroll taxes is a perennial suggestion by those concerned to reduce unemployment. Thus the *OECD Jobs Study* (1994) recommends that we should "Reduce non-wage labor costs, especially in Europe, by reducing taxes on labor..." (p. 46). The European Commission's White Paper on Employment proposes a reduction in payroll taxes in conjunction with an increase in taxes on energy. Another straightforward policy would be to lower payroll taxes and make up the shortfall by raising consumption taxes. Phelps (1994) argues that "such a substitution of tax instruments would achieve a major gain in employment and some gain in the general level of real wage rates as well" (p. 28). Presumably, such a switch would work equally as well in a non-European country, such as the United States, where the sum of payroll and income taxes is substantial.

The general argument for this switch goes as follows.[9] Payroll taxes apply only to labor income; consumption taxes apply to all income (which is spent). So a switch from the former to the latter raises the reward for working relative to not working and thereby reduces unemployment. More formally, we may write total real income in work net of taxes, Y, as

$$Y = \frac{W(1 - t_1)(1 - t_2)}{P(1 + t_3)} + \frac{Y_n(1 - t_2)}{P(1 + t_3)},$$

where W = labor costs, t_1 = payroll tax rate, t_2 = income tax rate, P = output price at factor cost, t_3 = consumption tax rate, Y_n = non-labor income. This may be rewritten as

$$Y = \frac{vW}{P}\left(1 + \frac{Y_n}{(1 - t_1)}\right),$$

where $v = (1 - t_1)(1 - t_2)/(1 + t_3) - (1 - t_1 - t_2 - t_3)$, the tax wedge, $y_n = Y_n/W$, the ratio of non-labor income to labor costs. Consider now the real income when unemployed. Y^u. This may be written as

$$Y^u = \frac{B(1 - t_2)}{P(1 + t_3)} + \frac{Y_n(1 - t_2)}{P(1 + t_3)}$$

$$= \frac{vW}{P}\left(b + \frac{y_n}{1 - t_1}\right),$$

where $b = B/W(1 - t_1)$ = unemployment benefit/wage ratio. The definition of Y^u assumes that benefits are subject to income tax.

In most theories of wage determination, the wage cost which is set depends on Y/Y^u which is increasing in b, y_n, and t_1. Increases in b, y_n, and t_1 will, therefore, automatically raise equilibrium unemployment. So a reduction in t_1 and an equal increase in t_3 will leave the tax wedge, v, unchanged but will lower equilibrium unemployment so long as y_n is not zero.[10] How big is this effect? The crucial factor is the extent of non-labor income which is not subject to payroll tax. It is arguable that, for the typical person at risk of unemployment, this non-labor income is extremely small. For example, in 1987/88, only 7 percent of unemployment entrants in Britain had savings of more than £3K, a sum which would produce an annual interest income of around 10 percent of unemployment benefit (Layard, Nickell and Jackman 1991, Table A6). So it may be that this tax switching effect is simply too small to have any noticeable effect.

A more fundamental question is whether any of the taxes (payroll, income, or consumption) have an impact on labor costs in the long-run, or whether they are all eventually shifted onto labor. An obvious first approach to this issue is to see whether countries with high taxes have higher labor costs than those with low taxes. We must obviously correct for productivity which suggests that we correlate

$$\frac{W}{P} / \frac{Y}{N}$$

with tax rates across countries (W = labor costs, P = GDP deflator, Y = GDP, N = employment). But this procedure is open to objection. Real labor costs normalized on productivity is precisely equivalent to WN/PY, the share of labor. In a Cobb-Douglas world, for example, an increase in taxes might lead to a rise in W/P and a fall in N, with the share of labor unchanged. The proposed correlation will then understate the true impact of taxes because of the fall in N when labor costs rise. This suggests that we normalize real labor costs on Y/L where L is the labor force. Taking average values over the period 1980-90 for thirteen OECD countries[11] we obtain:

$$WL/py = 7.06 + 0.017t_1 + 0.033t_2 - 0.12t_3,$$
$$(0.6) \qquad (0.5) \qquad (0.9)$$
$$(R^2 = 0.13, \ N = 13, \ t \text{ ratios in brackets})$$

where t_1 is the payroll tax rate, t_2 is the income tax rate, t_3 is the consumption tax rate. Basically there is no relationship between tax rates and labor costs, indicating complete shifting onto labor. A similar result due to James Symons and Donald Robertson and based on changes is reported in OECD (1990, Annex 6A). Using changes between 1974 and 1986 across 16 OECD countries,[12] they obtain

$$\Delta \log W/P = -0.05 + 0.009\Delta t_1 + 0.33\Delta t_2 + 0.68\Delta t_3 + 0.97\Delta \log \text{PROD}.$$
$$(0.3) \qquad (0.6) \qquad (1.1) \qquad (5.3)$$

$(R^2 = 0.80, \ N = 16, \ t$ ratios in brackets; PROD is labor productivity)

Here again we see no significant effects of tax changes on real labor costs although the numbers suggest that consumption taxes have the biggest impact.

While these cross-section regressions are useful for looking at long-run tax shifting, only time-series analysis can shed light on the dynamics. First we report some further results in the same Annex due to Symons and Robertson, which are the average coefficients and t ratios emerging from individual time-series regressions for 16 OECD countries. Thus we have:

$$\log(W/P)_t = \text{const.} + 0.84\log(W/OP)_{-1} + 0.12\log(K/L)_t$$
$$(9.6) \qquad\qquad\qquad (1.4)$$
$$+ 0.46\Delta(t_1 + t_2 + t_3) + 0.07t_1 - 0.07t_2 + 0.26t_3.$$
$$(2.3) \qquad\qquad (0.3) \quad\; (0.2) \quad\; (0.1)$$

(average t ratios in brackets)

These results suggest there is no systematic long-run impact of taxes on labor costs but that the short-run effects are substantial. A one percentage point increase in the tax wedge (from whatever source) leads to a short-run increase in labor costs of around 1/2 percent which takes a long time to fade away. So even after four years, labor costs are still 1/4 percent higher. Such effects will lead to significant and persistent temporary increases in unemployment, particularly in the light of the fact that tax wedges have risen by 10 to 20 percentage points in the last 30 years in most OECD countries. In the long-run, however, these unemployment effects will disappear.

These significant and long-lasting temporary tax effects imply that, when looking at individual country data, it is very difficult to discriminate between the short and long-run impacts of the individual taxes. There is simply not enough information. Consequently, the impression given by the collection of individual country time series studies of wage determination is that the estimated tax effects are all over the place.

It is not worth repeating the summaries in Layard, Nickell and Jackman (1991) and OECD (1994) but we may consider one other example, namely the work of Tyrväinen reported in OECD (1994). This work focuses on the long-run effects of taxes by using the Johansen method to estimate long-run cointegrating relationships between labor costs, taxes, and other relevant variables. The long-run tax effects he obtains are given in Table 3.6. The first point that stands out is how big the tax effects are. Whereas our previous evidence indicated zero long-run tax effects, here we have a substantial long-run impact of taxes. Second, in all but two of the countries, the tax effects are uniform across all taxes. Indeed, in no country is there any advantage in switching from payroll taxes to consumption taxes.[13]

Table 3.6

Labor Cost Responses to Changes in Tax Rates

	Semi-elasticity of labor costs with respect to:		
	Employers' payroll taxes (t_1)	Income taxes and employees' social security contributions (t_2)	Value-added and excise taxes (t_3)
Australia	0.5	0.5	0.5
Canada	0.8	0.8	0.8
Finlan	0.5	0.5	0.5
France	0.4	0.4	0.4
Germany	1.0	1.0	1.0
Italy	0.4	0.4	0.4
Japan	0.5	0.5	0.5
Sweden	0.0	0.0	1.0
United Kingdom	0.25	0.25	0.25
United States	0.0	1.0	0.0

Source: T. Tyrväinen. "Real Wage Resistance and Unemployment: Multivariate Analysis of Cointegrating Relations in 10 OECD Economies," The OECD Jobs Study: Working Paper Series. Shows $d\log(W/P)/dt_1$.

We have investigated these matters further in the context of our pooled regression equation of Table 3.2. The payroll tax rate, as an additional explanatory variable turns out to be insignificant (with a t-statistic of 0.4) though the total tax burden as percentage of GDP comes in with a small significant positive coefficient (though no effect on long-term unemployment). These results require further investigation.

On balance, we may perhaps conclude that taxes may have an adverse effect on unemployment in the long run, but any such effect is smallish, and that it relates to the burden of taxation in total and not to payroll taxes in particular.[14]

3.7. Work-Sharing And Early Retirement

Two final much-canvassed solutions to unemployment are reduced hours of work and early retirement. Advocates of these measures often seem to believe that there is some exogenous limit to the amount of work to be done. But history shows that, for a given institutional structure, the amount of work tends to adjust in line with the available supply of labor – leaving the equilibrium rate of unemployment unchanged. We can begin with some theoretical remarks, before supporting them with evidence.

3.7.1. Theoretical Issues

We shall first examine the underlying theory in a long-term context, using for illustration a simple efficiency wage model. Efficiency per worker hour is e, which depends on hourly wages (W_i) relative to the expected wage ($\hat{W}$) and on the unemployment rate: $e_i = e(W_i/\hat{W}, u)$. Output is given by $f(eHN)$ where H is hours per worker, which can be varied exogenously. Then the profits of the representative firm are

$$\pi_i = f(e_i H N_i) - \frac{W_i}{e_i} e_i H N_i \qquad (f' > 0, f'' < 0).$$

The problem is recursive and the firm can first choose W_i to minimize W_i/e_i. The optimum wage is then given by

$$e_i\left(\frac{W_i}{\hat{W}}, u\right) = e\left(\frac{W_i}{\hat{W}}, u\right).$$

Hence in general equilibrium (with $W_i = \hat{W}$) unemployment is determined by

$$e_i(1, u) = e(1, u).$$

This holds irrespective of hours.

This result arises because the change in hours affects both those making the wage comparison and the reference group with which the comparison is being made. In the long run both groups must be paid the same. However in the short run things could be different, especially if people are comparing their wage with what they think they "ought to" be paid – as in many models of real wage resistance. The problem here is that people's ideas of what they should be paid adjust only gradually to the reality of what they are paid. Thus

$$\Delta\log\hat{W} = \gamma(\log W_{-1} - \log\hat{W}_{-1}).$$

Suppose there is now a downward productivity shock. Sluggish adjustment of the reference wage will for a time prevent actual wages falling as much as is needed to preserve employment. In this case reduced hours can be an appropriate adjustment to temporary shocks. Indeed in general there can be no objection to allowing hours to act as shock-absorbers, as in Japan. But this is quite different from saying that lower hours will secure permanently higher employment. They will not, and they will also reduce the national output.

Similar arguments apply to the use of early retirement. Since labor market equilibrium requires a given unemployment rate, reductions in labor supply will simply reduce equilibrium employment. Employment will of course take a while to adjust down, and, until it does, there will be extra inflationary pressure in the economy – which eventually leads to the necessary fall in real aggregate demand (assuming nominal demand follows a steady path). However again a negative productivity shock together with real wage resistance will lead to less unemployment if the labor force is temporarily reduced.

3.7.2. Empirical Analysis

It is fairly simple to check on these basic lines of reasoning. We ran the following wage equation for each of our usual 19 OECD countries for the years 1952 to 1990:

$$\dot{w} = a_1\dot{w}_{-1} + (1 - a_1)\, \dot{p}_{-1} + a_2\, (w - p)_{-1} + a_3\log L + a_4\log N + a_5\log H$$

$$+ a_6t + \text{const},$$

where w is log hourly earnings in manufacturing, p is log consumption deflator, L is labor force, N employment, H is average weekly hours in manufacturing, and t is time. We then computed the average value of each coefficient (averaged across all countries) and its average t-statistic.

If our reasoning has been correct we would expect:

(i) $\log H$ to have no significant effect; and
(ii) a_3 to be insignificantly different from $(-a_4)$, indicating that it is the unemployment rate which affects wage pressure and the size of the labor force exerts no independent influence.

Both expectations were born out. The equation looked as follows, with average coefficients and average t-statistics:

$$w = 0.37w_{-1} + 0.63p_{-1} - 0.12(w - p)_{-1} - 2.10\log L + 1.82\log N$$
$$\quad (1.8) \qquad\qquad (0.7) \qquad\qquad (2.3) \qquad\quad (2.8)$$

$$- 0.16\log H + 0.008t + \text{const}.$$
$$\quad (0.1) \qquad\quad (1.4)$$

Hours have no significant effect and a cut in the labor force raises wage pressure in a way that can only be offset by an equivalent cut in jobs.

We again examine these effects also in the context of our pooled cross-section regression of Table 3.2. Average hours worked, as additional explanatory variable, had a small but statistically insignificant $(t = 1.1)$ negative effect on unemployment. A more rapid growth of the labor force was also associated with significantly $(t = 2.4)$ lower unemployment, but this result is not very plausible, and may reflect largely the rapid growth of the labor force in the United States.

3.8. Conclusions

We have found clear evidence that unemployment is strongly affected by how unemployed people are treated and by how wages are determined. There are also indications that problems of skill mismatch have exacerbated European unemployment. As regards employment protection, there is no clear evidence of whether it decreases the outflow rate from unemployment by more or less than it decreases the inflow rate. And there appears to be no long-term effect on unemployment rates from employment taxes or from work-sharing/early retirement.

Thus it is unhelpful to focus the discussion of unemployment on the concept of flexibility. Clearly lower benefits and less employment protection are examples of more flexibility. But active labor market policy, coordinated wage bargaining, and skill training are not exactly forms of flexibility.

It seems better to focus on the proper role of government in affecting unemployment. Clearly lower benefits of shorter duration would reduce unemployment, but these policies should be accompanied by more (not less) active labor market policy. Similarly governments would be ill-advised to encourage the dismantling of bargaining structures. And they ought certainly to ensure that most youngsters enter adult life with a basic level of competence.

Indeed if Europe's social chapter is to contribute to lower unemployment in Europe it needs to impose two further obligations on governments: a) to prevent entry to long-term unemployment (by replacing long-term benefits by active labor market policy), and b) to prevent young people ceasing their education (full-time or part-time) until they have acquired basic literacy, numeracy, and vocational competence.

4

Labor Market Institutions and Economic Performance

This 1999 article is one of the most cited textbook references in this field. Starting with the juxtaposition of the US vs. Europe, but also referring to significant intra-European differences in labor market success over the 1990s, Stephen Nickell and Richard Layard discuss and check the explanatory potential of a large set of core labor market institutions such as (a) the levels of taxes on labor, (b) the regulation of working conditions such as working time and leave, (c) trade union activity and collective bargaining as well as minimum wages, (d) unemployment benefit systems and active labor market policy, (e) education and skill formation and, finally, (f) home ownership. Relying on a comprehensive theoretical and empirical discussion within their unified analytical framework, they assess the impact of major labor market institutions on unemployment, productivity, and economic growth across countries. In many respects, their balanced judgments are still valid today. The article concludes that the key labor market institutions on which policy action should be focused are trade unions, where product market competition matters, and social security systems which should be reformed to establish a strong link between benefits on the one hand and active labor market policies on the other hand in order to move people from welfare to work. By comparison, Layard and Nickell emphasize time spent complaining about strict employment protection and minimum wages is probably wasted.

The original version of this chapter was published as: Nickell, S., Layard, R. (1999). Labour Market Institutions and Economic Performance, in: Ashenfelter, O. C. Card, D. (Eds.), Handbook of Labour Economics, Volume 3C, Amsterdam, 3029-3084. By permission of Oxford University Press.

4.1. Introduction

Barely a day goes by without some expert telling us how the continental European economies are about to disintegrate unless their labor markets become more flexible. Basically, we are told, Europe has the wrong sort of labor market institutions for the modern global economy. These outdated institutions both raise unemployment and lower growth rates. The truth of propositions such as these depends on which labor market institutions really are bad for unemployment and growth, and which are not. Our purpose here is to set out what we know about this question. One reason for doing this is to try and focus future attention on those institutions that really do make a difference, so that less time is wasted worrying about those that do not.

We restrict ourselves to the OECD countries. In Section 4.2., we show the substantial differences in performance across the different countries. As is well known, the US has had lower unemployment than many European countries, but by no means all. On productivity per hour worked, the US and core Europe are now at much the same level. But the US has had much lower productivity growth (per hour) than Europe. These are among the facts to be investigated.

In Section 4.3. we lay out the main institutional differences that might explain the facts. We focus on five main sets of institutions – the levels of labor taxation; the systems of employment protection; trade union activity and minimum wages; income support for the unemployed and active labor market policy; and education and skill formation. We then see how far these institutional differences are able to explain the cross-country range of differences in unemployment and productivity growth. In Section 4.4., we develop some theory as to how these factors might affect the outcomes, and in Section 4.5., we provide some general empirical evidence in the form of cross-sectional cross-country regressions. After this we look in detail at each of the five main kinds of institutions, assembling evidence from a variety of sources. Section 4.11. summarizes our conclusions.

The section on skills and education (Section 4.10.) goes rather further than the other sections, since it looks not only at unemployment but also at wage inequality. Some writers have tended to assume that in all countries the demand for skill has outrun the supply, and the only difference lies in the differential response of wages and employment (caused by institutional factors, e.g., Krugman 1994). Instead we first document the movements of demand and supply in different countries and show a greater problem in the US and the UK than elsewhere. Then we examine how this movement explains changes in unemployment rates and wage differentials. We also examine how far, in terms of levels, the distribution of skills alone can explain the level of wage inequality.

All the issues we discuss have been looked at many times before (see, e.g., Layard, Nickell and Jackman 1991) but not always within such a unified framework and much more in relation to unemployment than growth.

4.2. Economic Performance

It is commonplace to summarize the economic performance of countries by GDP per capita. This probably subsumes a bit too much, so here we split this variable into productivity and the employment/ population rate. Furthermore variations in the latter are generated by many factors of which perhaps the most interesting is the unemployment rate, because it is probably the least voluntary. Other important contributing factors include female participation rates and early retirement rates. With these, however, it is harder to say that more work is "better" whereas few would want to argue that about unemployment. The unemployed are looking for work, by definition, as well as being notoriously unhappy about not having it (Clark and Oswald 1994). In particular, the average unemployed person is much more unhappy, ceteris paribus, than the average person who is out of the labor force. This suggests that, on average, being out of the labor force is a different state from being unemployed and it is best not to combine the two. Nevertheless, it is clear that some individuals who are recorded as unemployed in some countries would be out of the labor force in others. For example, some of the large number of working age individuals on disability pensions in the Netherlands would probably be classified as unemployed in other countries.[1] In the light of this, we consider other aspects of labor input although our main focus will be on unemployment.

In Table 4.1, we present some measures of unemployment. The first point to notice is the enormous variation in rates across countries despite the fact that they are as close to being comparable as we can get.[2] Taking the long-term average from 1983-1996, the rates stretch from 1.8% in Switzerland to 19.7% in Spain. This variation means that,

Table 4.1

Unemployment Rates in the OECD (%)[a]

	1997 (Spring) Total	1983-1996 Total	1983-1988 Total	Short-term	Long-term	1989-1994 Total	Short-term	Long-term
Austria	4.5	3.8	3.6	na	na	3.7	na	na
Belgium	9.6	9.7	11.3	3.3	8.0	8.1	2.9	5.1
Denmark	6.3	9.9	9.0	6.0	3.0	10.8	7.9	3.0
Finland	15.4	9.1	5.1	4.0	1.0	10.5	8.9	1.7
France	12.5	10.4	9.8	5.4	4.4	10.4	6.5	3.9
Germany (W)	7.7	6.2	6.8	3.7	3.1	5.4	3.2	2.2
Ireland	11.7	15.1	16.1	6.9	9.2	14.8	5.4	9.4
Italy	8.2	7.6	6.9	3.1	3.8	8.2	2.9	5.3
Netherlands	5.7	8.4	10.5	5.0	5.5	7.0	3.5	3.5
Norway	4.8	4.2	2.7	2.5	0.2	5.5	4.3	1.2
Protugal	7.2	6.4	7.6	3.5	4.2	5.0	3.0	2.0
Spain	21.4	19.7	19.6	8.3	11.3	18.9	9.1	9.7
Sweden	10.9	4.3	2.6	2.3	0.3	4.4	4.0	0.4
Switzerland	4.0	1.8	0.8	0.7	0.1	2.3	1.8	0.5
UK	7.3	9.7	10.9	5.8	5.1	8.9	5.5	3.4
Japan	3.2	2.6	2.7	2.2	0.5	2.3	1.9	0.4
Australia	8.8	8.7	8.4	5.9	2.4	9.0	6.2	2.7
New Zealand	6.0	6.8	4.9	4.3	0.6	8.9	6.6	2.3
Canada	9.3	9.8	9.9	9.0	0.9	9.8	8.9	0.9
US	4.9	6.5	7.1	6.4	0.7	6.2	5.6	0.6

[a] These rates are OECD standarized rates with the exception of Austria, Denmark, and Italy. For Austria and Denmark we use national registered rates. For Italy we use the Bureau of Labor Statistics (BLS) "unemployment rates on US concepts." Aside from Italy, the OECD rates and the BLS rates are very similar. For Italy, the OECD rates appear to include the large numbers of Italians who who are registered as unemployed but have performed no active job search in the previous 4 weeks. Long-term rates refer to those unemployed with durations over 1 year. The data are taken from the OECD Employment Outlook and the UK Employment Trends, published by the Department of Employment and Education.

over the long term, around 30% of people in OECD Europe live in countries where unemployment is, on average, lower than the United States. However, at the precise time of writing, this number is much lower. Second, it is worth noting that the variation in short-term unemployment is substantially smaller than that in long-term unemployment. Indeed the latter seems to be a bit of an optional extra, the reason being that long-term unemployment, in contrast to the short-term variety, contributes very little to holding down inflation (OECD 1993).

As we have already indicated, alternative measures of labor input are also important, so we present a number of different aspects of this variable in Table 4.2. The overall measure of labor supply in column (7) is based on total hours worked per member of the population of working age and combines both annual hours per worker (column (3)) and the employment population ratio (column (5)). The enormous variation in this variable explains the large differences between GDP per hour and GDP per capita which we shall see in Table 4.3.

The cross country variation in employment/population ratios in column (5) is due to three main factors. First, variations in the participation of married women, which are very low in southern Europe and very high in Scandinavia and the United States (see column (2)). Second, variations in the retirement rates for men over the age of 55 (column (1)) and third, variations in the employment rates of prime age men (column (6)). These latter are generated by differing unemployment and disability rates. As we have already indicated, some of the non-participants in one place might well appear as unemployed in another depending on the structure of the benefit system. For example, if you have been out of work for a year in the United States or Italy, you will not be entitled to any benefits whether or not you say you are looking for work.

So there is no strong incentive to classify yourself as unemployed (looking for work) in the relevant survey. In countries with longer durations of benefit availability, the incentive to look for work and hence to be classified as unemployed is obviously stronger. It is, however, important not to make too much of this. The measured unemployment rates used here are all based on sample surveys which bear no official or unofficial relationship to formal unemployment registration and the benefit system. Thus, in Britain, for example, large numbers of individuals record themselves as unemployed on the survey based definition used here who are not counted in the official

Table 4.2

Measures of Labor Input in the 1990s

	Early retirement[a]	Participation[b]	Annual hours[c]	Growth rate (% pa)[d]	Emp./pop.[e]	Emp./pop.[f]	Total hours[g]	Self-employment[h]
	(1)	(2)	(3)	(4)	(5)	(6)	(7)	(8)
Austria	60	58.7	1610	0.4	67.3	86.8	51.6	6.7
Belgium	65	55.2	1580	0.3	56.1	87.4	42.6	14.3
Denmark	31	78.3	1510	0.3	75.0	86.6	54.5	6.8
Finland	55	70.0	1768	0.5	67.1	82.4	57.1	8.8
France	54	59.0	1654	0.7	59.8	87.9	47.4	9.1
Germany (W)	42	55.2	1610	0.5	65.2	87.0	50.0	8.0
Ireland	35	46.1	1720	0.9	53.2	80.3	44.8	12.8
Italy	64	43.3	1730	0.2	54.0	84.3	44.9	22.2
Netherlands	54	56.0	1510	0.7	62.2	86.5	45.2	8.1
Norway	27	70.8	1437	0.5	73.3	87.4	50.4	6.1
Portugal	33	62.0	2004	0.1	69.3	90.6	66.6	15.9
Spain	38	43.0	1815	0.7	47.5	81.5	41.6	17.5
Sweden	25	75.8	1485	0.3	75.6	88.2	52.0	7.1
Switzerland	18	67.6	1637	0.6	78.6	94.7	62.0	-

Table 4.2 (continued)

Measures of Labor Input in the 1990s

	Early retirement[a]	Participation[b]	Annual hours[c]	Growth rate (% pa)[d]	Emp./pop.[e]	Emp./pop.[f]	Total hours[g]	Self-employment[h]
	(1)	(2)	(3)	(4)	(5)	(6)	(7)	(8)
UK	32	65.3	1720	0.4	69.6	86.7	58.6	12.4
Japan	17	61.8	1965	0.6	73.4	95.9	69.2	11.6
Australia	37	62.3	1850	1.4	68.2	86.5	61.3	12.5
New Zealand	43	63.2	1812	0.7	68.0	86.6	59.8	14.7
Canda	35	67.7	1714	2.1	70.6	84.7	59.0	7.5
US	32	69.0	1919	0.8	73.1	88.2	68.2	7.7

[a] OECD Employment Outlook (1996, Table B, p.188). Defined as (100 less the percent participation rate in 1990 for males 55-64).

[b] OECD Employment Outlook (1996, Table K, p.197). Female labor force divided by the female working age population (15-64) in 1993. West Germany is for 1990.

[c] OECD Employment Outlook (1996, Table C, p. 190). Average annual hours worked per employee (1992). Austria is set equal to Germany, Ireland to UK, Denmark to Netherlands.

[d] OECD Employment Outlook. Growth rate of the population of working age, 1988-1993.

[e] OECD Employment Outlook (1996, Tables A,B). (Average of 1990 and 1994.) Employment/population ratio (whole working age population).

[f] OECD Employment Outlook (1996, Tables A,B). (Average of 1990 and 1994.) Employment/population ratio (males age 25-54).

[g] [(Average annual hours worked per employee x employment) / (2080 x population of working age)] x 100.

[h] OECD Jobs Study (1994a, Table 6.8). Percentage share of self-employment in total employment in the non-agricultural sector, 1990.

statistics and vice-versa. That is, a substantial number of people who receive unemployment benefit are perfectly happy to report in the survey that they are not actively searching for work (around 19% of the registered unemployed according to the 1995 UK Labour Force Survey).

On the hours front (column (3)), the numbers are dominated by the extent of part-time working and variations in weekly hours and annual holiday entitlements. Many countries in continental Europe have low annual hours actually worked even excluding part-time workers, essentially because of their low weekly hours and long annual holidays compared particularly to the US and Japan. And this does not imply that European workers would like to work more paid hours per year. Indeed, across the EC, more people would like to work *fewer* paid hours than would like to work more paid hours, holding constant the hourly rate of pay (European Economy 1995, Table 25a). This is probably due, at least in part, to higher marginal tax rates. Overall, we can see by comparing unemployment rates over the period 1989-1994 in Table 4.1 with the index of total labor input in column (7) of Table 4.2 that the latter is not the mirror image of the former. Norway, Germany, Sweden, and the Netherlands have a much lower total labor input than the United States and Portugal but their unemployment rates are all much the same. So it is probably worth investigating the impact of labor market institutions on some measures of labor input as well as on unemployment. However, we should emphasize again that the unemployment rate is an important measure of performance in the sense that more probably means worse. Total labor input, on the other hand, is not an unequivocal measure of performance. More does not necessarily mean better and can easily mean worse.

Turning now to measures of productivity performance, in Table 4.3, we list some measures of productivity levels. The obvious point here is the enormous difference between GDP per capita and GDP per hour worked. The latter is, of course, a pure productivity measure and here we see that the major countries of northern and central Europe are at a higher level than the United States, despite being well down in GDP per capita. This simply reflects the far lower level of labor input in most European countries that we have already noted. In the next table we turn to measures of productivity growth using both total factor and labor productivity measures. There are few outstanding features here (Table 4.4) with the exception of some tendency for those with low levels of productivity in Table 4.3 to have high growth rates

Table 4.3

Productivity Levels for the Whole Economy (1994) (US = 100)

| | GDP per capita | GDP per worker | GDP per hour worked | | |
| | | | (a) | (b) | (c) |
	(1)	(2)	(3)	(4)	(5)
Austria	79	87	-	-	100
Belgium	79	103	-	-	116
Denmark	81	80	-	-	96
Finland	64	75	82	78	80
France	76	92	109	104	114
Germany (W)	77	85	105	100	111
Ireland	60	82	-	-	86
Italy	73	98	111	105	87
Netherlands	73	89	124	118	114
Norway	86	87	118	112	108
Portugal	48	54	52	49	49
Spain	53	84	90	86	88
Sweden	68	72	91	98	98
Switzerland	94	82	97	92	106
UK	70	75	84	80	86
Japan	81	74	76	72	79
Australia	72	76	79	75	93
New Zealand	64	68	71	67	-
Canda	80	83	93	88	101
US	100	100	100	100	100

Sources: columns (1)–(4). Pilat (1996). Column (3) uses annual hours from OECD Employment Outlook (1996, Table C). Column (4) adjusts US hours from 1945 to 1950. Column (5) is from Crafts (1997, Table 5, column 1).

Table 4.4

Percentage Productivity Growth After the First Oil Shock

| | Whole economy (1976-1992) | | | Business sector (1986-1993) | |
| | Labor productivity | Labor productivity with hours | TFP with hours | Labor productivity | TFP |
	(1)	(2)	(3)	(4)	(5)
Austria	1.51	2.17	1.20	1.5	0.5
Belgium	1.03	2.21	2.00	1.7	0.9
Denmark	1.23	1.73	1.31	1.8	0.7
Finland	1.93	2.44	1.65	3.5	1.5
France	1.43	2.14	1.81	2.2	1.4
Germany (W)	1.38	2.04	1.91	1.6	1.0
Ireland	2.60	3.14	2.73	3.9	3.3
Italy	2.15	2.51	1.79	2.1	1.3
Netherlands	0.77	1.60	0.74	1.2	1.1
Norway	1.72	2.61	2.19	1.2	0.0
Portugal	2.76	2.79	1.28	–	–
Spain	1.42	2.12	2.18	2.2	1.0
Sweden	0.80	0.92	0.52	2.1	0.8
Switzerland	1.13	1.79	0.95	1.6	0.5
UK	1.76	2.30	1.66	1.9	1.5
Japan	3.09	3.51	1.60	2.2	0.8
Australia	0.91	1.13	0.74	0.9	0.4
New Zealand	-0.13	0.09	-0.33	–	–
Canda	1.35	1.76	0.57	0.9	0.2
US	1.17	1.08	0.22	0.9	0.6

Sources: columns (1), (2) from Summers-Heston with hours of work from OECD Employment Outlook, various issues. Column (3) uses the Centre for Economic Performance OECD dataset. Columns (4), (5) are from Englander and Gurney (1994a, Table 3). In Columns (2), (3), the hours correction involves substracting Δln(hours).

in Table 4.4 (except for New Zealand). The overall picture of performance in the OECD is quite a complex one. The United States has the highest GDP per capita but many countries of central and northern Europe appear to have higher levels of productivity. Broadly speaking these same countries have low levels of labor input, particularly in the form of low hours per year and low employment rates for women and older men. The employment/population ratios for prime age males are much the same in central and northern Europe as in the United States.

4.3. Labor Market Institutions

It is difficult to define precisely what we mean by labor market institutions, so we simply provide a list of those features of the labor market which we shall consider. The boundaries of this list are somewhat arbitrary. For example, we exclude product market regulations even though many of these are introduced at the behest of employees (e.g. regulations on shop opening hours). However, we include certain parts of the tax system, because they impact heavily on the operation of labor market even though they are not normally thought of as labor market institutions.

The "institutions" we consider are first, labor taxes; second, laws and regulations covering employees' rights; third, trade unions and the structure of wage bargaining including minimum wages; fourth, the social security system and the treatment of the unemployed; fifth, the system of education and training, and finally, barriers to regional mobility. We look at each of these in turn.

4.3.1. Taxes on Labor

Under this heading we include payroll taxes, income taxes, and consumption taxes. Of course, this is to some extent an arbitrary choice since some income taxes fall on capital income and some consumption taxes are paid by individuals who are out of the labor force. However, taxation on labor typically operates via the wedge between the real cost of a worker to an employer and the real consumption wage of the worker. Consider a representative firm in a closed economy producing GDP. Then real labor cost per worker is W/P where W is nominal labor cost per worker and P is the GDP deflator (at factor cost). The corresponding consumption wage, assuming workers consume GDP, is $W(1 - t_1)(1 - t_2)/P(1 + t_3)$ where t_1 is the payroll tax rate, t_2 is the income tax rate, and t_3 is the consumption tax rate. The tax wedge is $(1 - t_1)(1 - t_2)/(1 + t_3) \simeq [1 - (t_1 + t_2 + t_3)]$.

So, in general, we may expect the labor market consequences of taxation to operate via the sum of the three tax rates, $(t_1 + t_2 + t_3)$. However, there are some exceptions. For example, because unemployed individuals are not liable for payroll taxes, but do pay income and consumption taxes, the payroll tax rate alone (t_1) is sometimes considered important. Furthermore, the above analysis is based on proportional linear tax schedules. If, for example, the income tax schedule is progressive, then marginal tax rates may have an impact which is independent of the average tax rates and the degree of progressivity may be important.

So in Table 4.5, we present some information on tax rates across the OECD. In the first column, we have the payroll tax rate, defined as the ratio of labor costs to wages (less unity). In the second, we add to this the average income and consumption tax rates derived from aggregate tax and income data. Finally, in the third column we give an OECD estimate of the marginal tax wedge for an average production worker. In some cases, this is lower than the figures in the second column because, in column (3), the payroll tax is restricted to social security payments to public sector schemes, rather than the total of non-wage labor costs used in the other columns.

The key features of these numbers are first, the enormous variation in payroll tax rates stretching from Denmark, where the government levies no social security taxes on firms, to France and Italy with rates close to 40%. Second, while there is less variation in the other two columns, it is clear that the total rates in continental Europe are, with the exception of Switzerland and Portugal, higher by 10-20 percentage points than other OECD countries. This is mainly the consequence of higher levels of public expenditure in continental Europe than elsewhere, primarily focused on more generous social security and pension benefits and the public provision of health care and higher education.

Table 4.5

Tax Rates on Labor: 1980-1994

	Payroll tax rate (%) t_1 [a] (1)	Total tax wedge (%) $(t_1 + t_2 + t_3)$ [b] (2)	Marginal tax wedge (%) 1991-1992 [c] (3)
Austria	22.6	53.7	-
Belgium	21.5	49.8	66.3
Denmark	0.6	46.3	72.1
Finland	25.5	65.9	66.1
France	38.8	63.8	63.4
Germany (W)	23.0	53.0	63.8
Ireland	7.1	34.3	-
Italy	40.2	62.9	62.0
Netherlands	27.5	56.5	70.8
Norway	17.5	48.6	62.9
Portugal	14.5	37.6	-
Spain	33.2	54.2	53.4
Sweden	37.8	70.7	62.6
Switzerland	14.5	38.6	-
UK	13.8	40.8	50.4
Japan	16.5	36.3	22.2
Australia	2.5	28.7	43.5
New Zealand	-	34.8	-
Canda	13.0	42.7	-
US	20.9	43.8	38.5

[a] Centre for Economic Performance (LSE) OECD Dataset. Defined as the ratio of labor costs to wages (less unity). Note that this includes pension and other mandated payments by employers.

[b] Centre for Economic Performance (LSE) OECD Dataset. Defined as the sum of the payroll tax rate, the income tax rate, and the consumption tax rate. The latter are average rates derived from national income accounts including total tax receipts from different types of taxes. See "Data Sources" in Bean, Layard and Nickell (1986) for details.

[c] OECD Jobs Study (1994a, Table 9.1, last column (1991-1992)). Calculated by applying the tax rules to the average production worker. Includes employees' and employers' social security contributions, personal income taxes, and consumption taxes. Non-wage labor costs other than social security contributions are not included; neither are payroll taxes not earmarked for social security or social security contributions paid to the private sector.

4.3.2. Laws and Regulations on Employee Rights

Laws referring to the treatment of employees by companies include regulations on working hours, annual leave, health and safety, employee representation rights (on consultative committees, boards of directors, etc.), workers compensation insurance, fixed term contracts and employment security.[3] Aside from the last two items, these regulations are generally equivalent to an increase in labor costs although they may have additional effects on labor productivity. Regulations under the last two headings typically change the cost to employers of adjusting the size of their labor force. To give some idea of how these regulations vary across the OECD, we present a number of variables which attempt to capture overall labor standards and job security. In the first column of Table 4.6 is a labor standards index. This was produced by the OECD and refers to the strength of the legislation governing a number of aspects of the labor market. Each country is scored from 0 (lax or no legislation) to 2 (strict legislation) on five dimensions: working hours, fixed-term contracts, employment protection, minimum wages, and employees' representation rights. The scores are then summed, generating an index ranging from 0 to 10. The second column is the OECD employment protection index based on the strength of the legal framework governing hiring and firing. Countries are ranked from 1 to 20, with 20 being the most strictly regulated. These rankings are based on a variety of indicators set out in OECD (1994a). The picture generated by both these indices is one in which the countries of southern Europe have the toughest regulations and these tend to weaken as one moves further North (except for Sweden). Switzerland, Denmark, and the United Kingdom have the weakest regulations in Europe, comparable to those in place elsewhere.

In the third and fourth columns of Table 4.6, we present some additional information of a more specialized kind simply for background detail. In column (3) are the regulations on minimum paid annual leave (in addition to public holidays) and, in column (4), we have parental leave entitlement on the birth of a child. The overall impression here is one of minimal legal entitlement in the United States and the United Kingdom and relatively generous legal entitlements in continental Europe, with the exception of Italy. (While Italians are legally entitled to annual paid leave, its length is generally determined via collective bargaining.) Finally, it is worth remarking that while southern Europe has the most regulated labor markets in the OECD, it also has the highest rates of self-employment, which is more or less unregulated.

Table 4.6

Employee Rights

	Labor standards 1985-1993[a] (1)	Employment protection 1990[b] (2)	Minimum annual leave (weeks) 1992[c] (3)	Duration of parental leave (weeks) 1995[d] (4)
Austria	5	16	5	104
Belgium	4	17	4	(260)[e]
Denmark	2	5	5	28
Finland	5	10	5	156
France	6	14	5	156
Germany (W)	6	15	3	156
Ireland	4	12	3	18
Italy	7	20	None	46
Netherlands	5	9	4	40
Norway	5	11	4.2	52
Portugal	4	18	3-4.4	40
Spain	7	19	5	52
Sweden	7	13	5.4	78
Switzerland	3	6	4	14[f]
UK	0	7	None	40
Japan	1	8	2	52
Australia	3	4	4	52
New Zealand	3	2	3	52
Canada	2	3	2	38
US	0	1	None	12

[a] OECD Employment Outlook (1994b, Table 4.8, column 6) extended by author. This is a synthetic index whose maximum value is 10 and refers to labor market standards enforced by legislation on, successively, working time, fixed-term contracts, employment protection, minimum wages and employees representation rights. Each of these is scored from 0 (lax or no legislation) to 2 (strict legislation) and the scores are then added up.

[b] OECD Jobs Study (1994a, Part II, Table 6.7, column 5). Country ranking with 20 as the most strictly regulated.

[c] In addition to public holidays which range from 8 days in Switzerland to 13 in Austria. OECD Jobs Study (1994a, Part II, Table 6.12).

[d] OECD (1995, Table 5.1) and Ruhm (1996, Table 1).

[e] This is not comparable to the other numbers since it refers to the career break total, which can be allocated at will.

[f] 1988.

4.3.3. Trade Unions, Wage Bargaining, and Minimum Wages

Outside the United States, most workers in the OECD have their wages determined by collective agreements which are negotiated at the plant, firm, industry, or national level. In the first two columns of Table 4.7, we present the percentage of employees who belong to a trade union and an indicator of the percentage of employees covered by collective agreements (3 means over 70%, 2 means 25-70%, 1 is under 25%). The main point which emerges here is that even if the number of union members is very low, as in France and Spain, it is still possible for most workers to have their wages set by union agreements. This occurs because, within firms, non-union workers typically get the union negotiated rate and because, in many countries, union rates of pay are legally "extended" to cover non-union firms (see OECD, Jobs Study, Part II, 1994a, p. 15 for details).

Table 4.7

Trade Unions and Wage Bargaining (1988-1994)

	Union density 1%[a]	Union coverage index[b]	Union coordination[b]	Employer coordination[b]	Centralization[c]
	(1)	(2)	(3)	(4)	(5)
Austria	46.2	3	3	3	17
Belgium	51.2	3	2	2	10
Denmark	71.4	3	3	3	14
Finland	72.0	3	2	3	13
France	9.8	3	2	2	7
Germany (W)	32.9	3	2	3	12
Ireland	49.7	3	1	1	6
Italy	38.8	3	2	2	5
Netherlands	25.5	3	2	2	11
Norway	56.0	3	3	3	16
Portugal	31.8	3	2	2	7
Spain	11.0	3	2	1	7
Sweden	82.5	3	3	3	15
Switzerland	26.6	2	1	3	3
UK	39.1	2	1	1	6
Japan	25.4	2	2	2	4
Australia	40.4	3	2	1	8
New Zealand	44.8	2	1	1	9
Canada	35.8	2	1	1	1
US	15.6	1	1	1	2

[a] OECD Jobs Study (1994a, Table 5.8, column 3). Trade union members as a percentage of all wage/salary earners.

[b] Layard, Nickell and Jackman (1991, Annex 1.4) and OECD Employment Outlook (1994b, pp. 175-185). Union coverage is an index. 3 = over 70% covered, 2 = 25-70%, 1 = under 25%. Union and employer coordination in wage bargaining is an index with 3 = high, 2 = middle, 1 = low.

[c] Calmfors and Driffill (1988, Table 3). A ranking of the centralization of wage bargains with 17 being the most centralized.

An important aspect of union-based pay bargaining is the extent to which unions and/or firms coordinate their wage determination activities. For example, in both Germany and Japan, employers' associations are actively involved in the preparation for wage bargaining even when the bargaining itself may ostensibly occur at the level of the individual firm. Coordination may be distinguished from centralization which refers strictly to the level at which bargaining occurs; plant, firm, industry, economy. Of course, economy-wide bargaining, say, must be coordinated but highly coordinated bargaining need not be centralized (as in Japan or Switzerland). In the last three columns of Table 4.7, we present indices of union coordination and employer coordination, and a centralization ranking due to Calmfors and Driffill (1988). The coordination indices go from a low level of 1 to a high of 3. The most centralized economy has a score of 17, the least centralized a score of 1. The most coordinated and centralized economies are those of Scandinavia and Austria followed by continental Europe and Japan. The Anglo-Saxon economies, including that of Ireland, exhibit little or no coordination, despite having quite high levels of union density and coverage in some cases.

Since this notion of coordination is going to prove to be important, it is perhaps worth digressing at this point on the issue of whether coordination/centralization makes any significant difference to the workings of the labor market. To put it bluntly, is there any evidence that the distinctions between high and low levels of coordination/centralization are real ones? First, we have evidence that firm/industry level wages are more responsive to firm/industry level shocks in economies where wage bargaining is less coordinated/centralized. Thus, in Layard, Nickell and Jackman (1991, Chapter 4, Table 4), we see that in the United States, firm wages are highly responsive to firm-specific shocks, in Germany and the UK, their responsiveness is moderate, and in the Nordic countries, their responsiveness is negligible. A second piece of evidence on the distinctiveness of coordinated wage bargaining systems is the fact that average wages are far more responsive to the state of the labor market in countries where wage determination is coordinated (see Layard, Nickell and Jackman 1991, Chapter 9, Table 7). Finally, and not surprisingly, higher centralization/coordination is associated with lower levels of earnings inequality at given levels of union density and coverage (OECD 1997, Chapter 3, Table 3.B.l).

Turning now to minimum wages, the picture here is by no means uniform, because some countries have statutory minimum wages whereas others rely on extending collective bargaining agreements. The pattern across countries is set out in Table 4.8 and then, in Table 4.9, we report the ratio of the minimum wage to average earnings as well as an estimate of the percentage of workers at or near the minimum.

Table 4.8

The Pattern of Minimum Wages in the 1990s[a]

Statutory minimum wages	Extension of collective agreements	Statutory minima for selected industries[b]	Collective agreements covering most of the workforc
France	Belgium	Ireland	Austria
Netherlands	Germany	United Kingdom	Denmark
Portugal	Italy	(until 1993)	Norway
Spain	Austria		Sweden
United Kingdom			
New Zealand			
Canada			
United States			

[a] *Source*: Dolado et al (1996, Table 1); OECD Jobs Study, Part II (1994a, pp. 46-51); OECD (1997), p. 13).

[b] These cover a small minority of the labor force.

Table 4.9

The Significance of the Minimum Wage, 1991-1994

	Ratio of minimum to average wage	Percent of workers at or near minimum
Austria	0.62	4
Belgium	0.60	4
Denmark	0.54	6
Finland	0.52	
France	0.50	11
Germany	0.55	
Ireland	0.55	
Italy	0.71	
Netherlands	0.55	3.2
Norway	0.64	
Portugal	0.45	8
Spain	0.32	6.5
Sweden	0.52	0
United Kingdom	0.40	
New Zealand	0.46	
Canada	0.35	
United States	0.39	4

Source: Dolado et al. (1996, Table 1); OECD Jobs Study, Part II (1994, Chart 5.14).
Note: The minimum wage levels for the UK and Ireland refer only to a small group of "low pay" industries. Minimum wages were almost completely abolished in the UK in 1993. However, by 1999, the UK is set to have a universal statutory minimum wage.

A number of points are worth noting. First, since 1993, the United Kingdom has been the only country in the OECD without a minimum wage of any kind. Even before 1993, minimum wage rules covered only a small minority of workers and were never very effectively enforced. However, a statutory minimum wage is to be introduced by 1999. Second, there is substantial variation in the ratio of the minimum to the average wage, although the number of workers affected depends also on the spread of the earnings distribution. Thus it appears that no-one receives the minimum wage in Sweden despite the fact that it is over 50% of the average wage. By contrast, around 4% of the workforce in the United States is at or near the minimum wage even though it is less than 40% of the average. Third, there are crucial differences between countries on the application of minimum wage rules to young people. Thus, for example, in New Zealand and the Netherlands the minimum wage for those aged under 20 is only 60% or less of the adult rate. In the United States and France, by contrast, there is hardly any such adjustment (details can be found in Dolado et al. 1996, Table 1; OECD Jobs Study, Part II (1994a, p. 46)).

4.3.4. Benefit Systems and Active Labor Market Policies

The key features of the unemployment benefit system are the amount of benefit and the length of time for which the benefit is available. In the first two columns of Table 4.10, we present the replacement rate (the share of income replaced by unemployment benefits) and the duration of these benefits (4 years means indefinite duration). Benefit systems come in five main types: barely existent, as in Italy; miserly but indefinite, as in Britain, Ireland, Australia, and New Zealand; averagely generous but fixed term as in Japan and North America; generous but fixed term, as in Scandinavia; and generous and long-term or indefinite, as in much of continental Europe.

In addition to the level of benefits, the systems in place to get the unemployed back to work are also significant. In columns (3) and (4) of Table 4.10 we present a measure of the expenditure on active labor market policies and the number of unemployed per staff member in employment offices and related services. The former include expenditures for the unemployed on labor market training, assistance with job search, and employment subsidies. The variable itself is active labor market spending per unemployed person as a percentage of GDP per member of the labor force. Turning to the variable in column (4), the staff members concerned are those in employment offices plus those dealing with network and program management, and the administration of unemployment benefit. Generally speaking, the pattern of these two variables indicates a higher than average expenditure on the unemployed in most European countries with Spain and Ireland being notable exceptions.

Table 4.10

The Benefit System, 1989-1994

	Benefit replacement ratio (%)[a] (1)	Benefit duration (years)[a] (2)	Active labor market policies (1991)[b] (3)	Unemployment per staff member in employment offices (1992)[c] (4)
Austria	50	2	8.3	34
Belgium	60	4	14.6	44
Denmark	90	2.5	10.3	-
Finland	63	2	16.4	-
France	57	3	8.8	79
Germany (W)	63	4	25.7	39
Ireland	37	4	9.1	100
Italy	20	0.5	10.3	-
Netherlands	70	2	6.9	32
Norway	65	1.5	14.7	40
Portugal	65	0.8	18.8	51
Spain	70	3.5	4.7	191
Sweden	80	1.2	59.3	27
Switzerland	70	1	8.2	50
UK	38	4	6.4	72
Canada	59	1	5.9	68
US	50	0.5	3.0	-
Japan	60	0.5	4.3	93
Australia	36	4	3.2	89
New Zealand	30	4	6.8	76

[a] Mainly US Department of Health and Social Services, Social Security Programmes throughout the World, 1993. See Layard, Nickell and Jackman (1991, Annex 1.3) for precise details of the definitions. 4 years = indefinite.

[b] OECD Employment Outlook (1995). The variable is dated 1991 and measures current active labor market spending as % of GDP divided by current unemployment. Expenditure on the disabled is excluded.

[c] OECD Jobs Study, Part II (1994a, Table 6.16).

4.3.5. Skills and Education

In Table 4.11, we present an overall picture of the educational levels attained by the adult populations of most OECD countries. Of course, there are serious issues of comparability here which are hard to address although Table 4.12 gives some idea of the differences. Here we record the average scores by educational level in a uniform test of (quantitative) literacy which was taken by a random sample of the working age population in a variety of countries. While the scores for degree-level individuals are quite similar, the scores vary dramatically at the lowest education level, with Sweden's ISCED2 individuals actually doing better than those at ISCED5 (some College) in the United States.

Table 4.11

Educational Attainment (%) of the Adult Population, 1988[a]

	A		B/C		D		E	
	M	F	M	F	M	F	M	F
Austria	26.8	50.7	67.0	45.9	–	–	6.2	3.4
Blegum	64.0	70.8	21.4	17.2	–	–	14.0	12.0
Finland	73.7	73.9	15.3	16.6	–	–	11.0	9.5
Germany (W)	18.7	43.0	71.4	52.6	3.9	1.2	6.0	3.2
Italy	71.9	75.6	22.6	20.7	–	–	5.5	3.7
Netherlands	48.2	60.1	31.5	27.7	14.1	10.2	6.1	1.9
Norway	47.9	63.8	32.6	20.4	–	–	19.5	15.8
Portugal	87.4	89.0	8.4	6.3	0.8	2.5	3.4	2.0
Spain	67.3	73.9	24.3	19.5	4.3	4.5	4.1	2.1
Sweden	41.1	50.1	37.7	28.4	9.8	11.3	11.5	10.2
Switzerland	21.7	35.3	58.7	50.9	5.9	2.3	13.8	11.6
UK	48.2	72.1	35.3	13.1	–	–	16.6	14.8
Japan	32.6	37.1	42.8	46.3	5.3	11.6	18.9	4.4
Australia	41.2	55.2	37.5	14.7	11.1	23.7	9.6	5.5
Canada	33.6	32.5	30.4	33.9	21.8	23.3	14.1	10.3
US	22.9	23.0	36.2	41.7	18.4	19.0	22.4	16.3

[a] A, first stage secondary, end of compulsory schooling ≈ ISCED2; B/C, second stage or higher secondary ≈ ISCED3; D, non-degree level tertiary ≈ ISCED5; E, first degree or above ≈ ISCED6/7. ISCED, International Standard Classification of Education. For full details see OECD (1989, Chapter 2, Table 2.1 and Annex 2C). For ISCED definitions, see OECD Jobs Study, Part II (1994a, Annex 7B).

With this important caveat in mind, Table 4.12 appears to indicate that the countries of southern Europe have the lowest educational standards whereas middle Europe, Scandinavia, and North America have the highest.

Table 4.12

Average Literacy Test Scores by Education Level (1994)

	ISCED 2 minimal compulsory	ISCED 3 higher secondary	ISCED 5 non-degree tertiary	ISCED 6/7 degree	Total
Germany	2.42	2.97	3.11	3.39	2.84
Netherlands	2.52	2.69	–	3.27	2.74
Sweden	2.96	3.07	3.31	3.56	3.04
Switzerland	2.20	2.82	3.09	3.16	2.67
Canada	2.20	2.67	2.97	2.55	2.62
US	1.92	2.44	2.86	3.31	2.56

Source: Literacy, Economy and Society, OECD/Statistics Canada (1995, Table B9c). The average score is based on setting level 1 = 1, level 2 = 2, level 3 = 3, level 4/5 = 4 and uses the quantitative literacy test. Switzerland refers to the arithmetic average of French and German Switzerland. The literacy levels are based on marks in the literacy test with the same tests and mark schemes used in all the countries. ISCED levels are described in the notes to Table 4.11.

4.3.6. Barriers to Geographical Mobility

Barriers to mobility are clearly important for the functioning of an economy and many of these are institutional. In Table 4.13, we present some mobility data for a small number of countries, where the numbers reflect the percentage of the population who change region in each year. It is worth pointing out that, with the exception of Sweden, the regions are of comparable geographical size in each country, so the figures themselves are reasonably comparable.[4] What we find is that geographical mobility is lowest in southern Europe and about four or more times higher in Scandinavia and the United States. That people are very mobile in the United States is well known. The fact that mobility is also high in Norway and Sweden is quite surprising although encouraging people to move has long been a feature of labor market policy in these countries.

Table 4.13

Regional Mobility (% Who Change Region per Year)[a]

	1973-1979	1980-1987
Finland	1.8	1.5
France	-	1.3
Germany (W)	1.4	1.1
Italy	0.8	0.6
Norway	2.8	2.5
Spain	0.5	0.4
Sweden	4.4	3.7
UK	1.1	1.1
Japan	3.3	2.7
Australia	1.8	1.7
Canada	1.8	1.6
US	3.0	2.9

[a] Excludes persons who change country of residence.
Source: OECD Employment Outlook (1990, Table 3.3). For Spain, Bentolila and Dolado.

In Oswald (1996), it is suggested that one of the most significant barriers to mobility is home ownership because it is so much easier to move when living in rented accommodation. So, in Table 4.14, we present the percentage of households who are owner-occupiers, a variable which Oswald finds to be significantly correlated with unemployment, both across countries and across US States. The most notable feature of these data is the low level of owner-occupation in middle Europe with Austria, Germany, Switzerland, and the Netherlands being the four bottom countries.

Table 4.14

Percent of Households Who are Owner-Occupiers (1990)

Austria	54	Italy	68	UK	65
Belgium	65	Netherlands	45	Japan	59
Denmark	55	Norway	78	Australia	70
Finland	78	Portugal	58	New Zealand	71
France	56	Spain	75	Canada	63
Germany (W)	42	Sweden	56	US	64
Ireland	76	Switzerland	28		

Source: Oswald (1996, Table 3).

This completes our survey of labor market "institutions." Our next step is to look at the theoretical foundations of the relationship between labor market institutions and performance.

4.4. Unemployment, Growth, and Labor Market Institutions

In order to pursue fruitfully the relationship between labor market institutions and economic performance it is helpful to set out briefly some of the theoretical background on the interactions between growth, unemployment, and the labor market. We begin with a simple model of equilibrium unemployment.

4.4.1. The Determination of Equilibrium Unemployment

Consider an economy with a large number of identical firms. Wage setting goes on independently within each firm and workers in the ith firm are concerned with their employment prospects, N_i, and the excess of their net wages, $w_i(1 - \tau)$, over their outside opportunities, A. Note that w_i is labor cost per employee and τ is the sum of the payroll and income tax rates. Outside opportunities, A, we specify as

$$(1) \qquad A = \phi(n, s, c) \, w(1 - \tau) + (1 - \phi(n, s, c)) \, bw(1 - \tau),$$

where w is the aggregate labor cost per employee, b is benefit replacement rate (benefits relative to net wages), ϕ is the probability of working in an alternative job (or the proportion of the relevant period spent in working), and $(1 - \phi)$ is the probability of being unemployed. ϕ is increasing in the aggregate employment rate, n, and in the exogenous part of the separation rate out of employment, s. It is decreasing in the search effectiveness of the unemployed, c. The reasoning underlying these last two effects is as follows. If s increases, more people are leaving their jobs for exogenous reasons, there are more vacancies, and, *at given levels of aggregate employment*, it is easier for someone leaving the firm to get an alternative job, so ϕ goes up. Search effectiveness, c, covers the ability and willingness of the unemployed to make themselves available for unfilled vacancies. If search effectiveness increases at *given aggregate employment* (c increases), then a new entrant into unemployment finds it harder to get a new job because the existing unemployed provide more competition for the available vacancies.

So we assume that the representative worker's objective is to maximize $N_i^{\gamma} (w_i(1 - \tau) - A)$ where the worker knows that if he and his co-workers obtain a wage w_i, employment in the firm will be determined by profit maximizing behavior on the part of the firm, taking wages as given. The parameter γ measures the extent to which the worker takes account of the employment effects of the wage bargain. Purely individualistic bargaining would be associated with low levels of γ, collective bargaining with high levels of γ. The firm is, of course, keen to achieve as high a value of profit, π_i, as possible. Suppose that wages emerge by some mechanism of individual or collective bargaining as the solution to

$$\max_{W_i, N_i} \left[N_i^\gamma \; (w_i(1 - \tau) - A) \right]^\beta \pi_i,$$

subject to the firm choosing N to maximize profit at given w_i. The parameter β may be thought of as reflecting the power of the worker (s) in this bargain. Note that increased coordination on the part of workers within a firm is likely to increase both their power in the wage bargain, β, and their concern over total employment in the firm as captured by γ.

The first order condition for the above problem reduces to

(2)
$$\frac{w_i(1 - \tau)}{w_i(1 - \tau) - A} = \frac{\beta \gamma \eta s_\pi + (1 - s_\pi)}{s_\pi},$$

where s_π is the share of profits in value added and η is the wage elasticity of demand for labor. Since all firms are identical, $w_i = w$ and so using Equation (1), Equation (2) reduces to an equation for equilibrium unemployment, u^*, which has the form

(3)
$$\phi(1 - u^*, s, c) = 1 - \frac{\beta s_\pi}{(\beta \gamma s_\pi \eta + (1 - s_\pi))(1 - b)}.$$

In general s_π, η will depend on the level of employment in each firm and hence on u^*, but in the simple model where each firm has a Cobb-Douglas production function with labor exponent α and faces a product market demand curve with elasticity ε, then s_π, η are both constants. Indeed $s_\pi = 1 - \alpha k$, $\eta = (1 - \alpha k)^{-1}$ where $k = (1 - 1/\varepsilon)$. Then Equation (3) becomes

$$\phi(1 - u^*, s, c) = 1 - \frac{\beta(1 - \alpha k)}{(\gamma \beta + \alpha k)(1 - b)}$$

so

(4) $$u^* = f(s, c, b, \beta, \alpha k).$$

So equilibrium unemployment is decreasing in any factor which reduces the exogenous separation rate out of employment (s), increases the search effectiveness of the unemployed (c), lowers the benefit replacement ratio (benefits relative to *post-tax* earnings) (b), lowers the strength of workers in the wage bargain (β), or raises the elasticity of product demand facing the firm (ε, where $k = 1 - 1/\varepsilon$). It is also worth noting that equilibrium unemployment is decreasing in the extent to which workers take account of the employment effects of their actions when bargaining about wages (γ).

Most of our subsequent discussion of the impact of labor market institutions on unemployment comes under these headings but there are two notable absentees. The first is the payroll plus income tax rate, τ. Why does this not come in? Essentially because if benefits are indexed to post-tax earnings, b is unaffected by τ and hence the outside alternative A has the form $\overline{A}(1 - \tau)$ where $\overline{A}$ is independent of τ. So an increase in τ affects the opportunities both inside and outside the firm in exactly the same way and, so long as utility is isoelastic,[5] τ will not influence the labor cost outcome, w_i. Those who believe that taxes have an important impact on labor costs in wage bargains must rely on utility not being isoelastic (a weak reed) or on benefits being indexed to something other than post-tax earnings or on important non-labor income effects (see, e.g., Phelps 1994 and Pissarides 1996). These latter arise because while labor costs are subject to both payroll and income taxes, non-labor income is subject only to the second of these. So in the case where utility is not linear, the relevant term in the objective now has the form

$$v(w_i(1 - t_1 - t_2) + y_n(1 - t_2)) - [\phi v(w(1 - t_1 - t_2) + y_n(1 - t_2))$$
$$+ (1 - \phi)v(bw(1 - t_1 - t_2) + y_n(1 - t))],$$

where v is the utility function, t_1 is the payroll tax rate, t_2 is the income tax rate, and y_n is non-labor income. Now the taxes do not factor out even if it is isoelastic (so long as it is not linear). So an increase in the payroll tax rate, t_1, will influence the bargained labor cost, w_i, so long as v is not linear and y_n is not zero.

The second major area involving labor market institutions which is not covered by the simple model discussed above concerns the role of coordination by unions and employers *across firms*, and the related issue of centralization. In a unionized economy, coordination across firms makes a difference for a variety of reasons, generally concerned with the externality arising from the fact that bigger wage rises for one group makes other groups worse off (via consumer price increases, for example). See Calmfors (1993) for an extensive discussion. This externality is not internalized under decentralized, uncoordinated bargaining. However, if bargaining is completely coordinated, those who benefit from higher nominal wage increases are the same as those who are harmed by the consequent nominal price increases. This tends to reduce wage pressure and hence equilibrium unemployment.

A countervailing tendency, noted in Calmfors and Driffill (1988), is that bargaining at a higher level of centralization (industry versus firm, for example) tends to reduce the product demand elasticity facing the wage bargainers which will tend to raise wages and hence equilibrium unemployment (as in Equation (4)). This effect tends to be of lesser importance in more open economies but Calmfors and Driffill suggest this elasticity effect, when combined with the externality effect discussed above, leads to a "hump-shaped" relationship between centralization and unemployment in unionized economies.

4.4.2. Unemployment and Growth

There are many possible ways in which growth and unemployment may be related although generally speaking they are, of course, jointly determined endogenous variables. Consider first the ways in which *exogenous* increases in the rate of productivity growth may impact on unemployment. A typical mechanism where growth reduces unemployment operates via the so-called capitalization effect (see Pissarides 1990, Chapter 2). Here an increase in growth raises the present value returns from creating a new job slot (at a given level of employment) leading firms to open more vacancies. This, in the context of a matching model (see Mortensen and Pissarides 1999) will lead to reduced equilibrium unemployment.

A representative alternative, where growth raises unemployment, is based on the idea that higher growth is associated with more innovation and greater turbulence. Thus Aghion and Howitt (1991) present a model of growth via "creative destruction" which leads to a higher rate of labor reallocation and higher unemployment. Overall, therefore, this relationship can go either way (see Saint-Paul 1991 for some other mechanisms) and there is no evidence that it is either important or robust (see, e.g., Bean and Pissarides 1993).

Next, let us consider mechanisms which operate in precisely the opposite direction, that is ways in which exogenous increases in the equilibrium unemployment rate directly influence the rate of growth. Both Bean and Pissarides (1993) and Daveri and Tabellini (1997) present standard overlapping generations endogenous growth models of the "AK" type in which only the young work. Both these models have an equilibrium unemployment rate which is not directly influenced by exogenous shifts in the growth rate. However, because only the young work, a rise in equilibrium unemployment lowers the income of the young, lowers savings, and hence reduces the equilibrium growth rate. This mechanism is, however, not robust, since it relies on the old not working. A more uniform (and more realistic) spread of work through the lifecycle would tend to eliminate this effect.

Daveri and Tabellini (1997) have another mechanism. A rise in equilibrium unemployment lowers the marginal product of capital (because of the rise in the capital/labor ratio) which reduces returns and hence the savings of the young. This result depends critically on the positive impact of the interest rate on savings. While this may be theoretically robust, empirically it is quite the opposite. Leibfritz, Thornton and Bibbee (1997) present a summary of 14 single country studies of this relationship. There are four with a positive effect, four with a negative effect, two with some positive and some negative effects, and four with no effect. Bosworth (1993) and Masson, Bayoumi and Samieri (1995) have undertaken panel data investigations using a number of countries with the former finding a negative relationship and the latter a positive one. So, overall, there appears to be no very strong reason why factors which raise equilibrium unemployment should, of necessity, lower long-run growth rates.

4.4.3. Labor Market Institutions and Growth

While the two models we have just discussed do not provide strong backing for the view that factors which directly raise equilibrium unemployment will automatically reduce growth rates, they do both indicate that higher income taxes will reduce growth rates simply because they reduce savings. Of course, this depends on the taxes being spent on consumption. If they are spent by the government on productive investment, this particular result will no longer apply.

Turning to other factors, the endogenous growth literature (for a good survey, see Barro and Sala-i-Martin 1995) indicates that the most important mechanisms by which labor market institutions could affect productivity growth are via their impact on human and physical capital accumulation, on innovation (both technological and managerial), and on the rates at which low productivity companies close down and high productivity companies start up.

To summarize, therefore, it is theoretically plausible for any labor market institutions which influence equilibrium unemployment, consequently to influence the long-run labor productivity growth rate. Furthermore, the opposite also applies. Any labor market institutions which influence long run growth may, as a consequence, affect equilibrium unemployment. However, our analysis of the evidence suggests that neither of these two possibilities is likely to be of any great significance. This leaves us to consider the direct impact of labor market institutions on equilibrium unemployment and on long-run growth, treated separately.

With regard to lowering equilibrium unemployment, we expect this to be associated with any institution which reduces exogenous job separations, increases search effectiveness, reduces the level of benefits, lowers the strength of workers in the wage bargain, or raises the elasticity of product demand facing firms (i.e., raises the level of product market competition). Turning to raising equilibrium growth rates, this we expect to be associated with institutions which raise savings, raise human or physical capital accumulation, increase technological and managerial innovation, and raise the start-up rate of new companies.

4.5. Some Summary Regressions Explaining Growth and Labor Supply

Before we go into a detailed investigation of the relationship between labor market institutions, long-run growth, and unemployment, we set the empirical scene by presenting a few simple cross-country regressions. In Tables 4.15 and 4.16, we report some estimated equations explaining various aspects of unemployment and aggregate labor input. The idea here is to relate unemployment or labor input to the important labor market institutions. The only variables we do not consider are those which are highly specialized such as those covering annual and parental leave. Because these institutions influence *equilibrium* unemployment rates but we have *actual* rates for the dependent variable, we capture the difference between them by including the rate of change of inflation. This is consistent with a standard NAIRU framework. The variables which are reported in the main body of the table were those which are reasonably significant. In footnote a to the table, we report the coefficients on a further sequence of variables when they are added individually to the basic model in column (1). These are generally completely insignificant.

The regressions are based on two cross-sections dated 1983-1988 and 1989-1994. The dependent variables are some of the unemployment rates reported in Table 4.1 or the labor input variables in Table 4.2. The independent variables may be found in the tables above where we report their values for 1989-1994. The 1983-1988 values, many of which are different, are available from the authors. We choose to use 6-year averages in order to smooth out both the cycle and year-on-year noise. Finally, note that in the unemployment equations we use the log of unemployment as the dependent variable. This we do because there are good theoretical and empirical reasons for believing that wages are related to $\log a$ rather than u (Lipsey 1960; Nickell 1987; Blanchflower and Oswald 1994).

The independent variables have all been described in Section 4.2. and their impact on unemployment or labor input arises from the mechanisms described in the previous section (i.e., they impact on job separations, search effectiveness, benefits, bargaining strength, or the product demand elasticity). However it should be recognized that variations across country in labor input are going to be harder for our variables to explain than variations in unemployment, because labor input is also influenced by the disability system, the early retirement system, and factors influencing the participation rates of

Table 4.15

Regressions to Explain Log Unemployment Rate (%) (20 OECD Countries, 1983-1988 and 1989-1994)[a]

	Total unemployment (1)	Long-term unemployment (2)	Short-term unemployment (3)
Total tax wedge (%)	0.027 (4.0)	0.023 (1.6)	0.028 (3.5)
Employment protection (1-20)		0.052 (1.4)	-0.061 (2.8)
Union density (%)	0.010 (2.3)	0.010 (1.0)	0.0031 (0.5)
Union coverage index (1-3)	0.38 (2.7)	0.83 (2.3)	0.45 (2.1)
Coordination (union + employer) (2-6)	-0.43 (6.1)	-0.54 (3.6)	-0.34 (3.8)
Replacement rate (%)	0.013 (3.4)	0.011 (1.3)	0.031 (2.6)
Benefit duration (years)	0.10 (2.2)	0.25 (2.7)	0.045 (0.8)
Active labor market policies[b]	-0.023 (3.3)	-0.039 (2.8)	-0.097 (1.2)
Owner occupation rate (%)	0.013 (2.6)	-0.0007 (0.1)	0.01 (2.7)
Change in inflation (% pts. p.a.)	-0.21 (2.2)	-0.30 (1.6)	-0.29 (2.7)
Dummy for 1990-1994	0.15 (1.5)	0.30 (1.8)	0.092 (1.0)
R^2	0.85	0.84	0.73
N (countries, time)	40 (20, 2)	38 (19, 2)	38 (19, 2)
Hausman test of the random effects of restriction X^2_{10}	6.35	4.52	6.86

[a] Estimation is by GLS random effects (Balestra-Nerlose) using two time periods (1983-1988, 1989-1994). t ratios in parentheses. If we add the following variables, one at a time, to column (1), their coefficients are: payroll tax rate (%), 0.014 (0.5); employment protection, 0.011 (0.6); labor standards. 0.0011 (0.02); real interest rate (%), 0.040 (1.0); centralization, (centralization) 2, 0.048 (0.5), 0.0005(0.1). For the 1989-1994 values of the independent variables, see the tables above. The 1983-1988 values are available from the author on request. The dependent variables are in Table 4.1.

[b] The variable is instrumented. Because the active labor market policies variable refers to percent of GDP normalized on current unemployment, this variable is highly endogenous. So we renormalized the current percent of GDP spent on active labor market measures on the average unemployment rate in 1977-1979 to create the instrument. Insofar as measurement errors in unemployment are serially uncorrelated, this will help with the endogeneity problem.

Table 4.16

Regressions to Explain Labor Input Measures (Table 11) (20 OECD countries, 1983-1988 and 1989-1994)[a]

	Employment/Population (%)		Total hours/population (index)
	Whole working age population (1)	Males aged 25-54 (2)	(3)
Total tax wedge (%)	-0.24 (2.0)	-0.15 (2.0)	-0.26 (1.6)
Employment protection (1-20)	-0.79 (2.7)	0.037 (0.2)	-0.64 (1.6)
Union density (%)	-0.012 (0.1)	-0.058 (1.0)	-0.15 (1.3)
Union coverage index (1-3)	-2.40 (1.0)	-2.00 (1.2)	-2.97 (1.0)
Coordination (union + employer) (2-6)	4.75 (4.0)	2.39 (3.2)	4.08 (2.5)
Replacement rate (%)	-0.067 (1.0)	-0.065 (1.5)	-0.057 (0.6)
Benefit duration (years)	-1.06 (1.8)	-0.57 (1.4)	-0.23 (0.3)
Active labor market policies[b]	0.10 (1.0)	0.036 (0.5)	-0.036 (0.3)
Owner occupation rate (%)	-0.19 (2.7)	-0.11 (2.3)	-0.066 (0.8)
Change in inflation (% pts. p.a.)	-1.21 (1.3)	-0.50 (0.7)	-1.69 (1.6)
Dummy for 1990-1994	3.16 (3.7)	-1.39 (1.9)	0.48 (0.5)
R^2	0.80	0.64	0.51
N (countries, time)	(20,2)	(20,2)	(20,2)

[a] Variables and definitions are in Tables 4.2 (Columns 5-7) and 4.1. Estimation is by GLS random effects using two time periods (1983-1988, 1990-1994), t ratios in parentheses.

[b] Active labor market policies are instrumented as in Table 4.15.

married women. Cross-country variables which capture all these factors are not included in the regressions (because they are not readily available) and, as a consequence, the labor input equations will tend to contain a lot more unexplained noise. Summarizing the results briefly, the overall tax burden on labor has a clear negative impact on both unemployment and labor input. Payroll taxes alone, however, have no additional effect (footnote a, Table 4.15).

Looking at rigidities, there is no evidence that employment protection or labor standards (footnote a, Table 4.15) influence overall unemployment although the former raises long-term and reduces short-term unemployment. Employment protection does, however, appear to reduce the employment population ratio although this result is driven by high employment protection and low married women's participation in southern Europe (OECD 1994a, Table 6.9).

On the wage determination front, unions raise unemployment and reduce labor input. These effects are, however, offset if unions and employers can coordinate their wage bargaining activities. In the presence of the coordination variable, there is no role for centralization. Turning to benefits, both higher replacement ratios and longer durations of eligibility mean higher unemployment although there is no effect on labor supply, probably because higher benefits mean higher unemployment *and* higher participation. These effects can, however, be offset by active labor market policy. Finally, there is some evidence that owner occupation tends to raise unemployment, although whether this is a mobility barrier effect, as proposed by Oswald (1996), is another question. For example, there is no correlation across the twelve countries between the mobility numbers and the owner occupation numbers.

For purposes of comparison, it is worth reporting on a similar exercise undertaken by Scarpetta (1996), extended in Elmeskov, Martin and Scarpetta (1998). The main differences are that Scarpetta uses two fewer countries, uses an annual panel from 1983-1993, and captures the difference between actual and equilibrium unemployment by the deviation of output from trend generated by the HP filter. This last is a little bit risky since it is easy to over- or under-correct for the cycle using the HP filter, depending on how the arbitrary parameter is set. In terms of outcomes, the Scarpetta results are similar for the tax wedge, unionization, coordination, and benefits. The impact of active labor market policies is weaker. Employment protection has a significant effect on unemployment although it disappears when an index of centralization is included, so it is not totally robust.

We repeat the exercise for productivity growth in Table 4.17. Here we use a single cross-section, taking the average productivity growth over the period 1976-1992 as the dependent variable.[6] We omit union effects, because they are never remotely significant. The only clear-cut results are the positive impact of employment protection and the negative effect of the total labor tax rate. Both of these are completely wiped out once we control for convergence, using the initial productivity gap between the country concerned and the United States. We date this convergence variable prior to the start of the sample period to try and minimize measurement error bias. Nevertheless, if measurement error has some persistence at the country level, these convergence effects could be spurious. It is probably best to interpret these results as saying that employment protection and low total taxes are associated with high productivity growth but they happen to occur in countries which start off further behind.

To summarize, labor market institutions appear to have a strong association with unemployment, some association with labor input, and a weak association with productivity growth. We are now in a position to go more deeply into the various types of institution.

4.6. Labor Taxes

As we have already noted in Section 4.3., we expect the major impact of labor taxes to operate via the total tax wedge between product and consumption wages, namely the sum of payroll, income, and consumption tax rates. Some exceptions to this rule are first, for individuals earning the minimum wage, a switch from income tax to payroll tax will raise labor costs and reduce the demand for their services because the wage cannot adjust. Second, a switch from income tax to payroll tax will reduce the tax rate on non-labor income which will tend to reduce labor supply. Furthermore, on the growth front, since income taxes typically serve as direct taxes on capital income, they are more likely to have a more negative impact on productivity growth than payroll taxes. Third, a switch from income tax to consumption tax makes little odds to an individual who spends all her income. And since individuals most likely to become unemployed save little,[7] such a switch is unlikely to have much impact on labor costs and hence employment. However, this switch could obviously have a significant effect on savings behavior and hence influence growth.

Table 4.17

OECD Productivity Growth and Labor Market Institutions 1976-1992[a]

	Growth rates (%)					
	Labor productivity	Labor productivity With hours correction	TFP	Labor productivity	Labor productivity With hours correction	TFP
	(1)	(2)	(3)	(4)	(5)	(6)
Total tax rate (%)	-0.034 (2.2)	-0.031 (1.8)	-0.015 (1.2)	0.000 (0.1)	0.000 (0.0)	-0.006 (0.3)
Employment protection (1-20)	0.081 (2.8)	0.092 (2.8)	0.093 (3.4)	0.004 (0.1)	0.021 (0.6)	0.073 (1.9)
Replacement rate (%)	0.005 (0.5	0.008 (0.8)	0.008 (0.9)	-0.004 (0.6)	-0.000 (0.0)	0.006 (0.6)
Benefit duration (years)	-0.21 (2.0)	-0.13 (1.1)	0.087 (0.9)	-0.12 (1.6)	-0.046 (0.4)	0.11 (1.1)
Owner occupation rate (%)	0.014 (1.1)	0.011 (0.8)	0.014 (1.2)	0.001 (0.1)	0.000 (0.1)	0.010 (0.8)
Initial productivity gap				2.32 (3.9)	2.12 (2.7)	0.61 (0.8)
R^2	0.48	0.41	0.53	0.76	0.61	0.55
N	20	20	20	20	20	20

[a] Estimation is by OLS. If we add any of the union variables (density, coverage, coordination) they are jointly and severally totally insignificant in all the regressions as are labor standards and payroll tax rate. The dependent variables are columns (1)-(3) of table 4.12. The independent variables are the averages over the two time periods used in the unemployment regressions (Table 4.15). The initial productivity gap is measured by ln(US labor productivity, average 1973-1975) - ln(country labor productivity, average 1973-1975). The use of the average prior to the start of the productivity growth in 1976 is to reduce the usual measurement error bias problem which besets this variable.

There is also the possibility that marginal tax rates could have an effect independently of average tax rates. For example, a high level of tax progressivity ensures that wage increases become less valuable and so, in standard union models, wages are reduced (see Lockwood and Manning 1993). On the growth front, high tax progressivity reduces both effort incentives (Newell and Symons 1993) and education incentives, thereby reducing growth rates.

Finally, before turning to the empirical evidence it is worth noting that in steady state growth, even with unemployment, the growth rate of output per capita will be the same as the growth rate of labor productivity. So when we refer to evidence on "growth," this, in theory, implies the growth rate of both output per capita and productivity. In practice, it is not quite so straightforward because of the secular shifts in labor input per population member in many OECD countries over the post-war period. So when we refer to evidence on growth more generally, this typically means the growth of output per capita and the above caveat applies.

4.6.1. Differential Taxes

Unemployment

The key issue here is whether different taxes exhibit differential rates of shifting onto labor. There are a large number of time series wage equations for various countries which show different degrees of shifting onto labor for different taxes. There is no pattern to these numbers,[8] many of which are summarized in Layard, Nickell and Jackman (1991, p. 210) and OECD (1994a, p. 247). Some intensive cross-country investigations may be found in the work of Tyrväinen reported in OECD (1994a, Table 9.5) and in that of Robertson and Symons in OECD (1990, Annex 6A). In both these wide-ranging studies, there is no significant evidence that payroll, income, or consumption taxes have a differential impact on labor costs and hence on unemployment. As the OECD Jobs Study (1994a) remarks, "Changes in the mix of taxes by which governments raise revenues can be expected, at most, to have a limited effect on unemployment" (p. 275).

Productivity Growth

The main result here seems to be the existence of some evidence that personal income tax rates have a higher negative effect on growth rates in the OECD than other taxes (see, e.g., Dowrick 1993; Mendoza, Milesi-Ferretti and Asea 1997; Widmalm 1996).

4.6.2. Total Tax Rates

Unemployment

In OECD (1990, Annex 6), a simple test of the impact of tax rates on labor costs is carried out as follows. We have labor demand and labor supply equations of the form

$$N^D = f^1(w)K, \qquad\qquad N^S = f^2(w - T, z)L,$$

where N is employment, $w = \ln(\text{real labor cost})$, K is the capital stock, $T = (t_1 + t_2 + t_3)$, the total tax rate, L is the labor force, z is an exogenous factor. Then the reduced form wage equation is

$$w = g(T, K/L, z).$$

If w is independent of T in the long run, the labor market *behaves as if* labor supply is inelastic and taxes are all shifted onto labor. Employment, and hence unemployment is then unaffected by T in the long run. The following equation represents the average coefficients and t-statistics for individual time series regressions on 16 OECD countries (1955-1986).

$$w = 0.79w_{-1} + 0.18\ln(K/L) - 0.08T + 0.52\Delta T.$$
$$\quad (8.7) \qquad (2.0) \qquad\qquad (0.6) \qquad (2.6)$$

Thus total taxes, T, have no long-run effects on labor costs although they have a substantial and long-lasting short-run effect via ΔT (and the high level of persistence in wages). Consistent with this result is the work discussed in Gruber (1997) on the incidence of payroll taxation. Gruber studies the impact on wages and employment at the micro level of the sharp exogenous reduction in payroll tax rates (of around 25 percentage points!) which took place in Chile over the period 1979-1986. His analysis of a large number of individual firms indicates that wages adjust completely to this payroll tax shift and there is no employment effect whatever. This is, without question, one of the most reliable studies of labor tax incidence yet undertaken.

139

In contrast to this result the tax wedge effect appears significantly in the work of Scarpetta (1996) and in every unemployment and labor input equation in the previous section, although the overall effect on unemployment is not that great. For example, a reduction in the total tax rate of 5 percentage points, which is substantial, would reduce unemployment by around 13% (e.g., from 8 to 7%). Bigger effects on unemployment are found by Daveri and Tabellini (1997), who undertake a multi-country panel study of OECD countries and allow the coefficients on taxes to differ between three groups of countries. For two groups of countries (Scandinavia and Canada, US, Japan, UK (post-1980)), taxes have no significant impact but for one group (Australia, Belgium, France, Germany, Italy, The Netherlands, Spain, and UK (pre-1980)), the effects are substantial with an x percentage point rise in the overall labor tax rate leading to around an $x/2$ percentage point rise in the unemployment rate. This is enough to explain more or less all of the post-war rise in unemployment in most of these countries. Many others have found significant tax wedge effects on labor costs, and some have argued that the size of these tax wedge effects depends significantly on those labor market institutions connected with flexibility (see Daveri and Tabellini 1997; Leibfritz, Thornton and Bibbee 1997). In order to pursue this, we set out some results on the impact of the tax wedge on labor costs in Table 4.18. The first point to note is how wildly the numbers and the rankings fluctuate across the columns. This is basically due to variations in the other variables included in the labor cost equations and emphasizes the fragility of most of the results in this area. Second, in order to see if there is any relationship between tax wedge effects and labor market flexibility we regressed the average tax wedge effect on some institutional variables to obtain:

$$\text{Tax wedge effect} = \text{Constant} + 0.030 \text{ employment protection}$$
$$(0.9)$$
$$- 0.005 \text{ labor standards}$$
$$(0.1)$$
$$- 0.16 \text{ coordination (union + employer)}$$
$$(1.7)$$
$$+ 0.004 \text{ union density (average)}$$
$$(0.6)$$
$$N = 20, \ R^2 = 0.23$$

The independent variables are the same as those in the previous regressions and while most of the signs are consistent with the hypothesis, the negative impact of wage bargaining coordination is the only one which is significant (at the 10% level). So the evidence in favor of the hypothesis that flexibility reduces tax wedge effects is not strong. Overall, however, the balance of the evidence suggests that there is probably some overall adverse tax effect on unemployment and labor input. Its precise scale, however, remains elusive.

Table 4.18

Percentage Increase in Real Labor Cost in Response to a One Percentage Point Rise in the Tax Wedge[a]

	BLN (1)	T (2)	AP (3)	PSK (4)	Kvd W (5)	Average (6)
Austria	0			0		0
Belgum	3.4		0.37	0.95		1.57
Denmark	0		0.28	0		0.09
Finland	0.2	0.5	0.28			0.33
France	0.5	0.4	0.37	0	0.56	0.37
Germany (W)	0	1.0	0.37	0	0.72	0.42
Ireland	.14					1.4
Italy	0.3	0.4	0	0	1.03	0.35
Netherlands	0.4		0.37	0	1.15	0.48
Norway	0.2		0.28			0.24
Spain	1.0					1.0
Sweden	0.5	0.6	0.28	0.73	0.70	0.56
Switzerland	1.4					1.4
UK	1.3	0.25	0	0	0.58	0.43
Japan	0	0.5	0		1.19	0.42
Australia		0.5	0.37		1.64	0.84
New Zealand	0					0
Canada	1.5	0.8	0		0.59	0.72
US	0.1		0		0.43	0.18

[a] BLN, Bean, Layard and Nickell (1986, Tables 3 and 5) (except the number for Spain which is taken from Dolado et at. 1986); T, Tyrväinen (1995) as reported in OECD, Jobs Study (1994a, Table 9.5) (except Sweden's number which is from Helmlund and Kohn, 1995); AP, Alesina and Perotti (1997, Table 7, column 4); PSK. Padoa Schioppa-Kostoris (1992): KvdW, Knoester and Van der Windt, 1987. Some of these numbers were taken directly from Leibfritz, Thornton and Bibbee (1997. Table A1.5). The tax wedge definitions differ somewhat between columns: 1,2,4 use the sum of payroll, income, and consumption tax rates; 3, 5 omit the consumption tax rate.

Productivity Growth

The general conclusion in the quite extensive literature on taxation and growth is that there may be a negative relationship but it is not robust (see, e.g., Levine and Renelt 1992; Easterly and Rebelo 1993, Agell, Lindh and Ohlsson 1997). Indeed, Easterly and Rebelo (1993) argue that the reason why positive results sometimes show up is because of the positive correlation between the initial level of GDP per capita and total tax rates. So once convergence effects are controlled for, tax effects disappear, exactly as in our regressions in Table 4.17. However, the latest OECD estimates (Leibfritz, Thornton and Bibbee 1997, p. 10) indicate that a reduction of the total tax rate by 10 percentage points could have raised growth rates by as much as 0.5 percentage points. Furthermore, the reading of the evidence by Engen and Skinner (1996) reaches the same conclusion. Finally, it is worth noting that the really large estimates of the impact of taxation tend to come from simulated endogenous growth models (e.g., King and Rebelo 1990). The closer the investigation gets to the data, the smaller and more fragile are the estimated effects.

4.6.3. Marginal Tax Rates and Progressivity

Unemployment

The main argument here is that increased progressivity leads to lower wage demands (because wage increases are less valuable), lower inflationary pressure, and lower unemployment. Some evidence in favor of this hypothesis is reported in Tyrväinen (1994), Holmlund and Kohn (1995), and Lockwood and Manning (1993). However, Newell and Symons (1993) find that the change in unemployment between the 1970s and 1980s is a significantly *increasing* function of the change in marginal tax rates over the same period. They argue that this is essentially a labor supply effect.

Growth

Widmalm (1996) finds a significantly negative impact of progressivity on growth which is robust (in the sense of Levine and Renelt 1992). This is interpreted as an education effect. Newell and Symons (1993) also find that changes in marginal tax rates are negatively related to changes in growth rates from the 1970s to the 1980s. They interpret this as an effort effect.

4.6.4. Summary

There appear to be no important differential tax effects on unemployment but there is evidence that overall labor tax rates do influence labor costs in the long run and hence raise unemployment. There is a great deal of uncertainty about the size of this effect but a typical order of magnitude is where a 5 percentage point reduction in the aggregate tax wedge reduces unemployment by about 13% (e.g., from 8 to 7%). On the growth front, the results are not very robust. There is some indication that personal income taxes reduce growth rates but there is no strong and consistent evidence that total labor tax rates have any significant impact.

4.7. Labor Standards and Employment Protection

When studying labor market regulation, it is important to distinguish between rules which simply add to labor costs, such as mandatory sick pay, and rules which raise the cost of employment adjustment, such as employment protection legislation. In the former case, if wages adjust appropriately, the impact on the labor market is very limited. In the latter case, even if wages adjust fully to compensate for the legislation, the intertemporal pattern of labor demand may be very different.

First, we consider factors which add directly to labor costs but which do not affect hiring and firing costs. These include parental leave mandates, employee representation rights, rules on working time, health and safety regulations, mandatory sick pay. The key issue for unemployment is whether or not wages adjust to offset the extra labor costs. For productivity growth, it may be argued that too many rules and regulations inhibit innovative activity. On the other hand, employee rights to representation, for example, may induce a higher degree of management/worker co-operation which will enhance productivity performance. These are all empirical questions, so let us turn to the evidence.

4.7.1. Labor Standards

Unemployment
There are a small number of studies on the impact of various mandates and regulations on wages and employment. Thus Gruber and Krueger (1991) find that the costs of mandated workers compensation insurance in the United States are fully compensated by wage adjustments. Again Gruber (1994) indicates that the cost of laws mandating the inclusion of maternity coverage in company health insurance policies were fully compensated by reductions in the wages of married women aged 20-40. Ruhm (1996) studies parental leave entitle-

ment across European countries and finds again that there are wage adjustments when entitlements are substantial (>6 months) with no adverse employment effects. However, Bartel and Thomas (1987) find that environmental protection and health and safety regulation has reduced employment in small firms. So there are some bits and pieces of evidence, mostly pointing in the direction that labor legislation of this type has little impact on unemployment. And this is consistent with the fact that our labor standards index (Table 4.2) has no impact on unemployment in our cross-country regression. However, there is not really enough evidence here to be decisive.

Growth

Evidence here is also very thin. There seems no evidence of negative effects on productivity growth. Indeed the only germane evidence at all is that presented by Levine and Tyson (1990), where in a survey of studies, they find that what they call "representative" participation, where employees have representation on workers councils, consultative committees, or even boards of directors, has no significant impact on productivity performance.

4.7.2. Employment Protection

Unemployment

We turn now to the effects of job security regulations and laws concerning the use of fixed term contracts. It is obvious that employment protection will tend to reduce the separation rate from employment into unemployment, and reduce the exit rate from unemployment into work as firms become more cautious about hiring. This will tend to reduce short-term unemployment and raise long-term unemployment, exactly the pattern we see in Table 4.15. As for the overall impact of these offsetting effects, there appears to be very little on unemployment (footnote a, Table 4.15) confirming the results of Bentolila and Bertola (1990). As we have already noted in Section 4.5., there is a significant negative impact of employment protection on the employment population ratio, a fact reported in Lazear (1990). However, this correlation does not apply to prime-age men (Table 4.16, column (2)) and is basically driven by low female participation and high levels of employment protection in southern Europe (OECD, 1994a, Table 6.9). Whether there is, any particular causation running from the latter to the former remains an open question.[9]

Growth

One basic argument here is that employment protection laws slow down the reallocation from old and declining sectors to new and dynamic sectors, thereby reducing the growth rate (Hopenhayn and Rogerson 1993; Bertola 1994). A related argument, due to Saint-Paul (1997), is that the demand for new goods is more volatile than the demand for old goods. So more flexibility is required to produce new goods and countries with low levels of employment protection will specialize in their production.

However, these kinds of arguments carry less weight than they might, when it is recognized that firms can reduce employment by 10% per year or more, simply by relying on workers leaving. This is quite a rapid rate of adjustment although this applies only to continuing firms. A considerable proportion of the overall adjustment operates via the closure of old plants and the opening of new ones. If employment protection hinders this process, then it will still be damaging. However, there is no evidence that rates of job destruction and job creation are lower in central and southern Europe than anywhere else. Indeed, as we can see from Table 4.19, they are much the same in many European countries with high levels of employment protection as they are in the United States. This is explained by Bertola and Rogerson (1997) by the fact that while employment protection slows down the rate of job turnover, wage inflexibility at *the firm level* speeds it up. As Layard, Nickell and Jackman (1991, Chapter 4) note, firm wages are more responsive to firm-level shocks in the United States than they are in Europe, and this makes for increased job stability at the firm level. Nevertheless, this fact still indicates that despite the existence of employment protection, unprofitable jobs are closed down and profitable ones started up at a reasonable rate. On the other hand worker turnover is noticeably higher in North America than elsewhere which means that workers must rotate round existing jobs more rapidly. Whether or not this is particularly advantageous is not clear.

While rapid adjustment away from declining sectors is obviously good for growth, it is also true that job security may itself help to enhance productivity performance. There is a great deal of evidence that, in many sectors, substantive employee participation, where employees have some degree of autonomy in decision taking,[10] is associated with high productivity growth (see Levine and Tyson 1990, for a survey). Furthermore, the results reported in Levine and Tyson (1990) and Ichniowski, Shaw and Prennushi (1995) make it very clear that

145

Table 4.19
Job and Worker Turnover (% p.a.)[a]

| | Job turnover[b] | | | | | | | Worker turnover[c] | | | |
| | Total | | | | Continuing establishments | | | | | | |
	Years	Creation	Destruction	Turnover	Creation	Destruction	Turnover	Years	Accessions	Separations	Turnover
Austria	1991-1993				5.7	6.2	11.9	1985	21.9	19.9	41.8
Belgium	1983-1985	7.7	7.5	15.2				1984-1991[e]	29.0	29.0	58.0
Denmark	1983-1989	16.0	13.8	29.8	9.9	8.8	18.7	1984	40.0	37.0	77.0
Finland	1986-1991	10.4	12.0	22.4	6.5	8.7	15.2	1987	28.9	30.7	59.6
France	1984-1991	12.7	11.8	24.4	6.6	6.3	12.9				
Germany (W)	1983-1990	9.0	7.5	16.5	6.5	5.6	12.1	1984-1990	31.6	30.4	62.0
Ireland (manu.)	1984-1985	8.8	12.7	21.4	6.1	8.1	14.1				
Italy	1987-1992	11.0	10.0	21.0	7.3	6.2	13.5	1985-1991	34.5	33.6	68.1
Netherlands (manu.)	1984-1991	8.2	7.2	15.4			7.0	1990	11.9	10.1	22.0
Norway (manu.)	1985-1992	8.1	10.6	18.7	6.0	7.5	13.5				
Spain[d]	1993-1994	14.5	14.6	29.1	5.2	7.6	12.8	1993-1994	26.6	28.5	55.1
Sweden	1985-1992	8.7	6.6	15.3	8.0	9.6	17.6	1977-1981[e]	16.8	17.8	34.6
UK	1985-1992				6.0	2.7	8.7	1967-1985	37.2	37.6	74.8
Japan	1985-1992				8.6	5.3	13.9	1988-1992[f]	20.2	18.9	39.1
Australia (manu.)	1984-1985	16.1	13.2	29.3	7.1	4.6	11.7				
New Zealand	1987-1992	15.7	19.8	35.5	8.3	11.3	19.7				
Canada	1983-1991	14.5	11.9	26.4	11.2	8.8	20.0	1988	48.2	44.4	92.6
US	1984-1991	13.0	10.4	23.4	4.6	3.1	7.7	1985-1993			96.0
US (manu.)	1984-1988	8.2	10.4	18.6	6.7	7.7	14.4	1977-1981	45.2	46.0	91.2

[a] Job turnover (% of total employment, yearly average) = job creation + job destruction. Worker turnover (% of total employment, yearly average) = accession + separations.

[b] OECD Employment Outlook (1996, Table 5.1).

[c] OECD Employment Outlook (1996, Table 5.2); Contini et al. (1995, Tables 7.1, 7.2).

[d] Garcia Serrano (1998).

[e] Manufacturing.

[f] Continuing firms.

the role of participation is much enhanced by a number of complementary factors, notably incentive pay and employment security.

Employment security is important for two reasons. First, productivity improvements often depend crucially on the co-operation of workers, or even directly upon their ideas and suggestions. These will be withheld if individuals feel their jobs are at risk as a consequence. Second, substantive participation requires more training, and this is only worth providing if the employment relation is long-term. So there is no reason to be surprised that employment protection shows up with a positive coefficient in our simple productivity regressions (Table 4.17).

However, if the provision of employment security is good for productivity, why are most firms in the United States neither providing it nor agitating in favor of the introduction of "just-cause" legislation? The obvious argument here is based on adverse selection (see Levine 1991). If a single firm introduces employment security, it will attract dud workers and it then becomes too expensive to screen them out. If there are employment protection laws, this problem goes away. Furthermore, as the number of legal cases associated with employment separation in the US continues to increase, maybe this will change (see Flanagan 1987; Dertouzos and Karoly 1993). For, as Spulber (1989) remarks, "[r]ather than resorting to costly litigation in each instance of breach [of contract], it may be preferable to have standard penalties for breach which are established and enforced by a regulatory agency" (p. 60).

4.7.3. Summary

There is no evidence that stricter labor standards lead to higher unemployment, mainly because it appears that wages adjust to compensate. Employment protection slows down the flows through the labor market, raising long-term unemployment and reducing short-term unemployment with little evidence of any overall effect. As far as growth is concerned, there seems to be no evidence that either stricter labor standards or employment protection lowers productivity growth rates. If anything, employment protection can lead to higher productivity growth if it is associated with other measures taken by firms to enhance the substantive participation of the workforce.

4.8. Unions and Wage setting

One of the main differences between continental Europe and the United States is the fact that in continental Europe, most workers have their wages set as a result of collective agreements negotiated between trade unions and employers. This does not necessarily mean that most of these workers are union members. As we can see in Table 4.7, the two countries in the OECD with the lowest union membership are France (9.8%) and Spain (11%). The key point here is that within firms, unions or union-dominated works councils will negotiate pay even though many or even most of the employees are not members. Furthermore, in a number of continental European countries, union wage agreements in unionized firms are extended (by law) to non-union firms in the same locality (e.g., in Belgium and Germany).

Table 4.20

Coefficients on Union Membership in Individual Wage Regressions: 1985-1993 (%)

Austria	14,6
Germany (W)	3,4
Ireland	30,5
Italy	7,2
Netherlands	3,7
Norway	7,7
Spain	0,3
Switzerland	0,8
UK	14,7
Japan	47,8
Australia	9,2
New Zealand	8,4
Canada	4,8
US	23,3

The consequence of this is to make measured union membership wage effects particularly hard to interpret in some countries. In Table 4.20, we present a series of coefficients on union membership in individual wage regressions generated from International Social Survey Programme (ISSP) data by Blanchflower (1996). Several points are worth noting about these numbers. First, some important controls are missing, notably firm size, which helps explain the extraordinary Japan coefficient. Second, the numbers cannot, in most cases, be interpreted as the gap between union and non-union rates of pay (or the union mark-up). This is because, in many of the countries, the majority of non-union members are paid at union rates. This can be seen clearly from the fact that in Spain, Germany, and the Netherlands, for example, the estimated membership coefficients are very low despite the fact that unions are very powerful in all three countries. Nevertheless, the numbers in Table 4.20 are consistent with the view that unions raise wages, something which has been confirmed from numerous other data sources (see, e.g., Lewis 1986).

The extent to which unions can succeed in raising wages does not simply depend on the power of the union. It also depends on the extent of the firm's product market power. As the work of Stewart (1990), Abowd and Lernieux (1993), and Nickell, Vainiomaki and Wadhwani (1994) makes clear, union wage mark-ups are higher in firms with greater market power. Increased competition in the product market reduces the ability of unions to raise wages.

4.8.1. Unemployment

There is no question that because unions increase wage pressure, their existence will, ceteris paribus, raise unemployment. And the more workers they cover, the higher their impact (see Table 4.15). Our results indicate that if the proportion of workers covered by collective agreements rises from less than 25% to over 70%, unemployment is more than doubled. This, of course, is just based on a crude cross-section regression, but it gives some idea of the importance of union pay bargaining.

However, there is also no question that if unions and firms can coordinate their wage bargaining activities, they can overcome some of the externalities generated by decentralized collective bargaining, moderate wage pressure, and, thereby, reduce the unemployment consequences of trade union wage bargaining. Thus, using again the coefficients in Table 4.15, a move from no coordination to complete coordination will completely offset the unemployment impact of a move from zero union density and no union coverage to 100% union density and full coverage. Supporting evidence along the same lines may be found in OECD (1997, Chapter 3).

The problem for the fully unionized, fully coordinated economy is the potential fragility of the coordination element. Coordination has elements of instability for all the usual reasons displayed in standard oligopoly models. Individuals have an incentive to break away and this can only be prevented by the threat of social or economic punishment. Maintaining widespread union strength in individual firms while reducing coordination is a recipe for increased wage pressure and unemployment. This has been part of the problem in Sweden in the 1990s, the comparison with Norway being very instructive.

To summarize, therefore, unions generate wage pressure and cause unemployment although their overall impact is lower the greater the degree of product market competition faced by the firms. This positive effect of unions on unemployment can also be offset by coordination among both unions and employers. Such coordination is subject to a degree of fragility leading to the ever-present danger of its breaking down.

4.8.2. Growth

Unions may influence productivity growth for a number of reasons. First, by the standard hold-up mechanism, they may capture quasi-rents associated with firms' investments of various kinds. This reduces the level of such investments. Second, they may slow down the introduction of new technology and new working practices because they are wedded to restrictive working practices, which reduce the level of effort and enable the union to exercise control in the work place. This, of course, cuts both ways. A union which co-operates in the introduction of new technology or new work practices may actually enhance their impact by increasing the level of co-operative endeavor among the workforce.

The evidence on this issue is quite voluminous. On the hold-up mechanism, Van Reenen (1986) demonstrates that technological innovations by firms boost subsequent pay by more when unions are stronger. Furthermore the evidence reported in Nickell and Denny (1992) and the balance of the evidence surveyed in Addison and Hirsch (1989) suggests a negative impact of unions on investment. The evidence on R&D expenditure also appears fairly clear cut. Of the nine studies surveyed in Menezes-Filho, Ulph and Van Reenen (1995), seven exhibit a significant negative impact of unions on R&D expenditure. However, it is worth noting that when firm effects or industry effects are controlled, the negative relationship is much weakened.

On the overall impact of unions on productivity and productivity growth, the balance of the evidence for Britain and the United States suggests that this impact is negative (see Addison and Hirsch 1989, Fernie and Metcalf 1995). In particular, Bean and Crafts (1995) find that UK firms which have to deal with a multiplicity of unions are very badly affected. However, there is no evidence of union effects in cross-country growth regressions and in Englander and Gurney's (1994b) survey of the determinants of OECD productivity, there is not a single mention of trade unions.

Looking at more detailed micro studies of productivity, the impression given is one where, in many union plants, productivity is reduced by the activities of the union but it does not have to be so. It all depends on the response of management. For example, Cooke (1992) explains how participation programs generate significant productivity improvements in non-union firms or in union firms where the program is jointly administered by the firm and the union. If the management of a union firm pushes through a participation program on its own, it has no impact on productivity. Ichniowski and Shaw (1995) and Ichniowski, Shaw and Prennushi (1995) indicate how more non-union than union firms make use of participatory practices but those union firms which do introduce them do as well as non-union firms. Underlying this is the fact that workers and supervisors are typically strongly resistant to the introduction of new human resource management (HRM) practices in plants with a long story of adversarial industrial relations. Switching is then only induced by the threat of closure which suggests that unions are more likely to cooperate in productivity enhancing practices in bad times or when the firm faces a higher degree of product market competition. This story is wholly consistent with the surge in productivity in union plants in Britain after the very deep recession of 1981 (see Nickell, Wadhwani and Wall 1992).

4.8.3. Summary

Unions are important players in the economies of continental Europe. They generate wage pressure and hence unemployment although this effect can be, and in many countries is, offset by effective coordination in wage bargaining between different unions or between different employers. Effective coordination does, however, have a tendency to fragility. On the productivity front, unions, at least in the United States and Britain are, on average, negatively associated with productivity growth. But if management and unions can operate in a more co-operative fashion, then this negative association disappears. There is no evidence of negative union effects on growth in cross-country regressions which suggests that in the countries of continental Europe, unions and management, on average, operate in a more co-operative fashion and thereby avoid serious negative effects on productivity growth.

4.9. Minimum Wages

As we have already noted in Section 4.2., minimum wages of one form or another are widespread in the OECD where only the United Kingdom currently does without them completely. Their potential for influencing unemployment is obvious, their impact on productivity less so. Indeed, the only two serious arguments in this regard seem to be first, that minimum wages tend to raise overall productivity by eliminating low-pay, low-productivity jobs and, presumably, raising unemployment among the workers who would otherwise fill them. Second, minimum wages reduce skill differentials and hence the incentive to accumulate human capital.

4.9.1. Unemployment

This is a much-debated topic upon which there is little consensus as a reading of Card and Krueger (1995) and its various reviews in the July 1995 issue of *Industrial and Labour Relations Review* readily indicates. Our reading of the evidence is that minimum wages are typically set low enough not to have a significant impact on adult male unemployment. However, in countries where the minimum is not seriously adjusted for the under 25s (e.g., France and Spain) or which have very high payroll taxes (e.g., France and Italy), there is some evidence that youth unemployment rates are increased. Some suggest that wage floors, including the minimum wage, have had a significant impact on the unemployment rate of low-skill workers more generally. This is not clear, but we shall return to it when we discuss skills and training.

4.9.2. Growth

There are no serious hypotheses here except those noted above about minimum wages eliminating low productivity jobs and reducing training incentives. There is no solid evidence on the second of these and, as for the first, the problem is that low productivity jobs also tend to be eliminated if there is a shortage of low productivity people. For example, McKinsey Global Institute (1997) notes that in France, Toys 'R' Us stores employ 30% fewer people than in identical stores in the United States. This is put down to the minimum wage. However, even if there were no minimum wage in France, whether Toys 'R' Us would be able to find a large number of extra employees in France who would be prepared to work at very low wages is a moot point.

4.10. Social Security Systems and Active Labor Market Policies

The impact of the social security system on economic performance operates mainly via labor supply. Higher unemployment benefits are obviously liable to raise unemployment, and other elements of the social security system will influence the extent of disability and early retirement. To minimize these effects, it is clear that the system should be operated so that its main aim is to get people working. Systems which allow individuals who are able to work to collect benefit over long periods without serious pressure being applied to take up a job, will eventually have large numbers of customers. As for the impact of social security systems on productivity growth, we know of no evidence or hypotheses other than the vague notion that a social security system which is too generous will undermine entrepreneurial instincts or the equally vague notion that more generous social security encourages greater risk-taking and so enhances entrepreneurial instincts. So we shall have nothing further to say on this question.

4.10.1. Unemployment

The impact of a high benefit replacement ratio on unemployment is well documented (Layard, Nickell and Jackman 1991, p. 255/6; OECD, 1994a, Chapter 8) and is confirmed by the coefficient on the replacement ratio in Table 4.15. Another important feature of the benefit system is duration of entitlement. Long-term benefits generate long-term unemployment (see Table 4.15, column (2) or OECD, 1990, Chart 7.1B). Of course, it can be argued that countries might introduce more generous benefit systems when unemployment is a serious problem, so that in cross-country correlations, the causality runs from unemployment to benefits rather than the other way round. However, the micro-econometric evidence on the positive impact of benefit levels and entitlement duration on the duration of individual unemployment spells (Narendranathan, Nickell and Stern 1985, Meyer 1990) suggests that at least part of the observed cross-country correlation can be taken at face value.

The impact of a relatively generous benefit system might be offset by suitable active measures to push the unemployed back to work. Such policies seem to work particularly well when allied to a relatively short duration of benefit entitlement, reducing long-term unemployment while alleviating the social distress that might be caused by simply discontinuing benefits without offering active assistance toward a job. Their effects are well summarized in OECD (1993, chapter 2), and their significant impact in reducing long-term unemployment is illustrated in column (2) of Table 4.15.

While benefits affect unemployment, our evidence suggests that the benefit system seems to have little impact on overall labor input as shown in Table 4.16. There is a suggestion here that while high benefits lead to high unemployment, they also lead to high participation because they make participation in the labor market more attractive, participation being necessary to be eligible for the high benefits. This is consistent with a weak impact of benefits on employment/population ratios, because the higher unemployment effect and the higher labor market participation effect tend to cancel out.

4.10.2. Summary

Generous and long-lasting unemployment benefits will tend to raise unemployment. The effect can be offset by active labor market policies and strictly operated systems.

4.11. Skills and Education

While human capital accumulation is obviously important for productivity growth, the main purpose of this section is to explore the role of labor market institutions in the responses of different countries to the universal increase in the relative demand for skilled workers which has taken place in recent decades. It has been suggested that this shift has been responsible for the significant aggregate unemployment increases in Europe essentially because of the important rigidities generated by European labor market institutions, particularly unions and minimum wages (see, e.g., Krugman 1994). Just to see what we might expect to happen, consider the following basic model.

Suppose the production function has the form

$$(5) \qquad Y = F\big(K, [\delta N_1^{-p} + (1 - \delta) N_2^{-p}]^{-1/p}\big),$$

where Y is output, K is capital, N_1 is skilled labor, N_2 is unskilled labor. Then the labor demand equations will imply

$$(6) \qquad \frac{W_1}{W_2} = \frac{\delta}{1 - \delta} \left(\frac{N_2}{N_1}\right)^{1/\sigma},$$

even under imperfect competition in the product market. W_1 is the skilled wage, W_2 the unskilled wage and $\sigma = (1 - \rho)^{-1}$ is the elasticity of substitution. So if s is the share of skilled workers in the labor force and u_i is the unemployment rate of group i, (6) can be rewritten as

$$(7) \qquad \frac{W_1}{W_2} \left(\frac{1 - u_1}{1 - u_2}\right)^{1/\sigma} = \frac{\delta}{1 - \delta} \left(\frac{s}{1 - s}\right)^{-1/\sigma}.$$

In log changes, we thus have

$$(8) \qquad \sigma \Delta \ln(W_1/W_2) + \Delta \ln[(1 - u_1)/(1 - u_2)]$$

$$= \sigma \Delta \ln(\delta/(1 - \delta)) - \Delta \ln(s/(1 - s)),$$

where the right-hand side can be interpreted as the shift in the relative demand for skilled workers less the shift in the relative supply. If demand shifts outstrip supply shifts, this will translate into some combination of a relative wage movement and a relative unemployment movement pinned down by (8). Precisely how much will go into wages and how much into unemployment will depend on the wage setting mechanism for each skill group, i.e., how wages respond to

155

excess demand/supply in each of the labor markets. For example, if there is complete relative wage rigidity, all the shift in relative excess demand will go into unemployment changes. The nice feature of this simple framework is that we can estimate δ by the adjusted share of skilled labor in total labor cost, namely

$$\delta = W_1 N_1^{1/\sigma} \left[W_1 N_1^{1/\sigma} + W_2 N_2^{1/\sigma} \right]^{-1},$$

so we can easily measure the demand and supply shifts in (8) for given values of σ.

Before looking at these shifts, let us first investigate the wage and unemployment outcomes for the OECD countries. First, in Table 4.21, we report the unemployment rates for men which correspond to the educational attainment levels in Table 4.11. We restrict ourselves to men because they will be our main focus when we look at wage and unemployment changes. The results for women have exactly the same implications. The main feature of Table 4.21 is that for every country except Italy and Switzerland, the unemployment rates among the least educated are far higher than those for the most educated.

How have educational unemployment rates changed in recent years? In Table 4.22, we present some data which cover the last two decades for the top and bottom educational groups.

In all countries we see a large rise in unskilled unemployment from the 1970s to the 1990s. In many countries we have a substantial rise in skilled unemployment. However, in Germany, Norway, Sweden, and the United States, the increase in skilled unemployment is relatively slight as is the percentage point increase in unemployment as a whole. Overall, the pattern of the rise in US unemployment from the early 1970s to the early 1990s is very similar to that in Germany from the mid-1970s to the early 1990s. Of course, in the last couple of years there has been considerable divergence, although that is mainly cyclical.[11]

Table 4.21

Male Unemployment Rates by Education, 1991 (Age 25-64)

	ISCED2 Minimal compulsory	ISCED3 Higher secondary	ISCED5 Non-degree tertiary	ISCED6/7 Degree	All
Austria	4.7	3.0	-	1.3	3.2
Belgum	3.5	2.0	1.6	1.4	4.7
Denmark	13.0	7.9	5.2	4.6	8.8
Finland	10.2	9.0	4.1	2.8	8.2
France	8.9	4.9	2.6	2.8	6.0
Germany (W)	10.0	5.0	3.3	3.4	5.0
Ireland	16.9	8.5	5.4	3.0	15.9
Italy	3.3	4.0	-	3.4	3.4
Netherlands	4.0	2.5	-	-	3.4
Norway	7.6	4.8	2.9	1.8	4.6
Portugal	2.4	1.7	2.0	1.2	2.3
Spain	10.5	7.3	-	5.8	9.6
Sweden	2.6	2.7	1.3	1.1	2.3
Switzerland	0.4	0.8	0.8	2.3	0.9
UK	13.4	6.8	4.3	2.5	7.8
Australia	10.6	6.0	6.6	3.1	7.0
New Zealand	8.0	7.7	6.7	4.8	8.9
Canada	13.9	9.7	8.2	4.6	9.3
US	14.6	8.9	6.4	4.4	8.0

Source: OECD Jobs Study, Part II (1994a, Table 7.B.1). ISCED 0/1 is omitted. For full definitions, see Table 4.22.

Turning now to the wage changes, in Table 4.23 we see that while most countries except France saw a narrowing of educational wage differentials in the 1970s, the United Kingdom, the United States and, to some extent, Canada, saw a substantial widening of differentials in the 1980s and 1990s. In the case of Canada, however, this simply offset the dramatic narrowing that took place in the 1970s. So only in the case of the United Kingdom and the United States are educational wage differentials substantially wider now than they were in the early 1970s. These patterns reflect the changes in the overall earnings distribution over the same period.

Table 4.22

Male Unemployment Rates by Education (%)[a]

	1971-1974	1975-1978	1979-1982	1983-1986	1987-1990	1991-1993
France						
Total			5.2[b]	6.7[c]	7.2	8.1
High ed.			2.1	2.5	2.6	4.2
Low ed.			6.5	9.0	10.8	12.1
Ratio			3.1	3.6	4.1	2.9
Germany (W)						
Total		2.8	3.4	6.3	4.9	4.1[d]
High ed.		1.5	2.0	3.3	2.9	2.2
Low ed.		5.2	7.6	13.9	12.1	10.7
Ratio		3.5	3.8	4.2	4.2	4.9
Italy						
Total (M + F)		7.2	8.2	10.5	11.8	11.2[d]
High ed.		12.3	12.2	13.1	13.1	12.5
Low ed.		4.4	4.8	6.4	8.1	7.5
Ratio		0.4	0.4	0.5	0.6	0.6
Netherlands						
Total (M + F)		5.5[e]	7.1[f]	13.1[g]	6.9[h]	6.8
High ed.		2.9	3.4	6.2	5.2	5.0
Low ed.		5.7	8.3	18.0	9.9	9.9
Ratio		2.0	2.4	2.9	1.9	2.0
Norway						
Total (M + F)	1.2[g]	1.9	2.1	2.7	3.9	5.7
High ed.	1.0	0.8	0.9	0.8	1.5	2.6
Low ed.	1.9	2.2	2.9	3.8	6.0	8.8
Ratio	1.9	2.8	3.2	4.8	4.0	3.4
Spain						
Total		6.1	11.7	18.5	15.3	15.1
High ed.		4.5	7.9	11.0	8.8	9.0
Low ed.		7.7	13.5	21.4	17.7	20.0
Ratio		1.7	1.7	1.9	2.0	2.2
Sweden						
Total	2.8	1.9	2.4	3.1	1.8	5.8
High ed.	1.3	0.8	0.9	1.1	1.0	2.8
Low ed.	3.2	2.4	3.1	4.1	2.4	6.9
Ratio	2.5	4.0	3.4	3.7	2.4	2.5
UK						
Total	2.9[k]	4.4	7.7	10.5	7.5	10.8[d]
High ed.	1.4	2.0	3.9	4.7	4.0	6.2
Low ed.	4.0	6.4	12.2	18.2	13.5	17.1
Ratio	2.9	3.2	3.1	3.9	3.4	2.8

Table 4.22 (continued)

Male Unemployment Rates by Education (%)[a]

	1971-1974	1975-1978	1979-1982	1983-1986	1987-1990	1991-1993
Canada						
Total	6.9	6.6[i]	10.3[a]	7.8	11.6	
High ed.	2.6	2.4	4.3	3.4	5.1	
Low ed.	8.2	8.3	12.5	11.3	16.1	
Ratio	3.2	3.5	2.9	3.2	3.2	
US						
Total	3.6	5.5	5.7	7.3	5.1	6.0
High ed.	1.7	2.2	2.1	2.7	2.1	3.0
Low ed.	5.3	8.6	9.4	12.8	9.8	11.0
Ratio	3.1	3.9	4.5	4.7	4.7	3.7

[a] *Notes*: France: Low ed., no certification or only primary school certificate. High ed., 2 years university education or further education college degree or university degree (5.1% of labor force in 1968, 15.8% in 1990). Source: Enquête sur L'Emploi. INSEE. Data refer to males, age 15+. (West) Germany: Low ed., no formal qualification (39% of working age population 1976, 28% in 1989). High ed., degree (11.3% of working age population in 1976, 15.9% in 1989). Source: Buttler and Tessaring (1993), adjusted to be compatible with OECD standardized rate. Italy: Low ed., lower secondary or less (56% of labor force in 1977, 23.1% in 1992). High ed., upper secondary or higher (18% of labor force in 1977, 35.2% in 1992). Source: Annuario Statistico Italiano, ISTAT. M + F refers to males and females, age 25-64. Netherlands: Low ed., basic education or completed junior secondary school or junior vocational education (72.8% of labor force in 1975, 33.1% in 1993). High ed., completed vocational college or university (10.2% of labor force in 1975, 23.9% in 1993). Source: Dutch Central Bureau of Statistics. M + F refers to males and females, age 15-64. Norway: Low ed., primary level (64.5% of labor force in 1972, 16.3% in 1993). High ed., university level (9.9% of labor force in 1972, 26.3% in 1993). Source: Labour Market Statistics, Statistics Norway. Data refer to men and women, age 16-74. Spain: Low ed., illiterate or primary (75.8% of labor force in 1976, 40% in 1993). High ed., superior (university) 2.6% of labor force in 1976, 5.5% in 1993). Source: Spanish Labour Force Survey. Refers to males, age 16-64. Sweden: Low ed., pre-upper secondary school up to 10 years (59.7% of labor force in 1971, 30.6% in 1990). High ed., post-upper secondary education (7.9% of labor force in 1971, 21.7% in 1990). Source: Swedish Labour Force Surveys. Refers to males, age 16-64. UK: Low ed., no qualifications (55.7% of labor force in 1973, 28.2% in 1991). High ed., passed A levels (18+ exam) or professional qualification or degree (16.4% of labor force in 1973, 36.8% in 1991). Source: General Household Survey. Refers to males, age 16-44. Canada: Low ed., up to level 8 (23.3% of labor force in 1975, 7.3% in 1993). High ed., university degree (10.4% of labor force in 1975, 16.8% in 1993). Source: The Labour Force, Statistics Canada. Refers to males, age 15+. US: Low ed., less than 4 years of high school (37.5% of labor force in 1970, 14.5% in 1991). High ed., 4 or more years of college (15.7% of labor force in 1970, 28.2% in 1991). Source: Handbook of Labor Statistics, BLS. 1989 (Table 67). Statistical Abstract of the US (1993, Table 654). Refers to males, age 25-64. Ratio = low ed. unemployment / high ed. unemployment.

[b] 1982 only. [c] 1983, 1986. [d] 1991-1992. [e] 1975, 1977.
[f] 1979, 1981. [g] 1983, 1985. [h] 1990. [i] 1972-1974.
[j] 1973-1974. [k] 1979. [l] 1984-1986.

Table 4.23

Education Earnings Ratios for Men (Top Level/Bottom Level)

	Early 1970s	Late 1970s	Early 1980s	Mid/late 1980s	Early 1990s	% Annual Rate of Change	
						1970s	1980-1990s
Austria	–	–	–	–	1.17	–	–
Denmark	–	–	1.58	1.59	1.61	–	0.4
France	3.85	4.23	–	3.81	–	5.4	-5.2
Germany (W)	–	–	2.00	1.94	–	–	-1.2
Netherlands	–	–	1.96	1.86	–	–	-2.0
Norway	–	–	1.43	1.32	1.35	–	-1.0
Sweden	1.68	–	1.37	1.57	1.55	-4.4	1.8
UK	1.83	1.69	–	1.87	2.04	-2.8	3.4
Canada	2.09	1.69	–	1.90	2.08	-6.6	3.2
US	1.92	1.94	–	2.33	2.47	0.4	4.0
Japan	1.32	1.30	–	1.36	1.36	-0.4	0.4
Australia	2.03	1.87	1.74	1.70	1.79	-3.2	0.4

Source: OECD Jobs Study (1994a, part II, Table 7.A.I). The education ratios are E/level A = ISCED6/7/ISCED2 = degree level/minimal compulsory education level. See Table 4.11 for details. France is a complete outlier partly because level E appears to refer only to graduates of a Grand Ecole, which is a tiny elite subgroup of those with first degrees.

Three interesting questions emerge from these facts. First, why have the educational wage differentials widened so much more in Britain and the United States than in other countries, particularly in recent years?

Table 4.24

Changes in Demand and Supply of Skilled Workers (Equation (8))

	$\sigma\Delta\ln(\delta/1-\delta))$ change in relative demand	$\Delta\ln(s/(1-s))$ change in relative supply	Annual change (x100) in $\sigma\Delta\ln(\delta/1-\delta))-\ln(s/(1-s))$ (relative demand-relative supply)		
	$\sigma = 1$	$\sigma = 1$	$\sigma = 1$	$\sigma = 2$	$\sigma = 1/2$
	(1)	(2)	(3)	(4)	(5)
France 1984-1993	0.559	0.544	0.17	0.19	0.17
Germany (W) 1984-1993	0.175	0.241	-0.73	-1.51	-1.34
Italy 1977-1993	1.199	1.117	0.51	0.60	0.47
Netherlands	0.267	0.336	-1.36	-1.38	-1.36
Norway 1979-1993	0.875	0.862	0.09	-0.06	0.17
UK 1979-1991	1.126	0.984	1.29	2.24	0.65
Australia 1979-1990	0.429	0.443	-0.12	-0.32	-0.04
Canda 1997-1991	0.929	0.896	0.28	0.48	0.18
US 1980-1989	0.414	0.289	1.34	2.82	0.67

Source: Jackman et al. (1999, Annex 2 and Table 5) except for UK, Labour Force Survey and New Earnings Survey, and Germany, Clark (1997, Tables 5.1, 5.3). Definition of skilled workers (unskilled are the remainder). France: baccalaureat general and above. Germany: all exept those with basic/middle levels of schooling and no formal vocational training. Italy: upper secondary qualification or above. Netherlands: senior secondary qualification or above. Norway: secondary school II or above. UK: O levels (GCE) or above. Canada: some post-secondary education or above. US: some college or above. Australia: attended highest available secondary school or above.

Second, has the demand shift against the unskilled contributed substantially to the large increase in unemployment in some European countries over the last 20 years? Third, leaving aside France (see notes to Table 4.23), why are there such big cross-country variations in the wage differentials corresponding to similar education differentials? Note that these variations in educational pay differentials correspond quite closely to variations in the overall earnings distribution (see, OECD, 1993, Chapter 5).

The obvious place to start with these questions is the pattern of supply and demand. In Table 4.24, we present information on the recent changes in relative demand less changes in relative supply, corresponding precisely to Equation (8). In the first two columns we present changes in relative demand and supply under the assumption of a unit elasticity of substitution (see Jackman et al. 1999 for evidence in favor of this hypothesis). Then in the next three columns we have the average annual change in relative demand less relative supply for three different values of the elasticity of substitution. The numbers reveal immediately that the relative demand for skilled workers has outstripped the relative supply by far more in the United Kingdom and the United States than in any other country for which data are available. These numbers are consistent with those presented by Manacorda and Manning (1997). This seems quite enough to answer the first question without recourse to any special arguments about unions, minimum wages, and relative wage inflexibility.

All the available evidence suggests that the answer to the second question is no. While it has often been suggested that wage inflexibility has generated unemployment in Europe in response to relative demand shifts in favor of the skilled (see, e.g., Krugman 1994), there is no convincing evidence in favor of this view. As we might expect from the numbers in Tables 4.22 and 4.23, particularly the substantial rises in skilled unemployment in many countries, the evidence suggests that skill shifts account for only a tiny proportion of the rise in unemployment since the 1970s. Furthermore, there is no evidence that this proportion is lower in "flexible" Britain than anywhere else (see Card, Kramarz and Lemieux 1995; Nickell and Bell 1995, 1996; Jackman et al. 1999).

The last question is, perhaps, the most interesting, asking why earnings are so much more compressed in some countries than others. The standard answer to this question, set out persuasively in Blau and Kahn (1996), is that institutional factors in many countries (unions, minimum wages etc.) serve to raise pay at the bottom end and generate pay compression. However, the analysis which produces this kind of conclusion typically uses schooling as the international currency of skill, then shows that pay differentials across certain schooling levels are much higher in the United States than in Sweden, say, and concludes that the only explanation for this is that institutions generate pay compression (thereby raising unemployment).

Table 4.25

Average Test Scores and Earnings (Labor Force), 1990s[a]

	ISCED3/ISCED2		ISCED6-7/ISCED2	
	Test score ratio (1)	Earnings ratio (2)	Test score ratio (3)	Earnings ratio (4)
Germany (W)	1.054	1.133	1.40	1.94
Netherlands	1.092	1.188	1.30	1.86
Sweden	1.018	1.132	1.20	1.55
Switzerland	1.128	1.313	–	–
Canada	1.110	1.232	1.61	2.08
US	1.167	1.511	1.72	2.47

[a] ISCD2, first stage secondary-end of compulsory schooling; ISCED3, second stage or higer secondary. ISCED6-7, first degree or above. Columns (1) and (2) were provided by Per-Anders Edin (Uppsala) from data supplied by OECD. Column (3) is derived from Table 4.12. Column (4) is taken from Table 4.23. Test scores refer to scores in the OECD quantitative literacy test, reported in Literacy, Economy and Society (OECD, 1995). The tests and the marking system were identical across all countries.

As we have seen in Table 4.12, the use of schooling as a common currency may be a problem. An alternative hypothesis to explain why earnings differentials corresponding to apparently comparable schooling differentials differ so much, is that the schooling differentials are not comparable. Furthermore if a truly comparable measure of skill is used, the earnings differentials can readily be explained by the skill differentials. An investigation of this alternative hypothesis is presented in Table 4.25 and Figure 3.2 (see Chapter 3), where we use the scores in an OECD quantitative literacy test administered to a random sample of the working age population in a variety of countries. The test and the marking scheme were identical for each country. In Table 4.25 and Figure 4.1, we see that the earnings ratios associated with "comparable" education levels relate very closely to the test score ratios corresponding to these same "comparable" education levels. These results provide quite strong evidence in favor of the very simple hypothesis that variations in earnings distributions across countries correspond rather closely to variations in true skill distributions. Thus, Sweden has a very compressed earnings distribution relative to the United States, because it has a very compressed skill distribution.

There is no need to wheel on the all-purpose "European institutions" to explain the differences – supply and demand does fine (see Leuven, Oosterbeek and Van Ophen 1997 for further evidence).

Figure 4.1

The Relationship Between Earnings and Test Scores

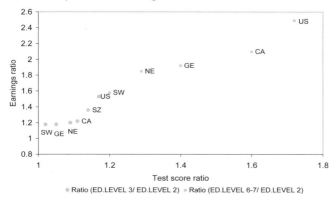

Ratio (ED.LEVEL 3/ ED.LEVEL 2) Ratio (ED.LEVEL 6-7/ ED.LEVEL 2)

4.11.1. Summary

The increase in the relative demand for skilled workers has been substantial in the last two decades across the OECD. The fact that relative demand has outstripped relative supply by much more in Britain and the United States than elsewhere helps to explain why relative skilled wages have risen by far more in those two countries. There is no evidence that relative demand shifts have played an important role in the overall rise in unemployment in many OECD countries. Finally, there is quite strong evidence that the compressed earnings distributions in some OECD countries relative to the United States are a consequence of equally compressed skill distributions. Most of the gross features of unemployment and wage distributions across the OECD in recent years seem explicable by supply and demand shifts and the role required of special institutional features such as unions and minimum wages is correspondingly minimal.

4.12. Conclusions

Consider each of the labor market features in turn.

Labor taxes. There is some evidence that overall labor tax rates have a short-run, and possibly a long-run, impact on unemployment rates. On the growth front the evidence is not robust and there is no strong reason for believing that total labor tax rates have any significant effect. Since major cuts in the tax burden are hard to achieve without significant social upheavals, such as moving health or pension provision into the private sector, an alternative strategy is to restructure the tax system so that things like health or pensions are paid for by a mechanism which largely mimics a private insurance system. This will add to the likelihood that such taxes are shifted wholly onto labor, thereby minimizing any negative effects on employment.

Labor standards and employment protection. There is no evidence that stricter labor standards or employment protection lead to higher unemployment. Employment protection does, however, raise long-term unemployment and lower short-term unemployment, by reducing the rate of flow out of and into unemployment. As far as growth is concerned, there is no reason to believe that stricter labor standards or employment protection lower productivity growth rates – indeed maybe the reverse.

Unions, wage setting, and minimum wages. The existence of strong trade unions can be expected to raise unemployment and lower growth rates except under certain circumstances. First, their harmful impact on unemployment can be offset if unions and firms can coordinate centrally over wage setting. Second, their harmful effect on growth rates can be offset if management and unions adopt a more co-operative and less adversarial stance. The difficulty here is the tendency for coordinating or co-operative endeavors to be unstable unless there are supporting institutions (such as local employers' federations in Germany).

A key factor forcing management and unions to adopt a co-operative stance is external competitive pressure. This suggests that encouraging high levels of product market competition is an important way of eliminating the negative effects of trade unions. This can be done both by standard competition policy and by removing anti-competitive product market regulation, which is a commonplace in much of the service sector in many OECD countries (see McKinsey Global institute, 1992, 1997 and Baily 1993, for example). Finally, the effects of minimum wages, at current levels, are minimal except perhaps in France.

Social security systems. Generous and long-lasting unemployment benefit entitlements remain commonplace in Europe and these generate higher unemployment. Strikingly, the only big difference between US unemployment and European unemployment is in long-term unemployment, and this is largely explained by the long period for which benefits are available in Europe with few strings attached. The impact of generous benefits can be offset by active labor market policies *and* a strictly operated system (e.g., a strict work test).

Skills and education. Institutional differences have not been very important in determining the unemployment and wage responses of different OECD countries to the substantial shifts in demand in favor of skilled workers. Different movements of supply and demand seem to explain most of the relevant features.

To conclude, the key labor market institutions on which policy should be focused are unions and social security systems. Encouraging product market competition is a key policy to eliminate the negative effects of unions. For social security the key policies are benefit reform linked to active labor market policies to move people from welfare to work. By comparison, time spent worrying about strict labor market regulations, employment protection, and minimum wages is probably time largely wasted.

5

Unemployment: Macroeconomic Performance and the Labor Market

In their introduction to the second edition of the 1991 book on "Unemployment: Macroeconomic Performance and the Labour Market" published in 2005, Richard Layard, Stephen Nickell, and Richard Jackman take stock of the research that has become available after the first edition of the seminal volume in 1991. They review the more recent developments in research, some of them inspired by the pioneering work of Layard and Nickell that set the agenda for subsequent theoretical and empirical work. Most of the new research reviewed, in particular at the micro level, however, basically confirms the findings of 1991 – as does the subsequent history. But the introduction to the second edition is not only highly relevant in academic terms – the authors also re-assess their original policy recommendations in the light of current political challenges and actual reforms implemented since the early 1990s. In fact, much has happened, in particular in terms of the activation of the unemployed and a general policy orientation moving beyond lowering unemployment and implementing policies that help mobilize labor supply.

5.1. The Determinants of Equilibrium Unemployment

The purpose of our book was to understand long-term shifts in the level of unemployment and hence to be able to explain why unemployment has been so much higher in some decades than others within countries, and why it is so much higher in some countries than others for very long periods.

The original version of this chapter was published as: Layard, R.,Nickell, S., Jackman, R. (2005). Introduction to New Edition, in: Layard, R.,Nickell, S., Jackman R. (Eds.), Unemployment: Macroeconomic Performance and the Labour Market, Oxford: Oxford University Press, XIII-XLI. By permission of Oxford University Press.

Since 1991, there have been a number of developments in the theoretical analysis of the long-run, equilibrium, level of unemployment. Particularly noteworthy are Ed Phelps' 1994 book (Phelps 1994), and the continuing work of Dale Mortensen and Chris Pissarides on flow models (summarized in Mortensen and Pissarides 1999; Pissarides 2000). Broadly speaking, theories of unemployment in the long run may be divided into those based on flow models and those based on stock models (Blanchard and Katz 1997 gives a general template for the latter). Luckily, all the models have the same broad implications, most of which may be found in the original edition of our book. But it is helpful to provide a brief summary here.

The long-run equilibrium level of unemployment is affected, first, by any variable which influences the ease with which unemployed individuals can be matched to available job vacancies and, second, by any variable which tends to raise wages in a direct fashion despite excess supply in the labor market. There may be variables common to both sets. Before going on to consider these variables in more detail, note that variables in the first group impact on the position of the unemployment/vacancy locus or Beveridge Curve, whereas those in the second do not do so in any direct fashion. However, this division is not quite as clear cut as it might appear at first sight (see below). What we can say is that any variable which shifts the Beveridge Curve to the right will increase equilibrium unemployment. So a shift of the Beveridge Curve is a sufficient but not necessary sign that equilibrium unemployment has changed.

We turn now to consider a series of variables which we might expect to influence equilibrium unemployment either because of their impact on the effectiveness with which the unemployed are matched to available jobs or because of their direct effect on wages. The unemployment benefit system directly affects the readiness of the unemployed to fill vacancies. Aspects of the system which are important are the level of benefits, their coverage, the length of time for which they are available, and the strictness with which the system is operated. Furthermore numerous government policies are concerned to increase the ability and willingness of the unemployed to take jobs. These are grouped under the heading of active labor market policies. Related to unemployment benefits is the availability of other resources to those without jobs. These include the returns on non-human wealth which may be increasing in the real interest rate (see Phelps 1994 for an extensive discussion).

Employment protection laws may tend to make firms more cautious about filling vacancies which slows the speed at which the unemployed move into work. However, the mechanism here is not clear-cut. For example, the introduction of employment protection laws often leads to an increased professionalization of the personnel function within firms, as was the case in Britain in the 1970s (Daniel and Stilgoe 1978). This can increase the efficiency of job matching. So, in terms of outflows from unemployment, the impact of employment protection laws can go either way. By contrast, such laws will clearly reduce involuntary separations and hence lower inflows into unemployment. So the overall impact on the Beveridge Curve, and hence on unemployment, is an empirical question. Furthermore, employment law may also have a direct impact on pay since it raises the job security of existing employees encouraging them to demand higher pay increases.

Anything which makes it easier to match the unemployed to the available vacancies will shift the Beveridge Curve to the left and reduce equilibrium unemployment. Factors which operate in this way include the reduction of barriers to mobility which may be geographical or occupational.

Turning now to those factors which have a direct impact on wages, the obvious place to start is the institutional structure of wage determination. Within every country there is a variety of structures. In some sectors wages are determined more of less competitively, but in others wages are bargained between employers and trade unions at the level of the establishment, firm, or even industry. The overall outcome depends on union power in wage bargains, union coverage, the degree of coordination of wage bargains, and the degree of competition in the product market. Generally, greater union power and coverage can be expected to exert upward pressure on wages, hence raising equilibrium unemployment, but this can be offset if union wage-setting across the economy is coordinated, or if there is a high level of product-market competition.

The final group of variables which directly impacts on wages falls under the heading of real wage resistance. The idea here is that workers attempt to sustain recent rates of real wage growth when the rate consistent with stable employment shifts unexpectedly. For example, if there is an adverse shift in the terms of trade, real consumption wages must fall if employment is not to decline. If workers persist in attempting to bargain for rates of real wage growth which take no account of the movement in the terms of trade, this will tend to raise unemployment. Exactly the same argument applies if there is an unexpected fall in trend productivity growth or an increase in labor taxes. For example, if labor tax rates (payroll tax plus income tax plus consumption tax) go up, the real post-tax consumption wage must fall if the real labor costs per employee facing firms are not to rise. Any resistance to this fall will lead to a rise in unemployment. This argument suggests that increases in real import prices, falls in trend productivity growth, or rises in the labor tax rate may lead to a temporary increase in unemployment. However, it may be argued that changes in labor taxes may have a permanent impact on unemployment depending on the extent to which the taxes are shifted onto labor. A key issue here is the extent to which benefits or the value of leisure adjust in proportion to post-tax earnings (see Pissarides 1998, for example).

To summarize, the variables which we might expect to influence equilibrium unemployment include the unemployment benefit system, active labor market policies, the real interest rate, employment protection laws, barriers to labor mobility, union structures and the extent of co-ordination in wage bargaining, product market competition, labor taxes, and unexpected shifts in the terms of trade and trend productivity growth. Our next step is to see how this list looks from the vantage point of 2003.

5.2. Evidence on the Factors Influencing Equilibrium Unemployment

The Unemployment Benefit System. The evidence that the structure of the unemployment benefit system influences equilibrium unemployment is now very strong, with Holmlund (1998) providing a good summary. On the level of benefits, micro evidence based on policy changes is contained in Carling, Holmlund, Vejsiu (1999), Hunt (1995) and Harkman (1997) and from experiments in Meyer (1995). Cross-country macro evidence is available in Scarpetta (1996), Elmeskov, Martin and Scarpetta (1998) and Nickell and Layard (1999, see Chapter 4). The average of their results indicates a 1.1 percentage point rise in equilibrium unemployment for every 10 percentage point rise in the benefit replacement rate.

Concerning the duration of benefits, there is fairly clear micro evidence that shorter benefit entitlements leads to shorter unemployment durations (see, for example, Ham and Rea 1987; Katz and Meyer 1990 and Carling et al. 1996). Variations in the coverage of unemployment benefits are large (see OECD 1994, Table 8.4) and there is a strong positive correlation between coverage and the level of benefit (OECD 1994, part II). Bover, Garcia-Perea and Portugal (2000) present evidence from Spain and Portugal that individuals covered by the benefit system exit unemployment much more slowly than the uncovered. Finally, there is strong evidence that the strictness with which the benefit system is operated, at given levels of benefit, is a very important determinant of unemployment duration. Micro evidence for the Netherlands may be found in Abbring, Van Den Berg and Van Ours (1999). Cross-country evidence is available in the Danish Ministry of Finance (1999, Chapter 2) and in OECD (2000, Chapter 4).

Active Labor Market Policies (ALMPs). Multi-country studies, basically using cross-section information, indicate that ALMPs do have a negative impact on unemployment (Scarpetta 1996; Nickell 1997; Elmeskov, Martin and Scarpetta 1998). This broad brush evidence is backed up by numbers of micro-econometric studies (Katz 1998; Martin 2000; Martin and Grubb 2001; Calmfors, Forslund and Hemström 2002 are useful surveys) which show that under some circumstances, ALMPs are effective. In particular, job search assistance tends to have consistently positive outcomes but other types of measure, such as employment subsidies and labor market training, must be well designed if they are to be effective.

The Real Interest Rate. There is some evidence that high real interest rates are associated with high unemployment, notably in Fitoussi et al. (2000) and Blanchard and Wolfers (2000). Some researchers, however, find very weak effects, for example, Carruth, Hooker and Oswald (1998, Table 4.3), Phelps (1994, Table 17.2), Nickell (1998) and Nickell et al. (2002). Overall, real interest rate changes do not seem to have a very robust impact on equilibrium unemployment. Furthermore, the interpretation of this effect is particularly tricky given that many macroeconomic shocks (monetary policy shocks, for example) will impact on both real interest rates and unemployment, generating correlations between the two variables which are far from structural.

Employment Protection Laws. These are thought by many to be a key factor in generating labor market inflexibility. Despite this, evidence that they have a decisive impact on overall rates of unemployment is mixed, at best. The results presented by Lazear (1990), Addison and Grosso (1996), Elmeskov, Martin and Scarpetta (1998), Nickell and

Layard (1999, see Chapter 4) do not add up to anything decisive, although there is a clear positive relationship between employment protection and *long-term* unemployment.

Barriers to Labor Mobility. Oswald (1997) proposes that barriers to geographical mobility, as reflected in the rate of owner occupation of the housing stock, play a key role in determining unemployment. He finds that changes in unemployment are positively correlated with changes in owner occupation rates across countries, US states, and UK regions. He also presents UK evidence that owner occupation represents a significant mobility barrier, relative to private renting. However, Gregg, Machin and Manning (2002) find that while unemployment is significantly negatively related to private renting both across UK regions and across time in a regional fixed effects model, this relationship becomes significantly positive once other relevant regional characteristics are included.

Systems of Wage Determination. Surveys of the evidence make it clear that trade union power in wage setting has a significant positive impact on unemployment (Nickell and Layard 1999, see Chapter 4; Booth et al. 2000, around Table 6.2). However, if wage bargaining is highly coordinated, this will tend to offset the adverse effects of unionism on employment (see again Chapter 4; Booth et al. 2000, around Table 6.1; OECD 1997, Chapter 3).

Product Market Competition. Evidence on the role of product market competition in determining unemployment is very thin. Haffner et al. (2000) provides some evidence that product market competition increases the employment rate, but the major problem in this area is measuring the extent of competition.

Labor Taxes. There is now a great deal of evidence on the impact of labor tax rates on unemployment and employment, but the precise size of these effects remains hard to pin down (useful surveys include Disney 2000; Pissarides 1998; Nickell 2003; see also Chapter 4.6.). The balance of the evidence suggests that a 10 percentage point rise in the labor tax wedge raises unemployment by between 1 and 2 percentage points in the long run.

Real Wage Resistance. There is now strong evidence that rises in import prices will raise unemployment temporarily (see Nickell et al. 2002) but, perhaps more interesting has been the recent work on changes in the rate of productivity growth. The rise in trend productivity growth in the US in the second half of the 1990s contributed to the apparent fall in equilibrium unemployment over the same period (see, for example, Ball and Moffitt 2001) and generated a renewed interest in the real wage resistance effect. This topic originally rose to prominence after the fall in trend productivity growth in the first half of the 1970s (see, for example, Grubb, Jackman and Layard 1982, 1983). Overall, there is strong evidence that changes in trend productivity growth shifts unemployment temporarily in the opposite direction, via its impact on real wages (see Nickell et al. 2002).

This completes our discussion of the evidence on the factors influencing equilibrium unemployment. Next we look at policy recommendations.

5.3. Our Original Policy Conclusions and How Things Have Changed

In the last chapter of our book, we made a sequence of policy recommendations and non-recommendations. How do these stand up in the light of subsequent experience and research (for example, OECD Jobs Study 1994; Martin and Grubb 2001; OECD 1999, 2003)? Our key recommendations were as follows:

1) The treatment of the unemployed

Recommended:

   i) limit the duration of eligibility for benefits
   ii) strengthen job search tests
   iii) introduce active policies to increase employability
         a) targeted adult training
         b) high-quality placement service
         c) recruitment subsidies for the hard-to-place
         d) guarantees of activity for the long-term unemployed

Not recommended:

   i) general increase in public employment
   ii) work sharing, early-retirement subsidies.

2) Wage determination

Recommended:

> i) if unions are pervasive, encourage co-ordinated wage bargaining
> ii) if wage pressure remains excessive, introduce a tax-based incomes policy

3) Labor market interventions

Recommended:

> i) review but do not completely abolish employment protection laws

Not recommended:

> i) subsidized profit share schemes

4) Policies which the analysis indicates will reduce unemployment but not specifically recommended:

> i) increase product market competition
> ii) weaken trade unions
> iii) cut unemployment benefits

In the light of what has happened since, how relevant are these? Those recommendations under 1) (the treatment of the unemployed) stand up well in the light of subsequent events. By and large they are consistent with the recommendations following the *OECD Jobs Study* in 1994 and a variety of countries put one or more of them into practice during the 1990s. For example, a number of countries have adopted the principle of requiring long-term unemployed people to accept offers of activity if they wish to receive further financial support. In Denmark and the Netherlands an unemployed person is now offered activity within a year of becoming unemployed, and must accept it. In Britain the New Deal for Young People, working on the same principle, has eliminated long-term unemployment among young people with no increase in short-term unemployment (Blundell et al. 2003). In these three countries unemployment has fallen sharply at any given level of vacancies (Layard 2004). However, it is clear from the experiences of Finland and Sweden that ALMPs tend to be overwhelmed in the short-term by major adverse demand shocks (see Calmfors, Forslund and Hemström 2002, for example).

Turning to the non-recommendations, many countries have been unable to resist continuing with subsidized schemes to reduce labor supply, despite their having no long-run impact on unemployment rates, merely serving to reduce employment rates. However, it is becoming more widely recognized that such schemes generally make matters worse (see OECD 2003, Chapter 4).

The recommendations under 2) (wage determination) have fared less well. The second, regarding tax-based incomes policies, has been more or less completely ignored and is now off the agenda. Encouraging coordinated wage bargaining where union coverage is high has undoubtedly helped Ireland, the Netherlands, and Norway to attain or sustain low levels of unemployment. These days, however, following the recommendations of the OECD Jobs Study, "wage flexibility" is far more fashionable, involving decentralized wage determination, regional wage flexibility, abandoning extension rules, abandoning indexation, the legalization of private employment agencies, and making minimum wage laws more flexible. All but the first of these can be categorized as policies which weaken the power of trade unions. Decentralized wage determination, however, is not in this category. Indeed, there is a lot of evidence to suggest that uncoordinated wage bargaining when union coverage is high tends to raise unemployment. Of course, when union coverage is low, this will tend to lower unemployment and wage setting will more or less automatically be decentralized. Coverage is the key factor here, however, not decentralization.

The recommendation under 3) (labor market interventions), namely to review but not abolish employment protection laws, has been taken up in a number of European countries. More specifically, they have been weakened in the 1990s in Denmark, Finland, Germany, Italy, Netherlands, Portugal, Spain, and Sweden. Uniquely, France strengthened its unfair dismissal laws in the 1990s. The non-recommendation under 3), namely subsidized profit sharing schemes, is barely relevant. Such schemes have been introduced (in the UK for example) but mainly to try and raise productivity, not to reduce unemployment.

Finally, the policies under 4) have been discussed above with the exception of increasing product market competition. Some product market deregulation has been introduced in most OECD countries, particularly in sectors such as telecom, but overall, many aspects of competition policy are weak across most of Europe and barriers to entry are high, particularly in the major economies of Continental Europe. Notable exceptions in Europe include Denmark, Ireland, Sweden, and the UK (see Lynch and Nickell 2001 for example).

5.4. Explaining Changes in Unemployment in OECD Countries: Overview

In Chapter 9 of our book, we attempted to explain the patterns of OECD unemployment from the 1960s to 1990. Here, we look at what has happened since and discuss how these subsequent changes may be understood. In particular we analyze the time series variation in unemployment in twenty different OECD countries, looking specifically at why certain countries have managed to reduce unemployment substantially from the peaks of the 1980s whereas others have not. As well as setting out our own explanations, we also consider some other alternatives from the literature.

In Table 5.1, we present a picture of unemployment in the OECD since the 1960s. To maintain comparisons through time, the numbers for Germany refer only to Western Germany. Two interesting features of this pattern stand out. First, unemployment in the European Union in 2002 was 7.6 percent. This is higher than every non-European country in the list except Canada. So, in this sense, there remains a European unemployment problem, just as there was throughout the 1980s and 1990s. However, a closer look at the numbers reveals that of the fifteen European countries, a majority, namely nine, have unemployment rates which are now lower than in the United States. Fundamentally, the European unemployment problem is a problem of the Big Four countries of continental Europe (France, Germany, Italy, Spain) plus Belgium and Finland. By and large, the remainder no longer have a problem. Second, a specific group of European countries has succeeded in dramatically reducing unemployment from the very high levels attained in the 1980s. These are Denmark, Ireland, The Netherlands, Portugal, and the UK. One of our aims here is to explain why some countries have succeeded whereas others have failed.

Table 5.1

Unemployment (Standardised Rate) %

	1960-64	1965-72	1973-79	1980-87	1988-95	1996-99	2000-1	2002
Australia	2.5	1.9	4.6	7.7	8.7	7.9	6.5	6.3
Austria	1.6	1.4	1.4	3.1	3.6	4.3	3.7	4.3
Belgium	2.3	2.3	5.8	11.2	8.4	9.2	6.8	7.3
Canada	5.5	4.7	6.9	9.7	9.5	8.7	7.0	7.7
Denmark	2.2	1.7	4.1	7.0	8.1	5.3	4.4	4.5
Finland	1.4	2.4	4.1	5.1	9.9	12.2	9.4	9.1
France	1.5	2.3	4.3	8.9	10.5	11.5	9.0	8.7
Germany	0.8	0.8	2.9	6.1	5.6	7.4	6.4	6.8
Ireland	5.1	5.3	7.3	13.8	14.7	8.7	4.0	4.4
Italy	3.5	4.2	4.5	6.7	8.1	9.9	8.4	7.4
Japan	1.4	1.3	1.8	2.5	2.5	3.9	4.9	5.4
Netherlands								
	0.9	1.7	4.7	10.0	7.2	4.5	2.6	2.8
Norway	2.2	1.7	1.8	2.4	5.2	3.8	3.6	3.9
New Zealand								
	0.0	0.3	0.7	4.7	8.1	6.8	5.7	5.2
Portugal	2.3	2.5	5.5	7.8	5.4	6.0	4.1	5.1
Spain	2.4	2.7	4.9	17.6	19.6	19.4	13.5	
Spain*						15.8	11.0	11.4
Sweden	1.2	1.6	1.6	2.3	5.1	8.6	5.5	4.9
Switzerland								
	0.2	0.0	0.8	1.8	2.8	3.5	2.6	2.6
UK	2.6	3.1	4.8	10.5	8.8	6.8	5.2	5.1
USA	5.5	4.3	6.4	7.6	6.1	4.8	4.4	5.8

Notes. As far as possible, these numbers correspond to the OECD standardized rates and conform to the ILO definition. The exception here is Italy where we use the US Bureau of Labor Statistics "unemployment rates on US concepts." In particular we use the correction to the OECD standardized rates made by the Bureau prior to 1993. This generates a rate which is 1.6 percentage points below the OECD standardized rate after 1993. The rates referred to in Spain* refer to recently revised ILO rates.

To pursue these issues, we start by arguing that the current European unemployment problem is not simply a consequence of tight macro policies forced on much of Europe since the mid-1990s by the introduction of the single currency.

In Table 5.2, we look at macroeconomic data for the Eurozone. Early in the period, monetary policy was tight, domestic demand growth was relatively modest, unemployment was nearly 11 percent, and the inflation rate was falling. Monetary policy was eased during the late 1990s, domestic demand growth was buoyant, and unemployment started to fall. However, by early 2000, inflation started to move above the ECB target range (2 percent was the top of this range) even though unemployment was still in excess of 8 percent. As a consequence, monetary policy was tightened throughout 2000. Despite subsequent easing, particularly in late 2001, domestic demand fell rapidly from the second half of 2000 and unemployment started to rise from its low point of 7.9 percent in mid-2001[1]. Despite this, inflation remained above the ECB target range until 2004. The lesson

Table 5.2

Macroeconomic Patterns in the Eurozone, 1994-2003

	94	95	96	97	98	99	00(i)	00(ii)	00(iii)	00(iv)
Short-term interest rate (%)	5.3	4.5	3.3	3.3	3.5	3.0	3.5	4.3	4.7	5.0
Final domestic demand contribution to growth (annual %)	1.5	1.7	1.5	1.7	3.1	3.6	3.1	3.5	2.6	2.2
GDP growth (annual %)	2.4	2.2	1.4	2.3	2.9	2.8	3.8	4.2	3.2	2.7
Unemployment	10.9	10.6	10.9	10.9	10.3	9.3	8.7	8.5	8.3	8.1
Inflation (CPI)	2.8	2.6	2.3	1.7	1.2	1.1	2.1	2.1	2.5	2.7

	01(i)	01(ii)	01(iii)	01(iv)	02(i)	02(ii)	02(iii)	02(iv)	03(i)	03(ii)	03(iii)
Short-term interest rate (%)	4.8	4.6	4.3	3.4	3.4	3.4	3.4	3.1	2.7	2.4	2.1
Final domestic demand contribution to growth (annual %)	2.0	1.4	1.1	0.7	-0.2	-0.2	0.0	0.4	0.8	0.8	0.6
GDP growth (annual %)	2.4	1.5	1.3	0.5	0.5	0.9	1.0	1.1	0.7	0.1	0.3
Unemployment Rate (%)	8.0	7.9	8.0	8.1	8.3	8.4	8.5	8.6	8.7	8.8	8.8
Inflation (CPI)	2.3	3.1	2.5	2.5	2.6	2.1	2.1	2.3	2.3	2.0	2.0

Notes: The quarterly annual growth rates are based on the current quarter relative to the same quarter one year earlier. Final domestic demand is $C + I + G$ in obvious notation. These data are from the Bank of England databank.

from this episode is that in the Eurozone, the reduction in unemployment generated by monetary policy easing in the 1990s hit the inflation constraint in 2000 and *policy had to be tightened to control inflation*. This prevented Eurozone unemployment falling much below 8 percent. On the basis of these data, it is hard to see how average equilibrium unemployment in the Eurozone can be below 8 percent, this despite the fact that unemployment in most of the small Eurozone economies has been below this level for many years.

Having dealt with the macro-policy issue, we next look at some of the literature which attempts to explain the time series patterns of unemployment in the different countries. How far has it proved possible to explain the unemployment patterns shown in Table 5.1 by variations over time and across countries in the sort of labor market institutions discussed in the previous section? Cross-country variation in post-1980s unemployment is easy enough to explain by cross-country variation in labor market institutions (see, for example Scarpetta 1996; Nickell 1997; Elmeskov, Martin and Scarpetta 1998; Nickell and Layard 1999, see Chapter 4). More interesting and more tricky is to explain the time series variation from the 1960s onward.

There are several different approaches that have been used. First, there is a basic division between studies that use econometric techniques to fit the data and those which use calibrated models which typically distinguish between a stylized "European" economy and a stylized "United States" economy. Second, there is another division between those which focus on changes in the institutions and those which consider "shocks" or baseline factors which shift over time and are typically interacted with average levels of institutional factors.

Looking first at panel data econometric models which interact stable institutions with shocks or baseline variables, good examples include Chapter 9 of our book, Blanchard and Wolfers (2000), Bertola, Blau and Kahn (2001) and Fitoussi et al. (2000). All these focus on the time-series variation in the data by including country dummies. Our Chapter 9 presents a dynamic model of unemployment based on annual data where the baseline variables include wage pressure (a dummy which takes the value one from 1970), the benefit replacement ratio, real import price changes, and monetary shocks. Their impact on unemployment differs across countries, since it depends on time invariant institutions, with different sets of institutions affecting the degree of unemployment persistence, the impact of wage pressure variables including the replacement rate and import prices, and the effect of monetary shocks. The model explains the data better than individual country autoregressions with trends.

Blanchard and Wolfers (2000) use five year averages to concentrate on long-run effects. The shocks or baseline variables consist of the level of TFP growth, the real interest rate, the change in inflation, and labor demand shifts (essentially the log of labor's share purged of the impact of factor prices). With the exception of the change in inflation, these "shocks" are not mean-reverting, which is why we prefer the term baseline variables. These variables are driving unemployment, so that, for example, the fact that annual TFP growth is considerably higher in the 1960s than in the 1990s in most countries is an important reason why unemployment is typically higher in the latter period. Quite why this should be so is not wholly clear. Many mechanisms are discussed in Saint-Paul (1991) but there is no evidence that they are important or robust in Bean and Pissarides (1993) for example. Nevertheless, interacting these observed baseline variables with time-invariant institutional variables fits the data well. In an alternative investigation, Blanchard and Wolfers replace the observed shock variables with unobserved common shocks represented by time dummies. When these time dummies are interacted with time-invariant institutions, the explanatory power of the model increases substantially.

The basic Blanchard and Wolfers model is extended in Bertola, Blau and Kahn (2001) who include an additional baseline variable, namely the share of young people (age 15-24) in the population aged over 15. The model explains a substantial proportion of the divergence between US and other countries' unemployment rates (48 to 63 percent) over the period 1970 to 1995, although an even higher proportion is explained when the observed baseline variables are replaced by time dummies.

Fitoussi et al. (2000) proceed in a slightly different way. First they interact the baseline variables with country dummies and then investigate the cross-section relationship between the estimated country dummies and labor market institutions. The baseline variables include non-wage support (income from private wealth plus social spending) relative to labor productivity and the real price of oil as well as two in common with Blanchard and Wolfers (2000), namely the real rate of interest and productivity growth.

In all the four papers we have just discussed the explanation of long-run changes in unemployment has the same structure. The

179

changes depend on long-run shifts in a set of baseline variables, with the impact of these being much bigger and longer-lasting in some countries than others because of stable institutional differences. The persuasiveness of these explanations depends on whether the stories associated with the baseline variables are convincing. For example, the notion that a fall in trend productivity growth, a rise in the real price of oil, or a downward shift in the labor demand curve leads to a *permanent* rise in equilibrium unemployment is one which many might find unappealing.

Interesting alternatives, still in the context of the institutions/ shocks framework, are the broad-brush analyses discussed in Krugman (1994) and Ljungqvist and Sargent (1998). Krugman argues that rigid European labor market institutions have meant that, when faced with a significant rise in the relative demand for skilled workers in the 1980s, the economies of Europe suffered significant increases in aggregate unemployment. While there is some evidence that European rigidities have worsened the employment prospects of the unskilled (Puhani 2003), there is no evidence that the Krugman argument has any validity when it comes to explaining the dramatic rises in aggregate European unemployment in the 1980s. One obvious problem with the Krugman argument is the substantial rise in unemployment among skilled workers across most of Europe during the relevant period. Overall, the evidence suggests that skill shifts account for only a small proportion of the rise in European unemployment since the 1970s (see Card, Kramarz and Lemieux 1995; Nickell and Bell 1995, 1996; Jackman et al. 1999; see also Chapter 4 in this volume).

The idea in Ljungqvist and Sargent (1998) is that in "Europe," benefits are high with a long duration of eligibility whereas in the "United States," benefits are modest and of fixed duration. In a world where turbulence is low, the rate at which the unemployed lose their skills is low and the difference in the unemployment rates in "Europe" and the "United States" is minimal, because the chances of an unemployed person in "Europe" finding a job with wages exceeding the benefit level are high. In a world where turbulence is high, the unemployed lose their skills at a rapid rate. As a consequence the high level of benefits relative to past earnings and hence the high reservation wage in "Europe" now bites and unemployment is much higher than in the "United States." So we have a situation where the relevant institution, namely the benefit system, remains stable but the consequences are very different in a world of high turbulence from those in a world of low turbulence.

While this model captures a particular feature of the situation, in order for it to be a persuasive explanation of recent history it must pass two tests. First, we need evidence that turbulence has indeed increased and second it must explain why many countries in Europe now have relatively low unemployment. Indeed the variation in unemployment (and employment) rates across European countries is far larger than the difference between Europe and the United States. To justify the assumption of increasing turbulence, Ljungqvist and Sargent point to the increasing variance of transitory earnings in the United States reported by Gottschalk and Moffitt (1994). There has also been a rise in the transitory variance in the UK, noted by Dickens (2000). However these facts hardly add up to a full empirical test of the theory. For example, in Europe, TFP growth has been much lower since 1976 than it was in the earlier period and we might expect TFP growth to be positively associated with turbulence. Indeed, the *fall* in TFP growth is one of the main factors generating a rise in unemployment in Blanchard and Wolfers (2000). Furthermore, there is no evidence of any significant changes in the rates of job creation and job destruction over the relevant period (see Davis and Haltiwanger 1999). Finally, no evidence is presented which explains why the various European countries have such widely differing unemployment patterns. So while the Lungqvist/Sargent model may capture an element of the story, it hardly comes close to a full explanation.

Turning now to studies which simply rely on changing institutions to explain unemployment patterns, notable examples include Belot and Van Ours (2000, 2001) and Nickell et al. (2002). The former papers provide a good explanation of changes in unemployment in eighteen OECD countries, although in order to do so they make extensive use of interactions between institutions, something which has a sound theoretical foundation (see Coe and Snower 1997, for example). Their model is, however, static like that of Blanchard and Wolfers. The model developed by Nickell et al. (2002) uses annual data and, since they explain actual unemployment, they include in their model those factors which might explain the short-run deviations of unemployment from its equilibrium level. Following the discussion in Hoon and Phelps (1992) or Phelps (1994), these factors include aggregate demand shocks, productivity shocks, and wage shocks. More specifically, they include the following:

i) money supply shocks, specifically changes in the rate of growth of the nominal money stock (i.e. the second difference of the log money supply);

ii) productivity shocks, measured by *changes* in TFP growth or deviations of TFP growth from trend;

iii) labor demand shocks, measured by the residuals from a simple labor demand model;

iv) real import price shocks, measured by proportional changes in real import prices weighted by the trade share;

v) the (ex-post) real interest rate.

With the exception of the real interest rate, these variables are genuine "shocks" in the sense that they are typically stationary and tend to revert to their mean quite rapidly. This distinguishes them from the "baseline variables" used in Blanchard and Wolfers (2000), for example. On top of these variables, Nickell et al. (2002) then use such time series of the institutional variables as are available including employment protection, the benefit replacement rate, benefit duration, union density, coordination, and employment taxes. These variables are there to explain equilibrium unemployment. Using a dynamic panel data model, the time series patterns of unemployment are well explained. Based on dynamic simulations, it is found that the institutional variables which are included explain about 55 percent of the individual country changes in unemployment from the 1960s to the early 1990s. This is reasonable, particularly as the early 1990s was a period of deep recession in much of Europe.

Overall, therefore, there is some evidence that the sort of labor market institutions discussed in the previous section made a significant contribution to explaining the patterns of unemployment reported in Table 5.1. So, as a final step, let us see how these institutional variables have changed over time and what these changes can tell us about why the European Big Four countries have performed less well than most other countries on the unemployment front in the 1990s.

5.5. Specific Changes in Labor Market Institutions and their Impact on Unemployment

In this section we look at changes in benefit systems, wage determination, employment protection, and labor taxes in the last decades of the 20th Century and see what they can tell us.

5.5.1. The Unemployment Benefit System

As we have seen, there are four aspects of the unemployment benefit system for which there are good theoretical and empirical reasons to believe that they will influence equilibrium unemployment. These are, in turn, the level of benefits, the duration of entitlement, the coverage of the system, and the strictness with which the system is operated. Of these, only the first two are available as time series for the OECD countries. The OECD has collected systematic data on the unemployment benefit replacement ratio for three different family types (single, with dependent spouse, with spouse at work) in three different duration categories (1st year, 2nd and 3rd years, 4th and 5th years) from 1961 to 1999 (every other year), see OECD 1994, Table 8.1 for the 1991 data. From this we derive a measure of the benefit replacement ratio, equal to the average over family types in the 1st year duration category and a measure of benefit duration equal to [0.6(2nd and 3rd year replacement ratio) + 0.4(4th and 5th year replacement ratio)] ÷ (1st year replacement ratio). So our measure of benefit duration is the level of benefit in the later years of the spell normalized on the benefit in the first year of the spell. A summary of these data is presented in Tables 5.3 and 5.4.

Table 5.3

Unemployment Benefit Replacement Ratios, 1960-95

	1960-64	1965-72	1973-79	1980-87	1988-95	1999
Australia	0.18	0.15	0.23	0.23	0.26	0.25
Austria	0.15	0.17	0.30	0.34	0.34	0.42
Belgium	0.37	0.40	0.55	0.50	0.48	0.46
Canada	0.39	0.43	0.59	0.57	0.58	0.49
Denmark	0.25	0.35	0.55	0.67	0.64	0.66
Finland	0.13	0.18	0.29	0.38	0.53	0.54
France	0.48	0.51	0.56	0.61	0.58	0.59
Germany (W)	0.43	0.41	0.39	0.38	0.37	0.37
Ireland	0.21	0.24	0.44	0.50	0.40	0.35
Italy	0.09	0.06	0.04	0.02	0.26	0.60*
Japan	0.36	0.38	0.31	0.29	0.30	0.37
Netherlands	0.39	0.64	0.65	0.67	0.70	0.70
Norway	0.12	0.13	0.28	0.56	0.62	0.62
New Zealand	0.37	0.30	0.27	0.30	0.29	0.30
Portugal	-	-	0.17	0.44	0.65	0.65
Spain	0.35	0.48	0.62	0.75	0.68	0.63
Sweden	0.11	0.16	0.57	0.70	0.72	0.74
Switzerland	0.04	0.02	0.21	0.48	0.61	0.74
UK	0.27	0.36	0.34	0.26	0.22	0.17
US	0.22	0.23	0.28	0.30	0.26	0.29

Source: OECD. Based on the replacement ratio in the first year of an unemployment spell averaged over three family types. See OECD (1994), Table 8.1 for an example.
* This number refers to the "mobility" benefit, paid to those who become unemployed as a result of a collective layoff. Most Italian unemployed do not fall under this category.

Table 5.4

Unemployment Benefit Duration Index, 1960-95

	1960-64	1965-72	1973-79	1980-87	1988-95	1999
Australia	1.02	1.02	1.02	1.02	1.02	1.00
Austria	0	0	0.69	0.75	0.74	0.68
Belgium	1.0	0.96	0.78	0.79	0.77	0.78
Canada	0.33	0.31	0.20	0.25	0.22	0.42
Denmark	0.63	0.66	0.66	0.62	0.84	1.00
Finland	0	0.14	0.72	0.61	0.53	0.63
France	0.28	0.23	0.19	0.37	0.49	0.47
Germany	0.57	0.57	0.61	0.61	0.61	0.75
Ireland	0.68	0.78	0.39	0.40	0.39	0.77
Italy	0	0	0	0	0.13	0
Japan	0	0	0	0	0	0
Netherlands	0.12	0.35	0.53	0.66	0.57	0.64
Norway	0	0.07	0.45	0.49	0.50	0.60
New Zealand	1.02	1.02	1.02	1.04	1.04	1.00
Portugal	-	-	0	0.11	0.35	0.58
Spain	0	0	0.01	0.21	0.27	0.29
Sweden	0	0	0.04	0.05	0.04	0.02
Switzerland	0	0	0	0	0.18	0.31
UK	0.87	0.59	0.54	0.71	0.70	0.96
US	0.12	0.17	0.19	0.17	0.18	0.22

Source: OECD. Based on [0.06 (replacement ratio in 2nd and 3rd years of a spell) + 0.04 (replacement ratio in 4th and 5th year of a spell)] ÷ (replacement ratio in 1st year of a spell).

The key feature of these data is that in nearly all countries, benefit replacement ratios have tended to become more generous from the 1960s to the late 1970s, the exceptions being Germany, Japan, and New Zealand. Italy had no effective benefit system over this period for the vast majority of the unemployed. After the late 1970s, countries moved in different directions, Italy introduced a benefit system and those in Finland, Portugal, and Switzerland became markedly more generous. By contrast, benefit replacement ratios in Belgium, Ireland, and the UK have fallen steadily since the late 1970s or early 1980s.

It is unfortunate that we have no comprehensive time series data on the coverage of the system or on the strictness with which it is administered. This is particularly true in the case of the latter because the evidence we possess appears to indicate that this is of crucial importance in determining the extent to which a generous level of benefit will actually influence unemployment. For example, Denmark, which has very generous unemployment benefits, totally reformed the operation of its benefit system through the 1990s with a view to tightening the criteria for benefit receipt and the enforcement of these criteria via a comprehensive system of sanctions. The Danish Ministry of Labor is convinced that this process has played a major role in allowing Danish unemployment to fall dramatically since the early 1990s without generating inflationary pressure (see Danish Ministry of Finance 1999, Chapter 2). Just to see some of the ways in which systems of administration vary across country, in Table 5.5 we present indices of the strictness of the work availability conditions in various countries. These are based on eight sub-indicators referring to the rules relating to the types of jobs that unemployed individuals must accept or incur some financial or other penalty. We can see that countries with notably lax systems in the mid-1990s included Austria, Finland, France, Germany, Ireland, and the UK, although Ireland and the UK have significantly tightened their benefit operations since that time.

Table 5.5

Index of the Strictness of Work Availability Conditions, Mid-1990s

Australia	3.6	Japan	–
Austria	2.3	Netherlands	3.7
Belgium	3.1	Norway	3.3
Canada	2.8	New Zealand	2.7
Denmarka	3.0	Portugal	2.8
Finland	2.7	Spain	–
France	2.7	Sweden	3.7
Germany	2.6	Switzerland	–
Ireland	1.7	UK	2.6
Italy	–	US	3.3

Source: Danish Ministry of Finance (1999), The Danish Economy Medium Term Economic Survey, Figure 2.4 d. This refers to 1998. In the early 1990s, the corresponding number was 2.3.

Table 5.6

Expenditure on Active Labor Market Policies (%GDP)

(In brackets, we present the figure normalized on the percent unemployment rate)

	1985	1989	1993	1998
Australia	0.42 (0.051)	0.24 (0.039)	0.71 (0.065)	0.42 (0.053)
Austria	0.27 (0.075)	0.27 (0.084)	0.32 (0.080)	0.44 (0.098)
Belgium	1.31 (0.12)	1.26 (0.16)	1.24 (0.14)	1.42 (0.15)
Canada	0.64 (0.062)	0.51 (0.068)	0.66 (0.058)	0.50 (0.052)
Denmark	1.14 (0.13)	1.13 (0.12)	1.74 (0.17)	1.66 (0.32)
Finland	0.90 (0.18)	0.97 (0.26)	1.69 (0.10)	1.40 (0.12)
France	0.66 (0.065)	0.73 (0.078)	1.25 (0.11)	1.30 (0.11)
Germany	0.80 (0.11)	1.03 (0.18)	1.53 (0.19)	1.26 (0.14)
Ireland	1.52 (0.087)	1.41 (0.096)	1.54 (0.099)	1.54 (0.21)
Italy	-	-	1.36 (0.13)	1.12 (0.095)
Japan	0.17 (0.065)	0.16 (0.070)	0.09 (0.036)	0.09 (0.022)
Netherlands	1.16 (0.11)	1.25 (0.15)	1.59 (0.24)	1.74 (0.42)
Norway	0.61 (0.23)	0.81 (0.17)	1.15 (0.19)	0.90 (0.27)
New Zealand	0.90 (0.25)	0.93 (0.13)	0.79 (0.083)	0.63 (0.084)
Portugal	0.33	0.48	0.84 (0.15)	0.78 (0.15)
Spain	0.33 (0.015)	0.85 (0.050)	0.50 (0.022)	070 (0.037)
Sweden	2.10 (0.88)	1.54 (1.10)	2.97 (0.34)	1.97 (0.24)
Switzerland	0.19 (0.079)	0.21 (0.12)	0.38 (0.095)	0.77 (0.22)
UK	0.75 (0.067)	0.67 (0.093)	0.57 (0.054)	0.34 (0.054)
US	0.25 (0.035)	0.23 (0.044)	0.21 (0.030)	0.17 (0.038)

Source: OECD Employment Outlook, 2001.

A further aspect of the structure of the benefit system for which we do not have detailed data back to the 1960s are those policies grouped under the heading of active labor market policies (ALMP). We do, however, have data from 1985 which we present in Table 5.6.

The purpose of these is to provide active assistance to the unemployed which will improve their chances of obtaining work. In Table 5.6 we see that, by and large, the countries of Northern Europe and Scandinavia devote most resources to ALMPs. It might be hypothesized that they do this because high expenditure on ALMPs is required to offset their rather generous unemployment benefit systems and to push unemployed individuals into work. Such additional pressure on the unemployed is less important if benefits are very low relative to potential earnings in work.

5.5.2. Systems of Wage Determination

In most countries in the OECD, the majority of workers have their wages set by collective bargaining between employers and trade unions at the plant, firm, industry, or aggregate level. Unfortunately, we do not have complete data on collective bargaining coverage (the proportion of employees covered by collective agreements) but the data presented in Table 5.7 give a reasonable picture. Across most of Continental Europe, including Scandinavia but excluding Switzerland, coverage is both high and stable. As we shall see, this is either because most people belong to trade unions or because union agreements are extended by law to cover non-members in the same sector. In Switzerland and in the OECD countries outside Continental Europe and Scandinavia, coverage is generally much lower, with the exception of Australia. In the UK, the US, and New Zealand, coverage has declined with the fall in union density, there being no extension laws.

Table 5.7

Collective bargaining coverage (%)

	1960	1965	1970	1975	1980	1985	1990	1994
Austria	n.a.	n.a.	n.a.	n.a.	n.a.	n.a.	99	99
Australia	85	85	85	85	85	85	80	80
Belgium	80	80	80	85	90	90	90	90
Canada	35	33	36	39	40	39	38	36
Denmark	67	68	68	70	72	74	69	69
Finland	95	95	95	95	95	95	95	95
France	n.a.	n.a.	n.a.	n.a.	85	n.a.	92	95
Germany	90	90	90	90	91	90	90	92
Ireland	n.a.	n.a.	n.a.	n.a.	n.a.	n.a.	n.a.	n.a.
Italy	91	90	88	85	85	85	83	82
Japan	n.a.	n.a.	n.a.	n.a.	28	n.a.	23	21
Netherlands	100	n.a.	n.a.	n.a.	76	80	n.a.	85
New Zealand	n.a.	n.a.	n.a.	n.a.	n.a.	n.a.	67	31
Norway	65	65	65	65	70	70	70	70
Portugal	n.a.	n.a.	n.a.	n.a.	70	n.a.	79	71
Spain	n.a.	n.a.	n.a.	n.a.	68	70	76	78
Sweden	n.a.	n.a.	n.a.	n.a.	n.a.	n.a.	86	89
Switzerland	n.a.	n.a.	n.a.	n.a.	n.a.	n.a.	53	53
United Kingdom	67	67	68	72	70	64	54	40
United States	29	27	27	24	21	21	18	17

These data were collected by Wolfgang Ochel. Further details may be found in Ochel (2001).

In Table 5.8, we present the percentage of employees who are union members. Across most of Scandinavia, membership tends to be high. By contrast, in much of Continental Europe and in Australia, union density tends to be less than 50 percent and is gradually declining. In these countries there is, consequently, a wide and widening gap between density and coverage which it is the job of the extension laws to fill. This situation is at its most stark in France, which has the lowest union density in the OECD at around 10 percent, but one of the highest levels of coverage (around 95 percent). Outside these regions, both density and coverage tend to be relatively low and both are declining at greater or lesser rates. The absence of complete coverage data means that we have to rely on the density variable to capture the impact of unionization on unemployment. As should be clear, this is only half the story, so we must treat any results we find in this area with some caution.

Table 5.8

Union Density (%)

	1960-64	1965-72	1973-79	1980-87	1988-95	1996-98	Extension laws in place (a)
Australia	48	45	49	49	43	35	√
Austria	59	57	52	51	45	39	√
Belgium	40	42	52	52	52	-	√
Canada	27	29	35	37	36	36	X
Denmark	60	61	71	79	76	76	X
Finland	35	47	66	69	76	80	√
France	20	21	21	16	10	10	√
Germany (W)	34	32	35	34	31	27	√
Ireland	47	51	56	56	51	43	X
Italy	25	32	48	45	40	37	√
Japan	33	33	30	27	24	22	X
Netherlands	41	38	37	30	24	24	√
Norway	52	51	52	55	56	55	X
New Zealand	36	35	38	37	35	21	X
Portugal	61	61	61	57	34	25	√
Spain	9	9	9	11	16	18	√
Sweden	64	66	76	83	84	87	X
Switzerland	35	32	32	29	25	23	√ (b)
UK	44	47	55	53	42	35	X
USA	27	26	25	20	16	14	X

Notes:
(i)   Union density = union members as a percentage of employees. In both Spain and Portugal, union membership in the 1960s and 1970s does not have the same implications as elsewhere because there was pervasive government intervention in wage determination during most of this period.
(ii)   (a) Effectively, bargained wages extended to non-union firms typically at the behest of one party to the bargain.
        (b) Extension only at the behest of both parties to a bargain. For details, see OECD (1994), Table 5.11.
Source: Ebbinghaus and Visser (2000).

Table 5.9

Co-ordination Indices (Range 1-3)

	1960-64		1965-72		1973-79		1980-87		1988-95		1995-99
	1	2	1	2	1	2	1	2	1	2	2
Australia	2.25	2	2.25	2	2.25	2.36	2.25	2.31	1.92	1.63	1.5
Austria	3	2.5	3	2.5	3	2.5	3	2.5	3	2.42	2
Belgium	2	2	2	2	2	2.1	2	2.55	2	2	2
Canada	1	1	1	1	1	1.63	1	1.08	1	1	1
Denmark	2.5	1.5	2.5	3	2.5	2.96	2.4	2.54	2.26	2	2
Finland	2.25	1.5	2.25	1.69	2.25	2	2.25	2	2.25	2.38	2.5
France	1.75	2	1.75	2	1.75	2	1.84	2	1.98	1.92	1.5
Germany (W)	3	2.5	3	2.5	3	2.5	3	2.5	3	2.5	2.5
Ireland	2	2	2	2.38	2	2.91	2	2.08	3	2.75	3
Italy	1.5	1.94	1.5	1.73	1.5	2	1.5	1.81	1.4	1.95	2.5
Japan	3	2.5	3	2.5	3	2.5	3	2.5	3	2.5	2.5
Netherlands	2	3	2	2.56	2	2	2	2.38	2	3	3
Norway	2.5	3	2.5	3	2.5	2.96	2.5	2.72	2.5	2.84	2
New Zealand	1.5	2.5	1.5	2.5	1.5	2.5	1.32	2.32	1	1.25	1
Portugal	1.75	3	1.75	3	1.75	2.56	1.84	1.58	2	1.88	2
Spain	2	3	2	3	2	2.64	2	2.3	2	2	2
Sweden	2.5	3	2.5	3	2.5	3	2.41	2.53	2.15	1.94	2
Switzerland	2.25	2	2.25	2	2.25	2	2.25	2	2.25	1.63	1.5
UK	1.5	1.56	1.5	1.77	1.5	1.77	1.41	1.08	1.15	1	1
US	1	1	1	1	1	1	1	1	1	1	1

Notes: The first series (1) only moves in response to major changes, the second series (2) attempts to capture all the nuances. Co-ordination 1 was provided by Michèle Belot to whom much thanks (see Belot and van Ours 2000, for details). Co-ordination 2 is the work of Wolfgang Ochel, to whom we are most grateful (see Ochel 2000a).

5.5.3. Employment Protection

In Table 5.10, we present an employment protection index for each country. Features to note are the wide variation in the index across countries and the fact that, in some countries, the basic legislation was not introduced until the 1970s.

Table 5.10

Employment Protection (Index, 0-2)

	1960-64	1965-72	1973-79	1980-87	1988-95	1998
Australia	0.50	0.50	0.50	0.50	0.50	0.50
Austria	0.65	0.65	0.84	1.27	1.30	1.10
Belgium	0.72	1.24	1.55	1.55	1.35	1.00
Canada	0.30	0.30	0.30	0.30	0.30	0.30
Denmark	0.90	0.98	1.10	1.10	0.90	0.70
Finland	1.20	1.20	1.20	1.20	1.13	1.00
France	0.37	0.68	1.21	1.30	1.41	1.40
Germany (W)	0.45	1.05	1.65	1.65	1.52	1.30
Ireland	0.02	0.19	0.45	0.50	0.52	0.50
Italy	1.92	1.99	2.00	2.00	1.89	1.50
Japan	1.40	1.40	1.40	1.40	1.40	1.40
Netherlands	1.35	1.35	1.35	1.35	1.28	1.10
Norway	1.55	1.55	1.55	1.55	1.46	1.30
New Zealand	0.80	0.80	0.80	0.80	0.80	0.80
Portugal	0.00	0.43	1.59	1.94	1.93	1.70
Spain	2.00	2.00	1.99	1.91	1.74	1.40
Sweden	0.00	0.23	1.46	1.80	1.53	1.10
Switzerland	0.55	0.55	0.55	0.55	0.55	0.55
UK	0.16	0.21	0.33	0.35	0.35	0.35
USA	0.10	0.10	0.10	0.10	0.10	0.10

Notes: These data are based on an interpolation of the variable used by Blanchard and Wolfers (2000), to whom we are most grateful. This variable is based on the series used by Lazear (1990) and that provided by the OECD for the late 1980s and 1990s. Since the Lazear index and the OECD index are not strictly comparable, the overall series is not completely reliable. The 1998 number is taken from Nicoletti, Scarpetta and Boylaud (2000), Table A3.11 (1st column rescaled).

5.5.4. Labor Taxes

The important taxes here are those that form part of the wedge between the real product wage (labor costs per employee normalized on the output price) and the real consumption wage (after tax pay normalized on the consumer price index). These are payroll taxes, income taxes, and consumption taxes. As we have seen, their combined impact on unemployment remains a subject of some debate despite the large number of empirical investigations. In Table 5.11 we present the total tax rate on labor for the OECD countries. All countries exhibit a substantial increase over the period from the 1960s to the 1990s although there are wide variations across countries. These mainly reflect the extent to which health, higher education, and pensions are publicly provided along with the all-round generosity of the social security system. Some countries have made significant attempts to reduce labor taxes in recent years, notably the Netherlands and the UK.

5.5.5. Labor Market institutions and the Successes and Failures of the 1990s

Having looked at some of the key factors which the evidence suggests have some impact on equilibrium unemployment, let us see how changes in these variables over the last two decades can contribute to our understanding of unemployment changes over the same period. In Table 5.12, we provide a picture of changes in the relevant variables with a tick referring to a significant move which will tend to reduce unemployment and a cross for the reverse. Double ticks and crosses reflect really big moves. A dash implies no significant change. Of course, this is a pretty crude business and a proper panel data analysis is arguable preferable. However, here we are able to take account of variables where we are unable to obtain long time series.

So we can ask the question, do the ticks and crosses bear any relationship to the unemployment changes reported in the final columns of the table? If we regress the unemployment change on the number of ticks and crosses we obtain:

Unemployment change (%) = 0.25 - 1.25 ticks + 1.21crosses $\left(\begin{array}{l} R^2 = 0.51 \\ N = 20 \end{array} \right)$
(80/87 to 00/01)   (3.1)   (2.2)

Or, in restricted form,

Unemployment change (%) = -0.42 -1.24 (ticks-crosses) $\left(\begin{array}{l} R^2 = 0.51 \\ N = 20 \end{array} \right)$
                     (4.3)

The restriction is easily accepted. So the number of ticks and crosses explains about half the cross-country variation in unemployment changes from the early 80s to the present day. We may reasonably conclude that the countries which had very high unemployment in the early 1980s and still have high unemployment today simply have too few ticks and/or too many crosses.

Table 5.11

Total Taxes on Labor Payroll. Tax Rate plus Income Tax Rate plus Consumption Tax Rate (%)

	1960-64	1965-72	1973-79	1980-87	1988-95	1996-2000
Australia	28	31	36	39	–	–
Austria	47	52	55	58	59	66
Belgium	38	43	44	46	49	51
Canada	31	39	41	42	50	53
Denmark	32	46	53	59	60	61
Finland	38	46	55	58	64	62
France	55	57	60	65	67	68
Germany (W)	43	44	48	50	52	50
Ireland	23	30	30	37	41	33
Italy	57	56	54	56	67	64
Japan	25	25	26	33	33	37
Netherlands	45	54	57	55	47	43
Norway	–	52	61	65	61	60
New Zealand	–	–	29	30	–	–
Portugal	20	25	26	33	41	39
Spain	19	23	29	40	46	45
Sweden	41	54	68	77	78	77
Switzerland	30	31	35	36	36	36
UK	34	43	45	51	47	44
USA	34	37	42	44	45	45

Note: These data are based on the London School of Economics, Centre for Economic Performance OECD dataset. They are average tax rates based on National Accounts. More details may be found in the Data Appendix of Nickell et al. (2002).

Table 5.12

From the Early 1980s to the Late 1990s - "Policy" Changes

	Replacement Rate	Benefit Duration	Benefit Strictness	ALMP	Union Coverage	Union Density	Co-ordination
Europe							
Austria	X	-	-	-	-	√	X
Belgium	√	-	-	-	-	-	X
Denmark	-	X	√	√√	-	-	X
Finland	X	-	-	-	-	X	√
France	-	X	-	√	X	-	X
Germany	-	X	-	√	-	-	-
Ireland	√	X	-	-	?	√	√
Italy	X	-	-	-	-	-	√
Netherlands	-	-	√	√	-	-	√
Norway	X	X	√	√	-	-	X
Portugal	X	X	-	√	-	√√	-
Spain	√	-	-	-	X	-	-
Sweden	X	-	-	-	-	-	X
Switzerland	XX	X	-	√	-	-	X
UK	√	X	√	X	√√	√	-
Non-Europe							
Australia	-	-	√	√	-	√	X
Canada	√	X	-	-	-	-	-
Japan	X	-	-	-	-	-	-
New Zealand	-	-	-	X	√√	√	XX
US	-	-	√	-	-	-	-

Table 5.12 (continued)

From the Early 1980s to the Late 1990s – "Policy" Changes

	Employment Protection	Labor Taxes	Total		Unemployment		Unemployment Change
			√	X	1980-87	2000-01	
Europe							
Austria	-	X	1	3	3.1	3.7	0.6
Belgium	√	-	2	1	11.2	6.8	-4.4
Denmark	√	-	4	2	7.0	4.4	-2.6
Finland	√	-	2	2	5.1	9.4	4.3
France	X	-	1	4	8.9	9.0	0.1
Germany	√	-	2	1	6.1	6.4	0.3
Ireland	-	√	4	1	13.8	4.0	-9.8
Italy	√	X	2	2	6.7	8.4	1.7
Netherlands	√	√	5	0	10.0	2.6	-7.4
Norway	√	-	3	3	2.4	3.6	1.2
Portugal	√	-	4	2	7.8	4.1	-3.7
Spain	√	-	2	1	17.6	13.5	-4.1
Sweden	√	-	1	2	2.3	5.5	3.2
Switzerland	-	-	1	4	1.8	2.6	0.8
UK	-	√	6	2	10.5	5.2	-5.3
Non-Europe							
Australia	-	?	3	1	7.7	6.5	-1.2
Canada	-	X	1	2	9.7	7.0	-2.7
Japan	-	-	0	1	2.5	4.9	2.4
New Zealand	-	?	3	3	4.7	5.7	1.0
US	-	-	1	0	7.6	4.4	-3.2

Notes:

√ implies "good" shift, X implies "bad" shift.

(i)   See Table 5.3. Replacement rate change (1980-87 to 1999) greater than 0.04 implies X, less than –0.04 implies √. Double X or √ for changes in excess of 0.25. The latter does not apply to Italy because the figure in the 1999 column refers to so few people.

(ii)   See Table 5.4. Duration index change (1980-87 to 1999) greater than 0.1 implies X, less than -0.1 implies √. Double X or √ for changes in excess of 0.5.

(iii)   See Table 5.5 and the discussion in OECD (2000), Chapter 4. Author's judgment based on this information.

(iv)   See Table 5.6. Change (1985/9 to 1993/8) greater than 0.2 implies √, less than –0.2 implies X. Double √ or X for changes in excess of 0.5. Bracketed amount must move in the same direction by 0.05.

(v)   See Table 5.7. Coverage change (1980 to 1994) greater than 0.1 implies X, less than –0.1 implies √. Double X or √ for changes in excess of 0.3.

(vi)   See Table 5.8. Density change (1980-87 to 1996-8) greater than 10 implies X, less than –10 implies √. Double X or √ for changes in excess of 30.

(vii)   See Table 5.9. Co-ordination (Type 2) change (1980-87 to 1995-99) greater than 0.5 implies √, less than –0.5 implies X. Double X or √ for changes in excess of 1.0.

(viii) See Table 5.10. Employment protection change (1980-87 to 1998) greater than 0.2 implies √, less than –0.1 implies X.

(ix)   See Table 5.11. Taxes change (1980-87 or 1988-95 to 1996-2000) greater than 0.07 implies X, less than –0.07 implies √.

5.5.6. Summary and Conclusions

Average unemployment in Europe in 2002 was relatively high compared with OECD countries outside Europe. The majority of countries in Europe in 2002 had lower unemployment than any OECD country outside Europe, including the US. These two facts are consistent because the four largest countries in Continental Western Europe namely, France, Germany, Italy, Spain (the Big Four), have very high unemployment and most of the rest have comparatively low unemployment. This variability is highly informative because the fifteen European countries which we study have more or less independent labor markets in practice, despite "free" movement of labor. Using this information we see how changes in the structure of the various labor markets explain a substantial proportion of the secular fluctuations in unemployment in the various countries. In particular, we pin down some of the particular factors which enable us to understand why some European countries have been able fully to recover from the unemployment disasters of the early 1980s whereas some have not.

5.6. Unemployment, Inactivity, and Happiness

Unemployment is one of the greatest evils in Western society. Since we wrote the book, a whole new science of well-being has developed which is able to identify the effect of altered circumstances upon a person's happiness. This shows that becoming unemployed is one of the worst experiences a person can have – similar in its impact to divorce or bereavement. This is found consistently both in cross-sectional and longitudinal studies [see, for example, Winkelmann and Winkelmann (1998, Tables 2 and 4); Helliwell (2007); Clark and Oswald (1994)].

In some circles it is fashionable to question the difference between unemployment and inactivity (outside the labor force). In consequence, it is argued, one should be studying employment rates not unemployment rates. Employment is of course a significant issue. But, if we are concerned with human misery and frustration, unemployment and inactivity are totally different. This point is so important that we reproduce below the findings from the German Socio-Economic Panel. Table 5.13 shows the changes in life-satisfaction for all the transitions between one year and the next. Similar findings appear in all other studies.

Table 5.13

Change in Life-Satisfaction (0-10) (Males Aged 20-64)

		Position this year		
		Employed	Unemployed	Inactive
Position last year	Employed	-	-1.2	-0.4
	Unemployed	1.1	-	0.4
	Inactive	0.6	-0.5	-

Source: Winkelmann and Winkelmann (1998), Table 2.

So unemployment is a very special problem. Moreover, it hurts as much after one or two years of unemployment as it does at the beginning (see Clark 2002). And even when you are back at work, you still feel its effects as a psychic scar (see Clark, Georgellis and Sanfey 1999). Moreover, even when they are in work, people fear unemployment, and when unemployment goes up, it has a major impact on the happiness of everybody, including those in work (see Di Tella, MacCulloch and Oswald 2001). These reasons explain why this book is about unemployment.

5.7. Last Words

Experience and research since our book was written confirm the accuracy of the analysis and the relevance of most of the policy conclusions. The experience of the last fifteen years shows that given sensible macroeconomic policies,[3] it is possible to ensure that unemployment remains fairly close to the full employment level. Four strategies seem particularly relevant (De Koning et al. 2003).

1. To prevent people drifting into long-term unemployment, there should be active policies to ensure that everyone gets offers of work or training within a year of becoming unemployed. The work should where possible be with regular employers, and secured if necessary by a recruitment subsidy. A modernized Public Employment Service is a key instrument in the business of channeling job offers to workers. It should be properly staffed and funded, with private agencies free to compete with it.

2. The welfare-to-work approach will not prevent long-term unemployment if individuals who receive offers from employers can instead choose to continue living on benefit. A system of complementary rights and responsibilities is needed where the citizen can expect high-quality help in finding work, but in return must take advantage of it or cease to draw benefits. Provided the state is channeling offers of work or work-related activity to everyone within the first year of unemployment that should be the maximum period for which benefits are paid to people who are not working or engaged in some work-related activity.

3. Further policies are needed to deal with regional unemployment. In particular, the decentralization of wage setting and measures aimed at improving the external environment where firms operate (e.g. the efficiency of public administration, the enforcement of the rule of law, etc.) are also essential. The decentralization of collective bargaining can be accompanied with measures encouraging regional labor mobility and encouraging take-up of relatively low-paid jobs, e.g., by providing in-work benefits to low-wage earners.

4. Labor supply reducing policies such as early retirement, as well as uncontrolled access to invalidity pensions, should be phased out as the welfare-to-work approach makes it possible to deal with redundancies without having to implement (high cost) early retirement for older workers. Ongoing or planned reforms of pension systems should also remove from public pension arrangements those features which discourage the participation of older workers.

6

Policies for Full Employment

Richard Layard's Section 1 of the Report "Policies for Full Employment" presented to the UK government in February 2003 sets up principles of sustainable and progressive employment policies. By referring to the experiences with employment policies in the UK, Denmark, and the Netherlands, the report draws conclusions for further labor market reforms in Europe. The "Layard Report," co-authored by Jaap de Koning, Stephen Nickell, and Niels Westergaard-Nielsen, not only emphasizes the role of appropriate activation policies based on rights and duties and effective "benefit conditionality" as the core instrument to overcome unemployment, but moves beyond combating unemployment as it tackles the issue of non-employment and inactivity in a wider sense and calls for a further mobilization of labor supply in order to increase employment. This is in contrast to policies of the 1970s and 1980s that aimed at keeping unemployment low by way of reducing labor supply of women, older workers, or migrants. The policy advocated in the report is bringing more people, in particular older workers and (single) mothers, into the labor market as a major tool to raise the level of employment. To achieve a longer working life, the report calls for the removal of early retirement incentives and better lifelong learning. For single mothers an expansion of child care, the abolition of incentives for inactivity, and better part-time opportunities are advocated.

European unemployment is too high, and employment is too low. Over 7½ percent of Europe's workforce is unemployed, and only two thirds of people aged 15-64 are in work. At the Lisbon summit in March 2000 the heads of government set the target that by 2010 the

This chapter comprises section 1 of: J. de Koning/R. Layard/S. Nickell/N. Westergaard-Nielsen (2003). Policies for Full Employment, UK Department for Work and Pensions. © Crown copyright 2004. Published with permission of the Department for Work and Pensions on behalf of the Controller of Her Majesty's Stationary Office.

employment rate should rise from 64 percent to at least 70 percent. And for older workers between 55 and 64 the employment rate should rise from 38 percent to at least one half. These are ambitious targets. They will require two big changes: more people must seek work, and among those seeking work a higher proportion must get a job. So we need higher participation, and (for full employment) we need a much lower unemployment rate.

Table 6.1

Unemployment Rates and Employment/Population Ratios, (%)

	Unemployment rate[a]	Employment/Population[b]	
	%	15-64	55-64
Austria	4.5	68	28
Belgium	8.0	60	26
Denmark	5.9	76	57
Finland	9.0	68	48
France	9.5	61	34
Germany	9.4	65	38
Greece	9.2	57	39
Ireland	4.6	65	48
Italy	8.5	56	29
Luxembourg	2.4	64	28
Netherlands	4.0	73	42
Portugal	6.6	68	51
Spain	11.2	59	40
Sweden	5.6	75	68
UK	5.0	73	53
EU	8.0	64	41
EU Target (2010)	NA	70	50
USA	6.1	72	59
Japan	5.2	68	62

[a] September 2003
[b] 2002

Can it be done? A mere glance at the experience of different European countries shows that it can. As Table 6.1 shows, four EU countries already exceed the overall target for 2010 (Britain, Denmark, the Netherlands, and Sweden). And seven of the 15 countries in the EU already have lower unemployment than the United States (the previous four plus Austria, Ireland, and Luxembourg). So there is no such thing as "the European unemployment problem." The fundamental problem is high unemployment in four of the five large countries. If high overall unemployment in Europe is to be reduced, these large countries will have to learn what they can from the experience of the rest of Europe. At the same time no European country can be satisfied with its current performance. In every country unemployment is higher than in the 1960s, and the participation rate (especially among older workers) is unsustainably low. There will have to be improvement on both points if Europe's employment target is to be met. More people should look for work, and those who look should be helped to look more effectively.

6.1. The Lump-Of-Labor Fallacy

But many people doubt whether more jobs will result if more people look for work. Indeed some people believe that the only way to reduce unemployment is to reduce the number of people looking for work – for example through early retirement. This is a profound error, and, unless people understand the process of job-creation, there is no chance of our hitting Europe's employment target.

The number of jobs is determined by the amount people want to buy – that is by aggregate demand. Aggregate demand is influenced by many factors, mostly outside the direct control of policy makers. However, monetary policy, in particular, is very important and is set so as to try and ensure that inflation remains low and stable. In a recession, aggregate demand is low and this is reflected in higher levels of unemployment. Monetary policy is then generally loosened in order to stimulate aggregate demand. As the economy recovers, at some stage it runs into labor shortages and inflationary pressure. In anticipation of rising inflation, monetary policy is then generally tightened. There is an unemployment problem if, at this point, unemployment is still high.

The key issue is how much unemployment remains when labor shortages become excessive and inflation therefore starts rising. This level of unemployment is known as the NAIRU (non-accelerating-inflation rate of unemployment). It is, if you like, the sustainable rate of unemployment and, if there is no trend in inflation up or down, it will also be the average rate of unemployment over a run of years. This rate of unemployment differs greatly between countries and over time, and depends on the institutions and policies existing at the time. It is these factors which determine the average unemployment rate – in other words they determine how many jobs there will be for a given total labor force. As we have said, at all times the number of jobs will depend on aggregate demand. But, because of the inflation constraint, aggregate demand will be restricted by the amount of available labor. So, over a run of years, the number of jobs will ultimately depend on the available supply of labor – that is, on the number of those who are ready and willing to take up jobs. This proposition is crucial, and many of the mistakes in employment policy come from a failure to understand it.

Consider for example policies to encourage early retirement. If we start at the sustainable rate of unemployment and labor supply is then reduced by early retirement, unemployment will fall at first. But then, as labor shortages bite, inflation will rise and aggregate demand and employment will be cut back until employment is back in line with the now reduced supply of labor. Alternatively, if we encourage more older people to work and labor supply increases, inflation will at first tend to fall, permitting a rise in aggregate demand and in the number of jobs. This is the direction in which Europe has to move if we are to support an ageing population from a reduced flow of births.[1] So it is quite wrong to think of the number of jobs as given, independent of the supply of labor. That is the lump-of-labor fallacy. If you think of the changes in employment and labor supply over the centuries it is quite obvious how wrong it is. And here is some further evidence from the recent past.

As Figure 6.1 shows, the supply of labor has grown at hugely different rates in different countries. But the number of jobs in each country has grown more or less in line with the growth in labor supply. Countries also differ in their levels of labor force participation. If the lump-of-labor theory were true, one might expect those with lower labor force participation rates to have lower unemployment. But, as Figure 6.2 shows, this is not so. If anything it is the other way round. One might also expect that countries which had lowered their participation rate most would have also lowered their unemployment most. Again, as Figure 6.3 shows, this is not so.

Figure 6.1

Percentage Growth in the Labor Force and Employment 1960-2000

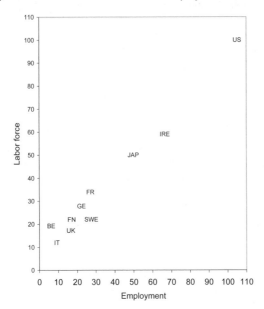

Figure 6.2

Labor Force Participation Rate (15-64) and Unemployment Rate, 2000 (%)

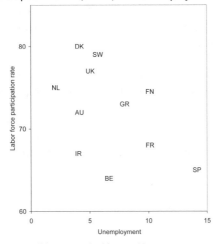

Source: For sources to all figures and tables, see Notes.

201

Figure 6.3

Change in Labor Force Participation Rate (15-64) and Change in Unemployment Rate. 1990s Compared with 1980s (% points)

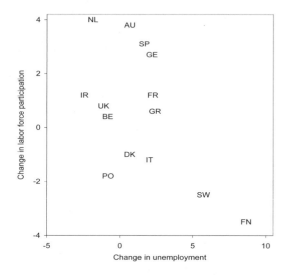

So the starting point is that, if we increase the supply of labor, we will increase employment. This has two implications. First, we can increase employment by increasing labor force participation (for example that of single mothers or older people). We return to this issue shortly. Second, we can increase employment by increasing the effective supply of labor from people who are already unemployed and searching unsuccessfully. We begin with the unemployment issue, because it is a source of major suffering and one of the greatest failings of contemporary European civilization.[2] Our analysis is based on the mass of evidence provided by the different experience of different countries.[3]

6.2. Unemployment When Vacancies Abound

The key evidence concerns the relation between unemployment and vacancies. When vacancies are high, unemployment should be relatively low – because it is easy for unemployed people to find work. Yet, strikingly, in France, West Germany, and Belgium vacancies in recent years have been extremely high by historical standards,[4] despite high unemployment. It is this high level of vacancies that helped to generate increasing European inflation in 2000/1, which led to higher interest rates and the end of the European recovery. The situation is shown in Figure 6.4. In all three countries vacancies in 2000/1 were far higher than in 1975. One would therefore expect that unemployment would have been lower than in 1975. But in fact it was more than double (except in Belgium). The main upward shift of unemployment relative to vacancies occurred in the 1980s. During that period a similar shift occurred in almost every European country. As Figure 6.5 shows, it occurred as well in Britain, Denmark, and the Netherlands. But in those countries something different then occurred in the 1990s. Unemployment fell back to close to its level in 1975. This reflected a structural shift, since vacancies did not rise compared with 1990 – if anything the reverse. So in those countries the unemployed became much more effective at filling vacancies, while in France, Germany, and Belgium they did not. Why was this?

There is no evidence of any major change in the mismatch between the characteristics of the unemployed and the characteristics of the jobs in any of the countries we are discussing.[5] So the change must have been a change in the matching process – in how unemployed people are treated.

6.3. How Unemployed People Are Treated

Even in the 1980s it was evident that unemployment differences between countries were influenced by how unemployed people were treated (Layard, Nickell and Jackman 1991). It was striking that the United States had virtually no long-term unemployed (with a duration of over a year), while Europe had almost as many long-term unemployed as short-term employed. The most obvious explanation was the long-duration unemployment benefits that existed in Europe but not the US. This relationship is depicted crudely in Figure 6.6, and it exists even when other factors are allowed for.[6]

Figure 6.4

Some High Unemployment Countries - During the 1990s Unemployment at Given Vacancies Did Not Fall

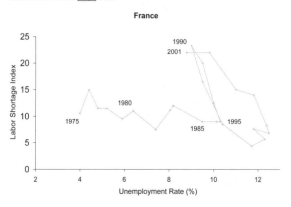

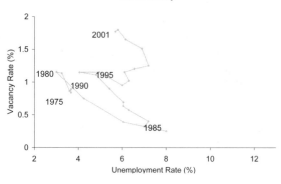

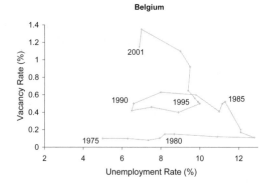

Figure 6.5

Some Low Unemployment Countries – During the 1990s Unemployment at Given Vacancies Fell

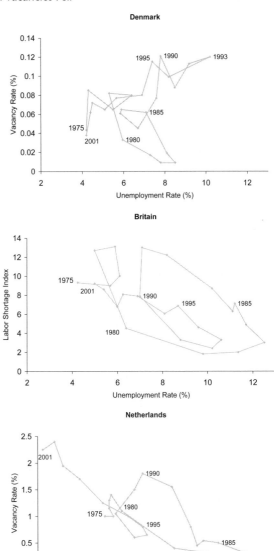

Figure 6.6

Long-term Unemployment and the Duration of Benefits

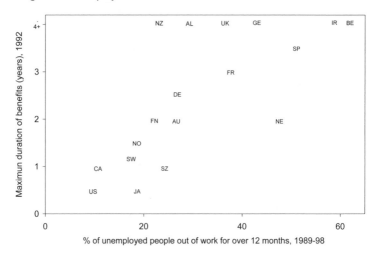

% of unemployed people out of work for over 12 months, 1989-98

The duration and level of benefits are one set of factors influencing unemployment. But even more important is the help which unemployed people get in finding work and the conditions which apply to the receipt of benefit. These two factors, active labor market policy and benefit conditionality, work best in conjunction with each other.

6.3.1. Benefit Conditionality

Clearly, one way to reduce long-term dependence on benefits is to make sure that benefits are used for their intended purpose – to support people who are not working and who really cannot find work. In other words, the right to benefits must be matched by an obligation to get a job if jobs exist. There must be a "test of willingness to work." As a 2000 OECD conference revealed, countries differ amazingly in the framework within which benefits are dispensed.[7] Experience shows that unemployed people are more available to fill employers' vacancies if

>	(i) benefits are paid through the same office as that where people are placed in work;
>	(ii) unemployed people have to attend regularly in person; and

(iii) unemployed people are expected after a period to be available for most types of work, even if this involves substantial journey times or even (as in a few countries) moving home with the help of a subsidy.

Thus the organization and effectiveness of the public employment service are crucial factors affecting the level of unemployment. The problem with imposing strict availability conditions is that these are difficult to apply unless the employment service is extremely active in helping people to get offers of work. So a "stricter benefit regime" to reduce "passive" dependence on benefits only makes sense if linked to an "active" labor market policy to help people back into work. The two should be complementary.

6.3.2. Active Labor Market Policy

This is the policy known as "welfare-to-work." The phrase comes from America, where it mainly applies to lone mothers. But the practice as applied to unemployed people has been mainly developed in Europe. Denmark, the Netherlands, and Britain all introduced major welfare-to-work policies in the 1990s. And in the last year or two France, Germany, and Spain have taken more limited steps toward greater conditionality.

In labor market policy there has to be a special focus on preventing long-term unemployment, since it is so destructive.[8] This means ensuring that everyone gets offers of work or training within a year or so of becoming unemployed, as required by the EU Luxembourg Guidelines. Britain, Denmark and the Netherlands do this for young people, but only Denmark and the Netherlands do it for people of all ages. The aim must if possible be to channel offers of work from regular employers, mainly in the private sector. But, to prevent long-term dependence on benefits, we need to ensure some worthwhile activity for everyone. It must be actively aimed at employability, so that, when we cannot secure a regular job, we should offer meaningful work with NGOs or socially-useful projects. The measure of success is the number who get regular work and keep it.

The right to offers of work will only work fully if linked to an obligation to accept one of the offers. Welfare-to-work must involve the principle of mutual obligation. The state has an obligation to ensure that offers of work are channeled to every unemployed person within a reasonable time after becoming unemployed. But in return the citizen should take advantage of those offers, and lose some or all of their benefit if they do not do so, unless there are medical reasons to the contrary. This principle should underpin active labor market policy across the EU.

6.3.3. Additionality

As always, there is the issue of whether such policies can really expand employment. Many people doubt whether active labor market measures can work owing to "displacement" and "substitution." In extreme form, these fears derive from the "lump-of-labor fallacy:" if the number of jobs is fixed and we enable Mr X to get one of them, then some other person must by definition go without work. In the very short-term of course the number of jobs is fixed. For example an employer may have a vacancy which would have gone to Mrs Y but instead the employment service induces the employer to take Mr X, who was hard to place. At that instant Mrs Y stays unemployed rather than getting a job. But by definition Mrs Y is inherently employable since she would normally have got the job. If she does not get it, she will look for another one. Employers will then find that there are more employable people in the market – they can more easily fill their vacancies. This will exert downward pressure on wages, and this will then make possible a higher level of employment at the same level of inflationary pressure. So eventually employment will rise. But by how much? Evidence on substitution and replacement is by its nature difficult to obtain. In the past it has been mainly got by asking questions to employers. When a subsidy is evaluated, employers are often asked the following:

1. Of the individuals subsidized, how many would you have hired anyway? ("Deadweight")
2. Of the remaining jobs subsidized, how many would have been filled by other recruits in any case? ("Substitution")
3. Of those remaining subsidized jobs which represent an increase in your own employment, how many were at the expense of your competitors? ("Displacement")

The net job creation resulting from the subsidy is then said to be the total number of subsidized jobs minus 1, 2, and 3.

Until recently this procedure has been used almost universally, and often implies that net job creation is only 20 percent of the total number of jobs subsidized. Yet these estimates of substitution and deadweight are based on a theory of the labor market which is never used for any other purpose. The theory being used is that, if somebody would have been employed in one place and that opportunity closes down, then unemployment increases permanently – by that amount. This makes no allowance for the possibility (discussed above) that people who find one channel of employment blocked will find another channel. The procedure is especially extraordinary when one considers that typically half the people supposedly sent into unemployment by the process of substitution are people who already have a job and would have simply been changing jobs.

Only recently have economists began to realize that the old assumptions about substitution are invalid. Lawrence Katz of Harvard University for example, has insisted on a more rational analysis of the main US wage subsidy program for youth, the Targeted Jobs Tax Credit. Until 1988 it covered disadvantaged young people aged 18-24, but from then onward it ceased to apply to people aged 23-24. This change provided a good controlled experiment, enabling one to isolate the effects which the subsidy had previously had on the employment of 23-24 year olds. The conclusion was that 40-52 percent of the subsidized jobs had represented net additions to employment (Katz 1998). This shows the crucial importance of analyzing active labor market policies within their overall setting. Interestingly, evaluations of more intensive job search assistance have never suffered from the problems discussed above. And they have generally shown good value for money. These can have the added advantage that extra effort is easily focused on those who really need it. This is an important element in any active labor market policy, and helps to reduce deadweight.

One further point on unemployed people. Throughout Europe, ethnic minorities are a growing proportion of the labor force and their unemployment rates are usually much higher than the average. Ethnic minorities need especial help and the same principle applies to them as to all citizens: the principle of rights and responsibilities. They, more than most, need the right to offers of work or training but they also have the responsibility to master the language of their adopted country and to use the offers that are available to them.

6.4. Older Workers

If we move from unemployed people to older workers and mothers, there are two issues which these groups share in common. First, there is the issue of distortions. Those not working may for that reason be receiving state benefits, in which case there is a cost to the rest of society and therefore a possibility that incentives are inefficiently distorted away from work. Second, there is the issue, arising from increased longevity and decreased birth rates, that we need to increase the numbers in work in order to pay for the growing numbers of dependent elderly. That said, the reasons for non-participation are very different for older people and for single mothers – and so are the policies needed to increase participation.

Among older people (55-64) only 43 percent are in the labor force and only 41 percent are working – making an unemployment rate of 6 percent, rather below the overall rate. The situation is very similar to what it was ten years earlier, but it is highly unsatisfactory. To find out what is causing it, we can learn a lot from the huge differences in participation rates and employment rates across countries and their time series variation (Blöndal and Scarpetta 1998). There are a number of key explanatory factors.

The first is the standard age of retirement at which state benefits become payable. The second is the use of unemployment benefits as a form of early retirement benefit, with none of the usual job-search conditions attached. And the third is the availability of invalidity or incapacity benefits, often not properly monitored to see whether the person still suffers from the problem they had when they first went on to benefit. (Some 15 percent of all men aged 55-64 are on invalidity benefit in Britain, Germany, Italy and 25 percent in the Netherlands, Blöndal and Scarpetta 1998, data on 1990). To achieve higher participation of older workers will require changes in all of these practices, and especially in the standard age of requirement.

But there must also be wider changes in society's attitudes and approaches to older people. From 2006 at the latest every European country must now introduce laws against age discrimination in employment. But this will only succeed if at the same time older workers become genuinely more attractive to employers through progressive updating of skills, either through workplace learning or independent study. Continuous learning and adequate job mobility in middle age are important to prevent workers become burned out or bored before their natural working life is over. One key handicap facing older workers is their low level of ICT skill and this must be urgently addressed (Gelderblom and de Koning 2002). More flexible pay for older workers could also help, as could lower social security payments levied on the employers of older workers.

6.5. Mothers

Among people of working age, mothers are the other main group who are often not working. The number of non-working mothers is falling rapidly, but must continue to fall if employment targets are to be met. For policy purposes it is important to distinguish between those whose choice is relatively undistorted (married mothers) and those who may be eligible for state benefits. The single mothers are the more serious problem and we shall focus on them especially (OECD 2001).

The first issue is the availability and conditionality of income support from the state. In some countries like Britain support is available without any job-search requirement. In some others job-search is required except when the children are very young. Generally participation is higher where job-search is required. A second issue is the availability of work with suitable hours. Where part-time work is readily available, some mothers who would not otherwise work will choose to do so. Then there is the question of leave. If a pregnant mother retains her right to return to her job, employment rates will be higher. And finally there is the issue of childcare – the more childcare is available, the more women will work.[9] If Europe wishes to achieve its employment targets, all these issues will have to be addressed.

6.6. Wage Flexibility And Regional Unemployment

We have focused so far on the supply side of the market, which in the long-run is the ultimate determinant of unemployment and employment rates. But the demand side is also very important. If wages are held too high, employers will not employ the available supply. There are two issues. One is the general level of real wages. At a given level of unemployment, these will be pushed too high if either the unemployed are not effectively supplying their labor (which we have already considered), or if there is autonomous wage push, due for example to union militancy or rises in import prices. Wage push is only likely in the context of unions and has been avoided in many of the smaller European countries by coordinated efforts of employers and unions (the Netherlands) or sometimes by the unions on their own (as at times in Sweden) or by employer solidarity (Portugal. The second and most serious problem concerns relative wages, across skills or regions. Across skills unemployment rates are much higher for unskilled people. One reason for this is a greater rigidity of wages at the bottom end. However, most legal minimum wages in Europe are low enough to cause no problem, and in some monopsonistic markets they may even raise employment. The more serious consequences of wage rigidity occur at the regional level, where overly high wages are a major cause of unemployment in Eastern Germany, Southern Italy, and Southern Spain.

Experience in the US and to a degree the UK suggests that marked differences in unemployment rates across regions can be reduced whenever two re-equilibrating factors are at work.[10] The first is wage adjustment. If unemployment is higher in one region than another, wages in the high-unemployment region decline vis-à-vis wages in the low-unemployment region. This attracts investment, which leads to more jobs in areas of high unemployment. The second re-equilibrating factor is regional labor mobility: there is net migration away from the high-unemployment regions.

In Continental Europe, these two re-equilibrating factors are often not allowed to operate properly. Centralized wage-setting institutions deter the emergence of significant regional wage differentials. At the same time, a number of factors – including state transfers to the high-unemployment areas – reduce the pressure to migrate. Thus, large regional labor market imbalances – the North-South divide in Italy and Spain or the West-East divide in Germany – are a prominent feature of the European landscape. Persistently high unemployment in some regions is also associated with low participation rates and a deterioration of the environment in which firms have to operate. In high-unemployment regions the public sector tends to pay more than the private sector (at least in terms of entry wages) and provides more job security. If it is difficult to get a public sector job when already employed in the private sector, this encourages "wait-unemployment" where people (sometimes the most educated people) queue for public sector jobs to become vacant.

In order to move these regions away from the high-unemployment, low-participation equilibria in which they are trapped, it is therefore necessary to act on both the demand and the supply side. On the demand side, it is necessary to pursue greater decentralization in collective bargaining; wages should be allowed to vary across regions so as to reflect more closely the differences in labor productivity and the cost of living. Decentralization in pay determination should extend to the public administration, and be accompanied by the introduction of incentives for higher productivity and hiring procedures which discourage queuing.

On the supply side, the task is to bring welfare-to-work principles into the cash transfers provided to non-employed individuals in these regions. A key requirement for this is to have unemployment benefits, rather than other instruments (like early retirement and invalidity pensions) which merely encourage non-participation in the labor market rather than supporting job search. Welfare-to-work should encourage regional labor mobility, but should circulate information on jobs available in more buoyant labor markets and sometimes also subsidize moving costs. Regional mobility should not necessarily involve long-range migration, as there are often areas within the high-unemployment regions that are more dynamic.

6.7. Employment Flexibility

Finally there is the thorny issue of employment protection. In public rhetoric it is common to attribute "high European unemployment" to high employment protection. But in fact employment protection is especially high in some European countries (like Portugal, Sweden, Norway, and the Netherlands) where unemployment is well below the U.S. level. The bulk of the economic evidence suggests that employment protection raises long-term unemployment (by reducing hiring), reduces short-term employment (by reducing firing), and has no clear effect on total employment (Bentolila and Bertola 1990, Bertola 1994). But specific policies to prevent the closure of enterprises are inefficient (Frederiksen and Westergaard-Nielsen 2002). The main danger of employment protection is that it strengthens the hand of workers in wage bargaining, leading to excessive wage pressure even when unemployment is high. Any effort to reduce employment protection should have this issue firmly in view.

6.8. Conclusion: Flexibility is Not Enough

Our conclusion is that for unemployment what really matters is
- how unemployed people are treated, and
- regional wage flexibility.

For the employment of older workers what matters is
- reduced subsidies to inactivity, used if necessary to finance employment subsidies
- lifelong learning
- an older official retirement age, where appropriate, and
- anti-discrimination legislation.

And for single mothers we need
- reduced subsidies to inactivity
- more child-care help, and
- more opportunities to work part-time.

Can these principles be usefully summarized as "more labor market flexibility?" It is a rather general phrase to describe a complex mix of policies, some of which involve less action by governments and some more.

7

A Final Note: Unemployment and the Current Recession

Once again unemployment is high. Can we handle the problem better this time that we did before? As this book shows, the answer is Yes.

In the 1980s the huge mistake, especially in Europe, was to permit the emergence of long-term unemployment. Once established, this is very difficult to eliminate. Long-term unemployed people so often become depressed and stigmatised, and thus separated from the labor market. They are therefore less likely to become re-employed than people recently disemployed. Thus, when vacancies reappear, these people are much less effective in filling them, and the rate at which vacancies get filled is lower the bigger the fraction of long-term unemployed. Since vacancies remain unfilled, the recovery quickly generates inflationary pressure and has to be aborted, even though unemployment is still high.

This analysis is central to our book and it is exactly what happened in many countries when the European boom finally arrived around 1990. But countries reacted very differently to this experience. In some there was a major reappraisal of how unemployed people are treated – aimed at preventing the separation of unemployed people from the labor market. Countries, like Denmark and the Netherlands introduced "activation policies" which insisted that, by the time people had been out of regular work for a year, they were actively involved in work or training as a condition of continued support. At the same time countries such as the UK tightened the conditionality attached to benefits. The result was a striking fall in the level of unemployment consistent with given vacancies. This is shown in Figure 7.1.[1] And unemployment in these countries in the 2007 boom was again much lower than in 1990.

Figure 7.1

Some Low Unemployment countries – during the 1990s unemployment at given vacancies fell.

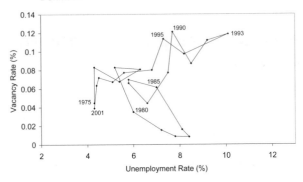

Denmark

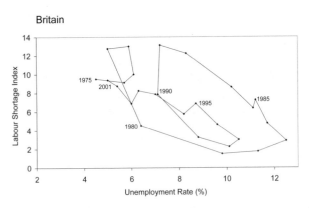

Britain

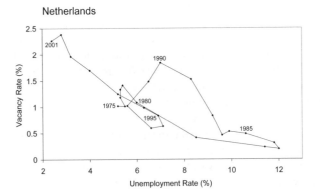

Netherlands

Figure 7.2

Some High Unemployment countries – during the 1990s unemployment at given vacancies did not fall.

France

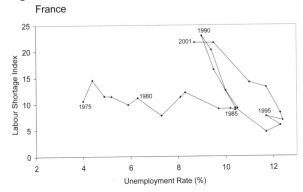

West Germany

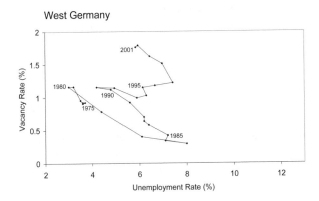

Belgium

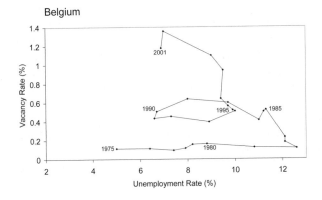

By contrast in France, and Belgium and in West Germany (before the Hartz reforms) there was much less change in how unemployed people were treated, and in consequence vacancies at given unemployment failed to fall (see Figure 7.2). In the 2007 boom unemployment was still as high in these countries as in 1990.

These were seminal experiences. In their light the OECD drastically modified the Job Strategy which it had first proposed in 1994.[2] The new strategy focussed heavily on the "activation strategy" as a key element in what is needed.

But if in a recession jobs are scarce, should we relax the drive toward welfare-to-work? This would be a major mistake. It may be true that in 2010 the main constraint on expanding demand is financial. But in the years that follow the main constraint will as usual be the danger of inflation. Except in hyper-inflation, core inflation depends on the tightness of the labor market. So the prospects of recovery depend crucially on our mobilising the unemployed and preventing them from losing contact with the labor market. But how?

7.1. The Job Guarantee

Our specific proposal is a policy to guarantee offers of work or training to every person within a year of becoming unemployed. This should be a duty of the state, and there should be a corresponding duty on the individual to take advantage of what is on offer.[3] Before the person reaches a year of unemployment there should be a gateway period where the Employment Service makes a major drive to get him or her into a regular job, if necessary with the aid of a targeted recruitment subsidy. But, if this drive fails, the guaranteed offer of work or training should come into play. For each beneficiary, this work should be temporary (6-12 months in length) and part-time (say 25 hours a week), and the individual would continue searching for a regular job at the same time. The work provided should be socially useful, requiring minimal training (like loft insulation, environmental improvement, painting and decorating, and home helps) organised at public cost by local authorities or voluntary bodies.

This arrangement will have three main effects. First, it will encourage those who do not want this work to find something better – a deterrent effect. There is no way to test a person's availability for work than by actually offering it to them. Second, for those who do take the work, it will provide a sense of doing something useful and a reason to get up in the morning – it will also deliver a useful product. It is important to stress this common sense point: one way the scheme cuts unemployment is by directly providing employment at the time. Its third effect is to increase the chances of subsequent employment. Not all schemes of direct temporary employment do that, but they can do so if the work is well-supervised and job search is maintained at the same time.[4]

Such proposals often attract criticism.

Criticism 1: "If the government is going to provide jobs, why not provide them in a 'non-distorting' way through general additions to aggregate demand?"

We have already given the answer. We need to target some demand directly at hard-to-place individuals, in order to reduce the proportion of unemployed people who are not effective as fillers of vacancies and who thus increase the NAIRU. In the short run, expenditure of this kind also has the normal effect on aggregate demand but, importantly, it also improves the supply side of the economy.

Criticism 2: "Targeted expenditure will largely displace other expenditure, and thus have little overall effect."

This is a misunderstanding. Suppose a recruitment subsidy increases employment of long-term unemployed workers at the expense of other workers. This again increases the supply potential of the economy. In the short run the money provided has the standard effects on aggregate demand (like a tax cut) but the point of it is to increase the supply potential. Similarly, if the central government finances local governments to do a project with unemployed people, the local government may cease to finance the project itself. If the result is a cut in local taxes, there will be the standard short-run boost to aggregate demand, but the point of the exercise is the increase in targetting.

Criticism 3: "These are good arguments but they do not apply in a recession."

We disagree. They are even more important when the danger of detachment from the labor market is so high. This makes the provision of fall-back jobs even more important. But what about the targeting of regular jobs? Many people do not realise how much turnover there is in the labor market even in a recession – the proportion of jobs filled in a year is at least one in five and very much higher than the number of people who become unemployed each year

We have focussed on this one proposal because it is the most important and could be largely self-financing. It should also be retained throughout the economic cycle. Another key requirement is wage restraint. This will require a dose of altruism on the part of insiders for the sake of the millions who would otherwise be left outside.

7.2. The Psychic Cost of Unemployment

As academics, we began working together on unemployment in the 1980s because we believed it was a great social evil, and not merely a source of economic inefficiency. That was before the science of well-being had become established. Not till the 1990s did we discover the evidence for our belief. By then there were large population surveys which asked people about their employment and other experiences, and also about how satisfied they were with their lives (or how happy/miserable they were). Some of these surveys like the German Socio-Economic Panel were longitudinal. From these surveys it emerged that unemployment was one of the clearest sources of personal misery, producing the same loss of happiness on average as divorce or bereavement. And the main cause of the reduced happiness was not the loss of income but the unemployment itself.[5] The surveys also showed the huge gain in happiness which occurred when a person returned to work.

The findings of these surveys are of enormous importance. First, they show the huge damage done by economic fluctuations – and the small or negligible societal gains from economic growth in advanced countries.[6] They thus turn on their head the priorities of mainstream modern macroeconomics.[7] Second, in terms of policy they stress the importance of reducing unemployment as a specific policy objective. Third, they reveal that in terms of experience almost any job is better than no job. This is so even if the unemployed (and those who lobby on their behalf) may not always want such jobs ex ante.

So the normative approach we adopted in the 1980s is now supported by the new science of well-being. And, as the previous chapter showed, the positive analysis we made then of the causes of unemployment has been broadly confirmed by the subsequent history of two decades. We rest our case.

Notes

Chapter 1

1   Non-employed job-seekers registered at employment exchanges.

2   The figures are standardized OECD figures for unemployed as a proportion of labor force (including self-employed), and read UK 13.1, France 7.7, Germany 7.6, Italy 6.6, and USA 7.2. They relate to 1984.

3   We have found that total factor productivity has no effect in our equations. This is quite explainable (Layard and Nickell 1986a).

4   One of the elements of wage pressure – real import prices – is not strictly exogenous since it depends on the real exchange rate. So the NAIRU described here is conditional on this variable. In the very long run we might expect the real exchange rate to adjust to maintain trade balance, and a very long-run NAIRU would allow for this. In practice, this would not make a very huge difference (Layard and Nickell 1986a).

5   The price equation is a re-estimated version of that in Layard and Nickell (l986a), and is derived by eliminating the demand variable σ from the employment equation of the form in their Table 4 and the first price equation in their Table 5. Small terms in Δ^3, Δl and Δk are omitted. All the relevant details may be found in Nickell (1987). Equation (1') corresponds to equation 24) in that paper. The wage equation is equation (7) below, with (7') being used to substitute for R. Small terms in $\Delta^3 u$ and its lags have been omitted. (1') and (7') were estimated jointly. The data are annual (1956-83) aggregates for Britain.

6   It is worth noting that, in order to generate stable inflation in the face of a reduction in wage pressure, real demand must rise. If the rise in demand is brought about, at least in part, by tax cuts, it is easy enough to achieve a zero fall in consumption wages. This point comes over clearly in the simulation in the Treasury Paper on Wages and Employment, 1985.

7   For a formal treatment of the models of wage determination being discussed here see Johnson and Layard (1986) and Nickell and Andrews (1983).

8   A simple model that captures these points is as follows. Suppose each worker in the ith firm yields net output $e\{W_i/W(1 - u)\}$ where $W(1 - u)$ is his expected earnings outside. The firm will choose the wage so that

$$e'\left\{\frac{W_i}{W(1 - u)}\right\}\frac{1}{W(1 - u)} - 1 = 0$$

9   In an extreme situation they could actually lose their jobs and be replaced by unemployed workers – as in Rupert Murdoch's fortress at Wapping.

10   The kind of model implied here is captured by the notion that the ith union chooses W_i to maximize expected rents $N_i\{u(W_i) - u(W)(1 - U)\}$ subject to

Notes

a perceived demand curve $N_i = f(W_i, I_{i,-1})$ where $I_{i,-1}$ is last year's inflow into unemployment from the firm. Taking the first-order condition and *then* setting $W_i = W$ and $I_{i,-1} = I_{-1}$ gives a national wage equation $W = g(U, I_{-1})$.

11   If so, there would still be a long-run natural rate of unemployment. For even if the wage equation was flat, the price equation has a slope. But the implied natural rate would be very sensitive to wage pressure (z).

12   Our wage equation confirms that the labor force (L) affects employment through its effect on wage behavior. We find that the log of the unemployment rate $(1 - N/L)$ is the best explanatory variable. If log N is entered in addition, it is insignificant. To see whether the labor force was generally significant in wage equations, David Grubb has estimated the following equations for 19 OECD countries on annual data 1952-82 (the coefficients and t-statistics are unweighted averages):

$$\dot{w} - \dot{w}_{-1} = 1.7 + 0.69(\dot{p} - \dot{w})_{-1} - 0.33(w - p)_{-1} - 1.91l + 2.00n - 0.17h + 0.26T,$$
$$\quad\quad\quad (3.0)\quad\quad\quad\quad\quad\quad (1.5)\quad\quad\quad\quad (1.6)\quad\quad (2.3)\quad\quad (0.2)\quad\quad (0.3)$$

where h is log hours per worker and T is time.

13   This is based on equation (3) of Table 1 in Nickell (1986). In estimating that equation (which is based on annual data), it was impossible to detect an effect of the $\Delta^2 p$ term. However, from the quarterly wage equation in Layard and Nickell (1986), we know that such an effect exists (albeit rather a small one, compared with that in the price equation), and we have used the estimate from that equation to obtain the coefficient on an equivalent annualized variable. The coefficients in the Nickell (1986) equation are consistently estimated despite the presence of an omitted variable $(p - p^e)$ since the latter is orthogonal to the instruments used in estimation.

14   They found that the doubling in the proportions of long-term unemployed since 1979 would predict about a 20 percent rise in the level of unemployment at given vacancies. We shall show below that in fact changes in duration explain rather more than this. There are two reasons why the proportions fall with duration. One is the way in which duration affects workers' morale and employers' perceptions (i.e., the duration-dependence of the chances of outflow for a given individual). The other is a selectivity effect – that the more motivated and desirable workers find jobs quicker, so that the proportion finding jobs is lower at long durations. To the extent that we are using the duration structure to explain the falling average outflow probability, we are assuming a constant level of true state-dependence and a constant distribution of characteristics among those becoming unemployed.

15   If the proportions p_t, leaving unemployment after duration t fall by a common multiple (λ) at all durations, the overall proportions leaving unemployment fall by more than λ. This applies in the steady state, and follows from the shift in the duration structure toward long durations. It can be illustrated easily in the case where the proportion leaving is λp up to duration T and $\lambda p'(< \lambda p)$ thereafter. Suppose an inflow of unity. The stock of unemployed is then

$$\frac{1}{\lambda p}\left(1 - e^{-\lambda p T}\right) + \frac{e^{-\lambda p T}}{\lambda p'} = \frac{1}{\lambda}\left\{\frac{1}{p} + e^{-\lambda p T}\left(\frac{1}{p'} - \frac{1}{p}\right)\right\} \quad \left(\text{with } \frac{1}{p'} > \frac{1}{p}\right)$$

when λ falls, this rises by a multiple exceeding $1/\lambda$. It follows that the average proportion leaving has fallen more than in proportion to λ. Figure 1.13 shows how the fall in the average proportion leaving can be decomposed into (1) the direct effect of changes in the ps and (2) the effect of changes in the duration structure (largely owing in turn to changes in the ps). Comparing the beginning and end-year, we can write the change in the average proportion leaving as

$$p_1 f_1 - p_0 f_0 = p_1(f_1 - f_0) + f_0(p_1 - p_0),$$

where p is the vector of ps and f the vector of proportions (f_t) with duration t. Looking at the right-hand side, the fall in the dotted line measures $p_1(f_1 - f_0)$, which is approximately half the total change.

16   This requires U_i/V_i to be the same everywhere. Two alternatives are less relevant:

(a) the ratio U_i/N_i but this does not take into account that the unemployed get employed by finding vacancies;

(b) the ratio $(U_i + N_i)/V_i$ but this does not take into account the fact that almost half of all vacancies are filled by the unemployed. Thus the fraction of unemployed who are looking for work exceeds the fraction of the employed looking for work by roughly the ratio N_i/U_i. If one knew exactly what fraction of employed workers were looking (λ_i), a good index might be $(U_i + \lambda_i N_i)/V_i$.

17   This is taken from Jackman and Roper (1987). For an alternative index see Nickell (1979).

18   The remarks are approximate and are based on the following line of thought. Suppose two regions, with region 1 the high-unemployment region: then, first,

$$mm = \frac{U_1}{U} - \frac{V_1}{V}.$$

If U_1/U falls, mm falls unless there are offsetting falls by V_1/V, which is unlikely.
Second,

$$SU = U_1 - \frac{V_1}{V}U.$$

So

$$\frac{dSU}{dU} = \frac{dU_1}{dU} - \frac{V_1}{V},$$

assuming V_1/V unaltered. This is positive if

$$\frac{dU_1}{L_1} > \frac{dU}{L}\frac{V_1/L_1}{V/L}.$$

Since $V_1/L_1 < V/L$ (since 1 is the high-unemployment region), $dU_1/dL_1 > dU/L$ is sufficient for $dSU/dU > 0$.

19   If one wished to argue that regional imbalance had worsened, one would need to argue that the share of *involuntary* unemployment in the North had risen. If we assume that voluntary unemployment is the same in all regions, this would require a huge growth in voluntary unemployment. An example is given in the table, where the total columns are actual and the other columns are hypothetical. Alternatively, we could assume more voluntary unemployment in the North (and smaller growth in voluntary unemployment in each region). But this seems implausible.

	South-East			North		
	Voluntary	Involuntary	Total	Voluntary	Involuntary	Total
1979	1	2	3	1	6	7
1985	7	3	10	7	11	18

20   That is, $\frac{1}{2}\sum |\Delta e_i|$ where e_i is the employment share. This shows the extent to which unemployment is moving from one sector to another.

21   See Layard and Nickell (1986a, Table 11), which also provides the source for similar remarks below about other z variables.

Notes

22   For a discussion of the benefit system see Layard (1986). See also Atkinson and Micklewright (1985).

23   The elasticities with respect to incomes in work were 0.96 and 0.87, respectively. This implies that, as incomes rise at a given replacement ratio, job-finding increases and thus unemployment falls. In time-series this proposition seems implausible.

24   For a fuller discussion of the shift in the u/v curve see Pissarides (1986).

25   Note that there are other effects on output through effects on productivity. Average effects on output via strikes cannot be large since in an average year only ¼ percent of man-days are lost that way.

26   The holiday argument is as follows. A worker will choose to be unemployed if, in the week in question, $u^i(W_c, H) < u^i(B_i, 0)$. The search argument adds in to the right-hand side an extra term reflecting the present value of the expected gain in future utility from searching rather than accepting a job at W_c.

27   Even in 1978, the duration of vacancies was as follows: skilled manual 6.2 weeks, semi-skilled and personal service 2.6 weeks, unskilled 1.5 weeks (Jackman, Layard and Pissarides 1984). Vacancy rates were similar in all occupations.

28   The limits were 1977-8, 10 percent; and 1978-9, 5 percent.

29   Pissarides and McMaster (1984). In 18 sectors real wages were regressed on log national vacancies and on log sector-specific vacancies, with six and five signs wrong respectively and the sum of the two effects always positive. But real wages were significantly affected by national vacancies in eight sectors and by sector-specific vacancies in three sectors only.

30   If wages are log normal, the mean exceeds the median and the median voters will gain from equalization (Ashenfelter and Layard 1983).

31   In January 1985, 28 percent of 16-year-olds were in the Youth Training Scheme and 13 percent in employment.

32   School education is dealt with in the fuller version of this paper (Layard and Nickell 1986b).

33   For a fuller discussion (up to 1979) see Layard (1982). See also Wells (1983) and Joshi, Layard and Owen (1985).

34   The index is

$$I_t = \sum_t \left(\frac{F_i}{M_i}\right)_{70} \frac{M_{i1}}{M_t},$$

where F is female person-hours, and M is male person-hours.

Chapter 2

1   For formal tests of whether unemployment follows a random walk see Blanchard and Summers (1986). However the results of this type of test depend critically on the time period chosen, suggesting that it may not be helpful to view a hundred years of unemployment as simply the result of a given time-invariant stochastic process.

2   Thus there is no reason to assume (as real business cycle theorists are wont to do) that only technology shocks can have persistent real effects. Our view of the world provides an alternative explanation of high persistence which has the merit of explaining not only output but also unemployment.

3   This is a different issue from whether insider power influences the NAIRU. Obviously trade union power affects the NAIRU – in any trade union model. Equally trade union behavior explains why employers do not hire new workers at less than the insider wage – because the union believes this will

4.   ultimately undermine its bargaining strength (Lindbeck and Snower 1988).

4.   This requires $d_1 - d_2 - d_3 < 0$. In the Layard and Nickell results this condition does indeed hold when the sum of their equations (5.1') and (5.2') is expanded around a 12 percent male unemployment rate, as prevailed in 1980-81.

5.   Such reforms could also be expected to raise b_1, the effect of unemployment on wage setting behavior, which would reduce the impact effect of a demand or supply shock (see equation (4)). Bean, Layard and Nickell (1986) provide empirical evidence on the link between corporatism and persistence as well as impact effects.

6.   The number of insiders would have an effect in efficiency wage models if individual efficiency was reduced when the firm recruited more workers, e.g.,

$$e = e(W/\overline{W}, \overline{c}u, N/N_{-1}) \qquad (e_3 < 0).$$

This seems improbable.

7.   Bargaining over employment is extremely rare, bargaining over productivity extremely common. The latter does not radically alter the picture (Jackman, Layard and Nickell 1988).

8.   Moreover in the real world of voting behavior there are many issues on which members vote, so that the wishes of the median number on one particular issue may not be decisive.

9.   The present value to being unemployed (V_u) if a person searches with unit effectiveness is

$$V_u = \frac{1}{1+r}\left[B + \frac{\phi}{\overline{c}}V_e + \left(1 - \frac{\phi}{\overline{c}}\right)V_u\right],$$

where r is the discount rate, ϕ the outflow rate from unemployment, $\overline{c}$ the effectiveness of those currently unemployed, V_e the present value of being employed elsewhere, and wages and benefits are assumed to be paid at the end of the period. V_e in turn is:

$$V_e = \frac{1}{1+r}\left(\overline{W} + sV_u + (1-s)V_e\right),$$

where s is the rate of separation into unemployment. Solving we find that

$$rV_u = (1 - \lambda)\overline{W} + \lambda B,$$

where $\lambda = (r + s)/(r + s + \phi/\overline{c})$ since $r \ll s$. Now in equilibrium $\phi u = s(1 - u)$. Hence, $\lambda \approx \overline{c}u/[1 - (1 - \overline{c})u] \approx \overline{c}u$.

10.   As regards workers, $\overline{\Omega}$ is unlikely to be exactly equal to A but it is certainly affected by both $\overline{W}$ and $\overline{c}u$. Note that the interior Nash solution only applies provided that both Ω^e and π^e exceed the outside option open to workers and firms respectively, assuming no agreement is reached. Unless there is full employment, Ω^e *will* exceed the workers' outside option, but a very high wage cannot be agreed on because the firm would rather sack the whole workforce and hire another one.

11.   Some regularity conditions on the distribution function are also required; see Gottfries and Horn (1987).

12.   In addition there is at least one other possible source of persistence in models with bargaining. Suppose that when unemployment rises, firms cease to be able to bargain over productivity. Demanning ensues. In a 2-sector model the NAIRU is now higher, unless the rise in real wages leads to sufficient increase in secondary sector employment; see Jackman, Layard and Nickell (1988).

Notes

Chapter 3

1   We also used the less conventional measure of "the change in inflation *relative* to its initial level" – to allow for the extra difficulty of reducing inflation when it is low. This was only marginally more significant than the conventional measure and barely affected the other coefficients. We also tried including the trade deficit since inflation can always be reduced by a real exchange rate appreciation; but it was insignificant and wrongly signed.

2   The other main influence was co-ordinated wage-bargaining. We reject the view that high employment was based on money illusion and repeated devaluation.

3   Because of cyclical effects on the scale of ALMP it is difficult to study the effect of ALMP on wage pressure (and thus unemployment) from time series data, as has often been tried (Calmfors and Nymoen 1990; Calmfors and Forslund 1991). The best evidence must come from cross-sectional comparisons such as our international comparisons or (when available) more microeconomic comparisons of the effects of institutional differences.

4   This draws heavily on the work of our colleagues Manacorda and Petrongolo (1995).

5   Since $\ln W_i = \log \alpha_i + \log\left(\frac{YLL_i}{LL_iN_i}\right)$.

6   There is also an important productivity argument. It is well known that a participatory environment is good for company productivity (see Nickell 1995a, Chapter 5) and that, as part of this environment, some degree of job security is required. If the remainder of the economy is governed by very loose employment protection laws, any employer who wishes to introduce some degree of job security for the above reasons may be so beset by adverse selection problems that he is unable to operate a participatory system. This mechanism could easily operate to the detriment of national productivity growth.

7   When analyzing labor demand dynamics on the basis of aggregate data, it is necessary to face up to some criticisms of this activity set out by Kramaz (1991), Caballero (1992), and Hamermesh (1992). Thus Hamermesh argues that "one cannot use aggregate dynamics to examine or compare the structures or sizes of adjustment costs" (p. 8). Since we intend to do just this, we must examine the arguments closely. Hamermesh looks at three types of adjustment cost structures, namely fixed costs, linear costs, and asymmetric quadratic costs. In each case he concludes that, in aggregate, the adjustment speed is related both to micro adjustments costs and to the cross-section variance of sectoral shocks. When looking across countries there is, therefore, the danger that any correlation between adjustment speeds and adjustment costs is corrupted by our inability to control for the variance of sectoral shocks. It is more or less impossible to obtain comparable measures of the variance of sectoral shocks because of the difficulty of obtaining consistent sectoral breakdowns across a large number of countries. However, this corruption will only be serious if the cross-section variance of shocks is strongly correlated with adjustment costs across countries. While we have no evidence on this, there seem to be no strong a priori arguments in favor of such a correlation, in which case the omission of this variable is not a problem. Finally, it is worth remarking that estimated labor market dynamics look very similar at the aggregate and at the firm level. For example, the dynamics of a United Kingdom aggregate annual employment equation have the form $n_t = 1.06n_{t-1} - 0.36n_{t-2} + etc.$, whereas a similar annual equation based on United Kingdom company data has dynamics $n_t = 0.83n_{t-1} - 0.14n_{t-2} + etc.$ (see Layard, Nickell and Jackman 1991, Chapter 9, Table 5; Nickell and Wadhwani 1991, Table III). Both exhibit a considerable degree of persistence, with shocks dying away at a very similar rate.

8   The results in OECD (1993), Table 3.5 indicate a strong positive relationship

between wages and long-term unemployment at given unemployment rates. Since long-term unemployment is negatively related to unemployment changes in the short-run, this asserts a positive relationship between long-term unemployment and hysteresis effects (negative effects of unemployment changes on wages).

9   This is the non-labor income argument. Hoon and Phelps (1995) also provide a real interest rate argument, which we do not consider here.

10   The effect will be enhanced if B is exogenous, rather than $B/W(1 - t)$. Typically, however, most countries (although not Britain) set the replacement ratio rather than the level of benefit.

11   These are Australia, Belgium, Canada, Denmark, France, Germany, Italy, Japan, Netherlands, Spain, Sweden, United Kingdom, United States.

12   These are those recorded in note 11 of chapter 3 plus Austria, Finland, Ireland, Norway and Switzerland minus Denmark and Spain.

13   So long as the tax base for these is the same. If, of course, it happens that the consumption tax base is larger, then a lower consumption tax rate would raise the same revenue and have a lesser impact on labor costs.

14   There is a separate question about the effect of changing the progressivity of the employment tax. If skill formation responds very little to relative wages, there is a strong case for a fiscally neutral shift towards greater progressivity, raising the demand for unskilled labor and reducing it for skilled (Layard, Nickell and Jackman 1991, Sections 6.5 and 10.3).

Chapter 4

1   In the Netherlands, the number of disability pensioners aged 15-64 in 1990 was over 15% of the labor force. This compares with around 5.5% in Germany and just over 4% in Britain and the United States.

2   To be unemployed, you have to be without work, to be ready to take up a job, and to have looked actively for work within the last 4 weeks.

3   Minimum wage legislation is discussed later in the section on wage determination although one of the index measures of labor standards we discuss here does include minimum wages.

4   For example in a simple gravity model, $M_{ij} = \theta(P_i P_j/D_{ij})^{1/2}$ where M_{ij} is the number migrating from region i to region j, P is population, D is distance. This implies $M_{ij}/P_i = \theta(P_j/P_i)^{1/2}$. So if all the regions within a country (but not across countries) have comparable levels of population, the geographical size of the regions should be the same across countries to ensure comparability of migration rates.

5   The general objective for non-linear utility has the form $[v(w_i(1 - \tau)) - v(\overline{A}(1 - \tau))]^\beta N_i^{\gamma \beta} \pi_i$. So long as $(1 - \tau)$ can be factored out, as it can if v is isoelastic, it will not influence the outcome.

6   Underlying this regression is a robust cross-country growth regression of the type described by Levine and Renelt (1992). The base regression is essentially one in which per capita output growth is explained by per capita input growth (i.e., investment, minus population growth, human capital growth) plus one or two other variables. The idea here is to investigate the extent to which labor market institutions influence per capita output growth either directly or *via per capita input growth*. So we replace these latter variables by the labor market institutions in order to allow them to have the maximum possible impact.

7   In 1987, over 50% of entrants into unemployment in Britain had no savings and only 15% had savings of more than £1000. This would generate an annual non-labor income of only a small proportion of the unemployment

Notes

8   benefit.
The problem in time series investigations is discriminating between permanent effects and temporary effects which persist for a long time.

9   A speculative hypothesis is that low participation rates among wives and strong employment protection for adult men are natural consequences of a culture which places a great deal of weight on the position of the (male) head of household. It comes as no great surprise that the unemployment rate among husbands in Italy is a mere 2% (OECD Jobs Study (1994a, Vol. I, Table 1.19)).

10   This must be distinguished from merely "representative" participation where, as we have already seen, there is no association with higher productivity growth.

11   Plus the fact that the "unification tax" of around 5% of West German GDP per annum has had a big impact on unemployment, mainly because the unions have been trying to offset the tax in their wage bargaining.

Chapter 5

1   Of course, the US economy turned down in 2001 and this would have had some impact on the Eurozone. However, we see that in 2000/2, GDP growth has exceeded the contribution of final domestic demand growth in every quarter, indicating a positive contribution of net trade (plus inventories) throughout. Furthermore, from the peak of GDP growth [2000(ii)] to the trough [2002(i)], GDP growth fell by 3.8 percentage points and the final domestic demand contribution fell by 3.3 percentage points. So the vast majority of the fall arises domestically.

2   One aspect of wage determination which we do not analyze here is minimum wages. This is for two reasons. First, the balance of the evidence suggests that minimum wages are generally low enough not to have much of an impact on employment except for young people. Second, only around half the OECD countries had statutory minimum wages over the period 1960 to 95. Of course, trade unions may enforce "minimum wages" but this is only a minor part of their activities. And these are already accounted for in our analysis of density, coverage and coordination.

3   Finland and Sweden in the early 1990s provide good examples of a situation where poor macroeconomic policy making, including a mishandled deregulation of the financial sector, generated adverse demand shocks which were so large that substantial and long-lasting unemployment was inevitable whatever labor market policies and institutions were in place. Of course, at the same time, Finland was hit by the collapse of the Soviet Union, a major trading partner. This made the situation a lot worse.

Chapter 6

1   On this and other aspects of labor market strategy required in Europe see Westergaard-Nielsen (2000).

2   As Clark and Oswald (1994) show, unemployment causes similar distress to divorce and bereavement. Other forms on non-employment have no such effect.

3   See Chapter 4 in this volume which analyzes the cross-sectional evidence, and Nickell et al. (2002) which analyzes the time-series. Both analyses reach similar conclusions. On cross-sectional evidence concerning benefit

228

conditionality see Danish Ministry of Finance (1999).

4   Different systems of measurement make it impossible to compare vacancy rates across countries. But they can be compared within countries over time. (No vacancy data are available for Italy.)

5   Mismatch can be mainly by skill or by region. In Britain there was some reduction mismatch but this was not the main factor reducing overall unemployment.

6   On this and other aspects of labor market strategy required in Europe see Westergaard-Nielsen (2000).

7   See OECD (2001). Labour Market Policies and the Public Employment Service: Proceedings of the Prague Conference, July 2000, Paris.

8   See for example de Koning (2001a) on the importance of preventing entry to long-term unemployment. It may also be desirable to have some automatic intervention for people who spend much of their time unemployed through a series of short spells of unemployment.

9   The employer will take the extra cost of this out of the wage-bill.

10   Layard, Nickell and Jackman (1991, Chapter 6). For the US, Blanchard and Katz (1992) stress the greater importance of mobility than of wage adjustment.

Chapter 7

1   For details, see Layard (2009).

2   Martin and Grubb (2001); OECD Employment Outlook (2005); Bassanini and Duval (2006).

3   We would prefer that for people over 25 the offer was of work (and not full-time training). For the superiority of "work-first" see Heckman, Lalonde and Smith (1999) and Bloom, Hill and Riccio (2001).

4   See, for example, Grogger and Karoly (2005) and Bivand et al. (2006).

5   See, for example, Winkelmann and Winkelmann (1998).

6   See, for example, Layard (2005) and Layard, Mayraz and Nickell (2010).

7   For example the work of Lucas and Prescott.

References

1. Introduction of the Editors

Bassanini, A., Duval, R. (2006). Employment patterns in OECD countries: Reassessing the Role of Policies and Institutions, OECD Social, Employment and Migration Working Paper No. 35.

Blanchard, O. (2007). A Review of Richard Layard, Stephen Nickell, and Richard Jackman's Unemployment: Macroeconomic Performance and the Labour Market, in: Journal of Economic Literature, 45(2): 410-18.

Bonin, H., Schneider, H. (2006). Workfare: Eine wirksame Alternative zum Kombilohn, IZA Discussion Paper No. 2399.

Eichhorst, W., Konle-Seidl, R. (2008). Contingent Convergence: a Comparative Analysis of Activation Policies, IZA Discussion Paper No. 3905.

Eichhorst, W., Zimmermann, K. F. (2007). And Then There Were Four ... How Many (and Which) Measures of Active Labor Market Policy Do We Still Need?, in: Applied Economics Quarterly, 53 (3): 243-72.

OECD (1994). The OECD Jobs Study – Facts, Analysis, Strategies, Paris: OECD.

Schmidt, C. M., Zimmermann, K. F., Fertig, M., Kluve, J. (2001). Perspektiven der Arbeitsmarktpolitik. Internationaler Vergleich und Empfehlungen für Deutschland, Berlin: Springer.

Zimmermann, K. F. (Ed.) (2003). Reformen jetzt! So geht es mit Deutschland wieder aufwärts, Wiesbaden: Gabler.

Zimmermann, K. F. (Ed.) (2006). Deutschland – was nun? Reformen für Wirtschaft und Gesellschaft, München: dtv.

2. Bibliography Chapters 1-7

Abbring, J. H., Van Den Berg, G. J., Van Ours, J. C. (1999). The Effect of Unemployment Insurance Sanctions on the Transition Rate from Unemployment to Employment, Tinbergen Institute, University of Amsterdam.

Abowd, J. M., Lemieux, T. (1993). The Effects of Product Market Competition on Collective Bargaining Agreements: the Case of Foreign Competition in Canada, in: Quarterly Journal of Economics 108(4): 983-1014.

Addison, J. J., Hirsch, B. T. (1989). Union Effects on Productivity, Profitability and Growth: Has the Long Run Arrived?, in: Journal of Labor Economics 7(1): 72-105.

Addison, J. T., Grosso, J.-L. (1996). Job Security Provisions and Employment: Revised Estimates, in: Industrial Relations 35(4): 585-603.

Agell, J., Lindh, T., Ohlsson, H. (1997). Growth and the Public Sector: a Critical Review Essay, in: European Journal of Political Economy 13(1): 33-52.

Aghion, P., Howitt, P. (1991). Growth and Unemployment, Discussion Paper No. 577, CEPR, London.

Akerlof, G., Katz, L. (1988). Workers' Trust Funds and the Logic of Wage Profiles. Mimeo, Berkeley and Harvard.

Akerlof, G., Yellen, J. (Eds.) (1986). Efficiency Wage Models of the Labor Market, Cambridge: Cambridge University Press.

Akerlof, G., Yellen, J. (1990). The Fair Wage/Effort Hypothesis and Unemployment. in: Quarterely Journal of Economics, 105(2): 255-83.

Alesina, A., Perotti, R. (1997). The Welfare State and Competitiveness, in: American Economic Review, 87(5), 921-39.

Alogoskoufis, C., Manning, A. (1988). On the Persistence of Unemployment, in: Economic Policy, 3(7): 427-69.

Arrow, K. (1974). General Economic Equilibrium: Purpose, Analytic Techniques, Collective Choice, in: American Economic Review 64(3): 1-10.

Ashenfelter, O., Layard, R. (1983). Incomes Policy and Wage Differentials, in: Economica, 50(198): 127-45.

Atkinson, A. B., Micklewright, J. (1985). Unemployment Benefits and Unemployment Duration, London: London School of Economics, Suntory-Toyota International Centre for Economics and Related Disciplines.

Atkinson, A. B., Micklewright, J. (1991). Unemployment Compensation and Labour Market Transitions: A Critical Review, in: Journal of Economic Literature, 29(4): 1679-727.

Bain, G. S. (Ed.) (1983). Industrial Relations in Britain, Oxford: Basil Blackwell.

Baily, M. N. (1993). Competition, Regulation and Efficiency in Service Industries, in: Brookings Papers on Economic Activity: Microeconomics, 1993(2): 71-159.

Ball, L., Moffitt, R. (2001). Productivity Growth and the Phillips Curve, in: Krueger, A., Solow, R. (Eds.), The Roaring Nineties: Can Full Employment Be Sustained?, New York, NY: The Russell Sage Foundation.

Barro, R. J., Sala-i-Martin, X. (1995). Economic Growth, New York, NY: McGraw-Hill.

Bartel, A. P., Thomas, L. G. (1987). Predation through Regulation: the Wage and Profit Effects of the Occupational Safety and Health Administration and the Environmental Protection Agency, in: Journal of Law and Economics, 30(1): 239-64.

Bassanini, A., Duval, R. (2006). Employment Patterns in OECD Countries: Reassessing the Role of Policies and Institutions, OECD Social, Employment and Migration Working Paper No. 35.

Batstone, E. (1984). Working Order, Oxford: Basil Blackwell.

Bean, C., Crafts, N. (1995). British Economic Growth since 1945: Relative Economic Decline ... and Renaissance, in: Crafts, N., Toniolo, G. (Eds.), Economic Growth in Europe since 1945, Cambridge: Cambridge University Press, 131-172.

Bean, C. R., Layard, R., Nickell, S. J. (1986). The Rise in Unemployment: a Multi-Country Study, in: Economica, 53(210): 1-22.

Bean, C., Pissarides, C. A. (1993). Unemployment, Consumption and Growth, in: European Economic Review, 37(4): 837-54.

Belot, M., van Ours, J. C. (2000). Does the Recent Success of Some OECD Countries in Lowering their Unemployment Rates Lie in the Clever Design of their Labour Market Reforms?, IZA Discussion Paper No. 147.

Belot, M., van Ours, J. C. (2001). Unemployment and Labor Market Institutions: An Empirical Analysis, in: Journal of Japanese and International Economics, 15(4): 1-16.

Bentolila, S., Bertola, G. (1990). Firing Costs and Labour Demand: How Bad is Eurosclerosis, in: Review of Economic Studies, 57(3): 381-402.

Bentolila, S., Dolado, J. (1991). Mismatch and Internal Migration in Spain, in: Padoa-Schioppa, F. (Ed.), Mismatch and Labour Mobility, Cambridge: Cambridge University Press, 182-236.

Bertola, G. (1994). Flexibility, Investment and Growth, in: Journal of Monetary Economics, 34(2): 215-38.

Bertola, G., Blau F. D., Kahn, L. M. (2001). Comparative Analysis of Labor-Market Outcomes: Lessons for the United States from International Long–Run Evidence, in:

References

Krueger, A., Solow, R. (Eds.), The Roaring Nineties: Can Full Employment Be Sustained?, New York, NY: Russell Sage Foundation.

Bertola, G., Rogerson, R. (1997). Institutions and Labour Reallocation, in: European Economic Review 41(6): 1147-71.

Bivand, P., Brooke, B., Jenkins, S., Simmonds, D. (2006). Evaluation of the StepUP Pilot: Final Report, Department of Work and Pensions Research Report No. 337.

Blanchard, O. (1986). The Wage Price Spiral, in: Quarterly Journal of Economics 101(3): 543-66.

Blanchard, O. (1988). Unemployment: Getting the Questions Right and Some of the Answers. MIT, Mimeo.

Blanchard, O., Katz, L. (1992). Regional Evolutions, in: Brookings Papers on Economic Activity, 23(1): 1-75.

Blanchard, O., Katz, L. (1997). What We Know and Do not Know about the Natural Rate of Unemployment, in: Journal of Economic Perspectives, 11(1): 51-73.

Blanchard, O., Layard, R. (1988). Layoffs by Seniority and Equilibrium Employment, London School of Economics, Centre for Labour Economics, Working Paper No. 1055.

Blanchard, O., Summers, L. H. (1986). Hysteresis and the European Unemployment Problem, MIT, Mimeo.

Blanchard, O., Wolfers, J. (2000). The Role of Shocks and Institutions in the Rise of European Unemployment: The Aggregate Evidence, in: The Economic Journal 110(462): C1-C33.

Blanchflower, D. (1996). The Role and Influence of Trade Unions in the OECD, CEP Discussion Paper No. 310.

Blanchflower, D., Oswald, A. (1994). The Wage Curve, Cambridge, MA: MIT Press.

Blau, F. D., Kahn, L. (1996). International Differences in Male Wage Inequality: Institutions versus Market Forces, in: Journal of Political Economy, 104(4): 791-837.

Bloom, H. S., Hill, C. J., Riccio, J. (2001). Modeling the Performance of Welfare-to-Work Programs: The Effects of Program Management and Services, Economic Environment, and Client Characteristics, New York, NY: Manpower Demonstration Research Corporation.

Blöndal, S., Scarpetta, S. (1998). The Retirement Decision in OECD Countries, OECD Economics Department Working Paper No. 202.

Blundell, R., Reed, H., Van Reenen, J., Shephard, A. (2003). The Impact of the New Deal for Young People on the Labour Market: a Four-Year Assessment. in: Dickens, R., Gregg, P., Wadsworth, J. (Eds.), The Labour Market Under New Labour, Basingstoke: Palgrave Macmillan, 17-31.

Booth, A., Burda, M., Calmfors, L., Checchi, D., Naylor, R., Visser, J. (2000). What Do Unions Do in Europe?, A Report for the Fondazione Rodolfo DeBenedetti, Milan.

Bosworth, G. P. (1993). Saving and Investment in a Global Economy, Washington, DC: The Brookings Institution.

Bover, O., Garcia-Perea, P., Portugal, P. (2000). Iberian Labour Markets: Why Spain and Portugal are OECD Outliers, in: Economic Policy, 15(31): 381-428.

Bruno, M., Sachs, J. (1985). Economics of Worldwide Stagflation, Cambridge, MA: Harvard University Press.

Budd, A., Levine, R., Smith, P. (1986). Unemployment, Vacancies and the Long-Term Unemployed, London Business School, Centre for Economic Forecasting, Discussion Paper No. 154.

Budd, A., Levine, P., Smith, P. (1987). Long Term Unemployment and the Shifting U/V Curve: A Multi-Country Study, in: European Economic Review, 31(1-2), 296-305.

Bulow, J., Summers, L. (1986). A Theory of Dual Labor Markets with Application to Industrial Policy, Discrimination, and Keynesian Unemployment, in: Journal of Labor Economics, 4(3): 376-414.

Caballero, R. J. (1992). A Fallacy of Composition, in: American Economic Review, 82(5): 1279-92.

Calmfors, L. (1993). Centralisation of Wage Bargaining and Economic Performance: a Survey, OECD Economics Department, Working Paper No. 131.

References

Calmfors, L., Driffill, J. (1988). Bargaining Structure, Corporatism and Macroeconomic Performance, in: Economic Policy, 3(6): 14-61.

Calmfors, L., Forslund, A. (1991). Real-Wage Adjustment and Labour Market Policies: The Swedish Experience, in: Economic Journal, 101(408): 1130-48.

Calmfors, L., Forslund, A., Hemström, M. (2002). Does Active Labour Market Policy Work? Lessons from the Swedish Experiences, Institute for Labour Market Policy Evaluation, Uppsala, Working Paper 2002: 4.

Calmfors, L., Nymoen, R. (1990). Real Wage Adjustment and Employment Policies in the Nordic Countries, in: Economic Policy, 5(11): 398-448.

Card, D., Kramarz, F., Lemieux, T. (1995). Changes in the Relative Structure of Wages and Employment: a Comparison of the United States, Canada and France, Industrial Relations Section, Princeton University, Working Paper No. 355.

Card, D., Krueger, A. B. (1995). Myth and Measurement: the New Economics of the Minimum Wage, Princeton, NJ: Princeton University Press.

Carling, K., Edin, P.-A., Harkman, A., Holmlund, B. (1996). Unemployment Duration, Unemployment Benefits and Labor Market Programs in Sweden, in: Journal of Public Economics, 59(3): 313-34.

Carling, K., Holmlund, B., Vejsiu, A. (1999). Do Benefit Cuts Boost Job Findings? Swedish Evidence from the 1990s, Swedish Office of Labour Market Policy Evaluation, Working Paper No. 8.

Carruth, A., Hooker, M., Oswald, A. (1998). Unemployment Equilibria and Input Prices: Theory and Evidence from the United States, in: Review of Economics and Statistics, 80(4): 621-28.

Clark, A. (2002). A Note on Unhappiness and Unemployment Duration, CNRS and DELTA, Mimeo.

Clark, A., Georgellis, Y., Sanfey, P. (1999). Scarring: the Psychological Impact of Past Unemployment, in: Economica, 68(270): 221-41.

Clark, A., Oswald, A. (1994). Unhappiness and Unemployment, in: Economic Journal, 104(424): 648-59.

Clark, D. (1997). Skills, Earnings Inequality and Unemployment, M.Ph. Economics Thesis, University of Oxford.

Coe, D. T., Snower, D. J. (1997). Policy Complementarities: the Case for Fundamental Labour Market Reform, CEPR Discussion Paper No.1585.

Commission of the European Communities (1995). Performance of the EU Labour Market: Results of an Ad-Hoc Labour Market Survey, Reports and Studies No. 3, Directorate-General for Economic and Financial Affairs, European Commission.

Contini, B., Pacelli, L., Filippi, M., Lioni, G., Revelli, R. (1995). A Study of Job Creation and Job Destruction in Europe, for the European Commission, Turin: DGV, R & P.

Cooke, W. N. (1992). Product Quality Improvement through Employee Participation: the Effects of Unionisation and Joint Union-Management Administration, in: Industrial and Labour Relations Review, 46(1): 119-34.

Crafts, N. F. R. (1997). Economic Growth in East Asia and Western Europe since 1950: Implications for Living Standards, in: The National Institute Economic Review, 162(1): 75-84.

Daniel, W. W., Stilgoe, E. (1978). The Impact of Employment Protection Laws, London: Policy Studies Institute.

Danish Ministry of Finance (1999). The Danish Economy: Medium Term Economic Survey, Copenhagen: Ministry of Finance.

Daveri, F., Tabellini, G. (1997). Unemployment, Growth and Taxation in Industrial Countries, Bocconi University, Mimeo.

Davis, S., Haltiwanger, J. (1999). Gross Job Flows, in: Ashenfelter, O. C., Card, D. (Eds.), The Handbook of Labor Economics, Vol. 3B, Amsterdam: Elsevier, 2711-805.

De Koning, J. (2001a). How Can We Make Active Policies More Effective? The Role of Organisation, Implementation and Optimal Allocation in Active Labour Market Policy, in: OECD (Ed.), Labour Market Policies and the Public Employment Service, Paris: OECD, 311-36.

De Koning, J. (2001b). Aggregate Impact Analysis of Active Labour Market Policy: a Lit-

References

erature Review, in: International Journal of Manpower, 22 (8): 707-35.

De Koning, J., Layard, R., Nickell, S., Westergaard-Nielsen, N. (2003). Policies for Full Employment, London: UK Department for Work and Pensions. [Chapter 6 in this volume]

Dertouzos, J. N., Karoly, L. A. (1993). Employment Effects of Worker Protection: Evidence from the United States, in: Buechtemann, C. F. (Ed.), Employment Security and Labor Market Behavior – Interdisciplinary Approaches and International Evidence, Ithaca, NY: ILR Press.

Dickens, R. (2000). The Evolution of Individual Male Earnings in Great Britain: 1975-95, in: Economic Journal, 110(460): 27-49.

Disney, R. (2000). Fiscal Policy and Employment 1: a Survey of Macroeconomic Models, Methods and Findings, IMF, Mimeo.

Di Tella, R., MacCulloch, R., Oswald, A. (2001). Preferences over Inflation and Unemployment: Evidence from Surveys of Happiness, in: American Economic Review, 91(1): 335-41.

Dixit, A., Stiglitz, J. (1977). Monopolistic Competition and Optimum Product Diversity, in: American Economic Review, 67(3): 297-308.

Dolado, J. J., Kramarz, F., Machin, S., Manning, A., Margolis, D., Teulings, C. (1996). The Economic Impact of Minimum Wages in Europe, in: Economic Policy, 23: 319-372.

Dolado, J. J., Malo de Molina, J. L., Zabalza, A. (1986). Spanish Industrial Unemployment: Some Explanatory Factors, in: Economica, 53(210(S)): S313-34.

Dowrick, S. (1993). Government Consumption: Its Effects on Productivity Growth and Investment, in: Gemmel, N. (Ed.), The Growth of the Public Sector - Theories and International Evidence, Aldershot: Edward Elgar, 136-52.

Easterly, W., Rebelo, S. (1993). Marginal Income Tax Rates and Economic Growth in Developing Countries, in: European Economic Review, 37(2-3): 409-17.

Ebbinghaus, B., Visser, J. (2000). Trade Unions in Western Europe, London: MacMillan.

Elmeskov, J., Martin, J. P., Scarpetta, S. (1998). Key Lessons for Labour Market Reforms: Evidence from OECD Countries' Experiences, Paris: OECD.

Engen, E. M., Skinner, J. (1996). Taxation and Economic Growth, NBER Working Paper No.5826.

Englander, A. S., Gurney, A. (1994a). OECD Productivity Growth: Medium-Term Trends, OECD Economic Studies, 22: 111-29.

Englander, A. S., Gurney, A. (1994b). Medium-Term Determinants of OECD Productivity, OECD Economic Studies, 22: 49-109.

Fahrer, J., Pease, A. (1993). The Unemployment/Vacancy Relationship in Australia, Reserve Bank of Australia, Economic Research Department, Discussion Paper No. 9305.

Fay, R. (1995). Enhancing the Effectiveness of Active Labour Market Policies, the Role of - and Evidence from - Program Evaluations in OECD Countries, Paris: OECD.

Fernie, S., Metcalf, D. (1995). Participation, Contingent Pay, Representation and Workplace Performance: Evidence from Great Britain, Centre for Economic Performance, London School of Economics, Discussion Paper No. 232.

Fitoussi, J-P., Jestaz, D., Phelps, E. S., Zoega, G. (2000). Roots of the Recent Recoveries: Labor Reforms or Private Sector Forces?, in: Brookings Papers on Economic Activity, 31(1): 237-91.

Flanagan, R. J. (1987). Labor Relations and the Litigation Explosion, Washington, DC: The Brookings Institution.

Franz, W. (1987): Hysteresis, Persistence and the NAIRU: An Empirical Analysis for the FRG, in: Layard, R., Calmfors, L. (Eds.), The Fight against Unemployment, Cambridge, MA: MIT Press, 91-122.

Frederiksen, A., Westergaard-Nielsen, N. (2002). Where Did They Go?, Department of Economics, Aarhus School of Business, CLS Working Papers 01-11.

Garcia Serrano, C. (1998). Worker Turnover and Job Reallocation: the Role of Fixed Term Contracts, in: Oxford Economic Papers, 50(4): 709-25.

Gelderblom, A., de Koning, J. (2002). ICT and Older Workers: no Unwrinkled Relationship, Paper for the EALE-conference, University of Paris, Pantheon Sorbonne, September 19-22.

Gottfries, N., Horn, H. (1987). Wage Formation and the Persistence of Unemployment, in: Economic Journal, 97(388): 877-84.

Gottschalk, P., Moffitt, R. (1994). The Growth of Earnings Instability in the US Labor Market, in: Brookings Papers on Economic Activity, 25(2): 217-72.

Gregg, P., Machin, S., Manning, A. (2000). Mobility and Joblessness, London: LSE Centre for Economic Performance.

Grogger, J., Karoly, L. (2005). Welfare Reform: Effects of a Decade of Change, Cambridge, MA: Harvard University Press.

Grubb, D., Jackman, R., Layard, R. (1982). Causes of the Current Stagflation, in: Review of Economic Studies, 49(5): 707-30.

Grubb, D., Jackman, R., Layard, R. (1983). Wage Rigidity and Unemployment in OECD Countries, in: European Economic Review, 21(1-2): 11-39.

Gruber, J. (1994). The Incidence of Mandated Maternity Benefits, in: American Economic Review, 84(3): 622-41.

Gruber, J. (1997). The Incidence of Payroll Taxation: Evidence from Chile, in: Journal of Labor Economics, 15(3): 72-101.

Gruber, J., Krueger, A. B. (1991). The Incidence of Mandated Employer-Provided Health Insurance: Lessons from Workers' Compensation Insurance, in: Bradford, D. (Ed.), Tax Policy and the American Economy, Vol.5, Cambridge, MA: MIT Press, 111-143.

Haffner, R. C. G., Nickell, S. J., Nicoletti, G., Scarpetta, S., Zoega, G. (2000). European Integration, Liberalisation and Labour Market Performance, in: Bertola, G., Boeri, T., Nicoletti, G. (Eds.), Welfare and Employment in a United Europe, Cambridge, MA: MIT Press, 147-236.

Hall, R. E. (1975). The Rigidity of Wages and Persistence of Unemployment, in: Brookings Papers on Economic Activity, 1975(2): 301-49.

Ham, J., Rea, S. (1987). Unemployment Insurance and Male Unemployment Duration in Canada, in: Journal of Labor Economics, 5(3): 325-53.

Hamermesh, D. S. (1992). Spatial and Temporal Aggregation in the Dynamics of Labour Demand, NBER Working Paper No. 4055.

Harkman, A. (1997). Unemployment Compensation and Unemployment Duration – What Was the Effect of the Cut in the Replacement Rate from 90 to 80 percent?, in: Harkman, A., Jansson, F., Kallberg, K., Öhrn, L. (Eds.), Unemployment Insurance and the Functioning of the Labour Market, Stockholm: The Swedish National Labour Market Board.

Heckman, J., Lalonde, R., Smith, J. (1999). The Economics and Econometrics of Active Labor Market Programs, in: Ashenfelter, O. C., Card, D. (Eds.), The Handbook of Labor Economics, Vol. 3A, Amsterdam: North-Holland, 1865-2097.

Helliwell, J. (2007). Well-Being and Social Capital: Does Suicide Pose a Puzzle?, in: Social Indicators Research, 82(3): 455-96.

Holmlund, B. (1998). Unemployment Insurance in Theory and Practice, in: The Scandinavian Journal of Economics, 100(1): 113-41.

Holmlund, B., Kohn, A. (1995). Progressive Taxation, Wage Setting and Unemployment - Theory and Swedish Evidence, Tax Reform Evaluation Report No.15, Stockholm: National Institute of Economic Research.

Holzer, H., Katz, L., Krueger, A. B. (1988). Job Queues and Wages: New Evidence on the Minimum Wage and Inter-Industry Wage Structure, NBER Working Paper No. 2561.

Hoon, H. T., Phelps, E. S. (1995). Taxes and Subsidies in a Labor-Turnover Model of the Natural Rate, Columbia University, Mimeo.

Hoon, H. T., Phelps, E. S. (1992). Macroeconomic Shocks in a Dynamized Model of the Natural Rate of Unemployment, in: American Economic Review, 82(4): 889-900.

Hopenhayn, H., Rogerson, R. (1993). Job Turnover and Policy Evaluation: a General Equilibrium Analysis, in: Journal of Political Economy, 101(5): 915-38.

Hughes, G., McCormick, B. (1981). Do Council Housing Policies Reduce Migration between Regions?, in: Economic Journal, 91(364): 919-37.

Hunt, J. (1995). The Effect of Unemployment Compensation on Unemployment Duration in Germany, in: Journal of Labor Economics, 13(1): 88-120.

Ichniowski, C., Shaw, K. (1995). Old Dogs and New Tricks: Determinants of the Adoption of Productivity Enhancing Work Practices, in: Brookings Papers on Economic Activity: Microeconomics, 1995: 1-65.

Ichniowski, C., Shaw, K., Prennushi, G. (1995). The Effects of Human Resource Management Practices on Productivity, NBER Working Paper No.5333.

Jackman, R., Layard, R. (1987). Innovative Supply-Side Policies to Reduce Unemployment, in: Minford, P. (Ed.), Monetarism and Macroeconomics, London: IEA, 93-114.

Jackman, R., Layard, R. (1991). Does Long-Term Unemployment Reduce a Person's Chance of a Job? A Time-Series Test, in: Economica 58(229): 93-106.

Jackman, R., Layard, R., Manacorda, M., Petrongolo, B. (1999). European versus US Unemployment: Different Responses to Increased Demand for Skill?, in: Layard, R. (Ed.), Tackling Unemployment, London: MacMillan, 201-30.

Jackman, R., Layard, R., Nickell, S. (1991). Unemployment, Oxford: Oxford University Press.

Jackman, R., Layard, R., Pissarides, C. (1984). On Vacancies, London School of Economics Centre for Labour Economics, Working Paper No. 165 (Revised).

Jackman, R., Layard, R., Savouri, S. (1987). Labour Market Mismatch and the Equilibrium Level of Unemployment to Vacancies, London School of Economics, Centre for Labour Economics, Working Paper No. 1009.

Jackman, R., Roper, S. (1987). Structural Unemployment, in: Oxford Bulletin of Economics and Statistics, 49(1): 9-36.

Jackman, R., Williams, C. (1985). Job Applications by Unemployed Men, London School of Economics, Centre for Labour Economics, Working Paper No. 792.

Johnson, G., Layard, R. (1986). The Natural Rate of Unemployment: Explanation and Policy, in: Ashenfelter, O. C., Layard, R. (Eds.), Handbook of Labor Economics, Amsterdam: North-Holland, 921-99.

Joshi, H. E., Layard, R., Owen, S. J. (1985). Why are More Women Working in Britain?, in: Journal of Labor Economics, 3(1): S147-S76.

Katz, L. F. (1998). Wage Subsidies for the Disadvantaged, in: Freeman, R., Gottschalk, P. (Eds.), Generating Jobs: how to Increase Demand for Less Skilled Workers, New York, NY: Russell Sage Foundation, 19-102.

Katz, L. F, Meyer, B. (1990). The Impact of Potential Duration of Unemployment Benefits on the Duration of Unemployment, in: Journal of Public Economics, 41(1): 45-72.

King, R. G., Rebelo, S. (1990). Public Policy and Economic Growth: Developing Neoclassical Implications, in: Journal of Political Economy, 98(5): S126-S150.

Knoester, A., Van der Windt, N. (1987). Real Wages and Taxation in ten OECD Countries, in: Oxford Bulletin of Economics and Statistics, 49(1): 151-69.

Kramarz, F. (1991). Adjustment Costs and Adjustment 'Speed', Paris: INSEE.

Krueger, A. B., Summers, L. (1988): Efficiency Wages and the Inter-Industry Wage Structure, in: Econometrica, 56(2): 259-94.

Krugman, P. (1994). Past and Prospective causes of High Unemployment, in: Economic Review, 1994(Q IV): 23-43.

Layard, R. (1982). Youth Unemployment in Britain and the US Compared, in: Freeman, R., Wise, D. (Eds.), The Youth Labor Market Problem, Chicago, IL: University of Chicago Press.

Layard, R. (1985). How to Reduce Unemployment by Changing National Insurance and Providing a Job-Guarantee, London School of Economics Centre for Labour Economics, Working Paper No. 218.

Layard, R. (1986). How to Beat Unemployment, Oxford: Oxford University Press.

Layard, R. (1995). The Road Back to Full Employment, Rudolf Meidner Lecture, Centre for Economic Performance, London School of Economics, Mimeo.

Layard, R. (2004). Good Jobs and Bad Jobs, CEP Occasional Paper No. 19.

Layard, R. (2005). Happiness. Lessons from a New Science, London and New York, NY: Penguin.

Layard, R. (2009), L'expérience du chômage: quelles leçons pour la France?, Travail et Emploi, No 118.

Layard, R., Bean, C. (1989). Why Does Unemployment Persist?, in: Scandinavian Journal of Economics, 91(2): 371-88. [Chapter 2 in this volume]

References

Layard, R., Mayraz, G., Nickell, S. (2010). Does Relative Income Matter? Are the Critics Right?, in: Diener, E., Helliwell, J., Kahneman, D. (Eds.), International Differences in Well-Being, New York, NY: Oxford University Press, 139-65.

Layard, R., Metcalf, D., Nickell, S. (1978). The Effects of Collective Bargaining on Relative Wages, in: British Journal of Industrial Relations, 16(3): 287-302.

Layard, R., Nickell, S. (1986a). Unemployment in Britain, in: Economica, 53(210): 121-69.

Layard, R., Nickell, S. (1986b). The Performance of the British Labour Market. Discussion Paper No. 249, London School of Economics Centre of Labour Economics.

Layard, R., Nickell, S. (1987). The Labour Market, in: Dornbusch, R., Layard, R. (Eds.), The Performance of the British Economy, Oxford: Oxford University Press, 131-79. [Chapter 1 in this volume]

Layard, R., Nickell, S., Jackman, R. (1991). Unemployment: Macroeconomic Performance and the Labour Market, Oxford: Oxford University Press.

Layard, R., Nickell, S., Jackman, R. (1996). Combatting Unemployment: Is Flexibility Enough?, in: OECD (Ed.), Macroeconomic Policies and Structural Reform, Paris: OECD, 19-49. [Chapter 3 in this volume]

Layard, R., Nickell, S., Jackman, R. (2005). Unemployment: Economic Performance and the Labour Market, Oxford: Oxford University Press, XII-XLI. [Chapter 5 in this volume]

Lazear, E. P. (1990). Job Security Provisions and Employment, in: Quarterly Journal of Economics, 105(3): 699-726.

Leibfritz, W., Thornton, J., Bibbee, A. (1997). Taxation and Economic Performance, Economics Department, OECD, Working Paper No. 176.

Leuven, E., Oosterbeek, H., van Ophen, H. (1997). International Comparisons of Male Wage Inequality; Are the Findings Robust?, University of Amsterdam, Mimeo.

Levine, D. I. (1991). Just-Cause Employment Policies in the Presence of Worker Adverse Selection, in: Journal of Labor Economics, 9(3): 294-305.

Levine, D. I., Tyson, L. D. A. (1990). Participation, Productivity, and the Firm's Environment, in: Blinder, A. (Ed.), Paying for Productivity, Washington, DC: The Brookings Institution, 183-244.

Levine, R., Renelt, D. (1992). A Sensitivity Analysis of Cross-Country Growth Regressions, in: American Economic Review, 82(4): 942-63.

Lewis, H. G. (1963). Unionism and Relative Wages in the US, Chicago, IL: University of Chicago Press.

Lewis, H. G. (1986). Union Relative Wage Effects: a Survey, Chicago, IL: University of Chicago Press.

Lindbeck, A., Snower, D. (1984). Involuntary Unemployment as an Insider-Outsider Dilemma, Institute for International Economic Studies, University of Stockholm, Seminar Paper No. 282.

Lindbeck, A., Snower, D. (1988). Cooperation, Harassment, and Involuntary Unemployment: an Insider-Outsider Approach, in: American Economic Review, 78(1): 167-88.

Lipsey, R. G. (1960). The Relation between Unemployment and the Rate of Change of Money Wage Rates in the United Kingdom 1892-1957: a Further Analysis, in: Economica, 27(105): 1-31.

Ljungqvist, L., Sargent, T.J. (1998). The European Unemployment Dilemma, in: Journal of Political Economy, 106(3): 514-50.

Lockwood, B., Manning, A. (1993). Wage Setting and the Tax System: Theory and Evidence for the United Kingdom, in: Journal of Public Economics, 52(1): 1-29.

Lynch, L., Nickell, S. (2001). Rising Productivity and Falling Unemployment: Can the US Experience be Sustained and Replicated?, in: Krueger, A. B., Solow, R. (Eds.), The Roaring Nineties: Can Full Employment be Sustained?, New York, NY: The Russell Sage Foundation, 538-78.

Malinvaud, E. (1982). Wages and Unemployment, in: Economic Journal, 92(365): 1-13.

Manacorda, M., Manning, A. (1997). Just Can't Get Enough, More on Skill-Biased Change and Unemployment, London: London School of Economics, CEP.

Manacorda, M., Petrongolo, B. (1995). The Race between the Supply and Demand of

References

Skills: Some Evidence from OECD Countries, London: London School of Economics, CEP.

Martin, J. (2000). What Works among Active Labour Market Policies?, in: OECD (Ed.), Evidence from OECD countries, OECD Economic Studies No.30, Paris: OECD, 79-112.

Martin, J. P, Grubb, D. (2001). What Works and for Whom: A Review of OECD Countries' Experiences with Active Labour Market Policies, Paris: OECD.

Masson, P. R., Bayoumi, T., Samieri, H. (1995). Saving Behaviour in Industrial and Developing Countries, in: Staff Studies for the World Economic Outlook, Washington, DC: IMF.

McKinsey Global Institute (1992). Service Sector Productivity, Washington, DC: McKinsey Global Institute.

McKinsey Global Institute (1997). Removing Barriers to Growth and Employment in France and Germany, Washington, DC: McKinsey Global Institute.

Mendoza, E. G., Milesi-Ferretti, G. M., Asea, P. (1997). On the Ineffectiveness of Tax Policy in Altering Long-Run Growth: Harberger's Superneutrality Conjecture, in: Journal of Public Economics, 66(1): 99-126.

Menezes-Filho, N., Ulph, D., Van Reenen, J. (1995). R & D and Union Bargaining: Evidence from British Companies and Establishments, University College London, Mimeo.

Metcalf, D., Nickell, S. (1978). The Effects of Collective Bargaining on Relative Wages, in: British Journal of Industrial Relations, 16(3): 287-302.

Metcalf, D. (1986). Labour Market Flexibility and Jobs: a Survey of Evidence from OECD Countries with Special Reference to Great Britain and Europe, London School of Economics, Centre for Labour Economics, Working Paper No.870.

Meyer, B. (1995). Lessons from the US Unemployment Insurance Experiments, in: Journal of Economic Literature, 33(1): 91-131.

Meyer, B. D. (1990). Unemployment Insurance and Unemployment Spells, in: Econometrica, 58(4): 757-82.

Micklewright, J. (1984). Male Unemployment and the Family Expenditure Survey 1972-1980, in: Oxford Bulletin of Economics and Statistics, 46(1): 31-53.

Minford, P. (1985). Unemployment: Cause and Cure, Oxford: Basil Blackwell.

Modigliani, F., Monti, M., Drèze, J., Giersch, H., Layard, R. (1987). Reducing Unemployment in Europe: The Role of Capital Formation, in: Layard, R., Calmfors, L. (Eds.), The Fight against Unemployment, Cambridge, MA: MIT Press, 10-47.

Mortensen, D. T., Pissarides, C. A. (1999). New Developments in Models of Search in the Labor Market, in: Ashenfelter, O. C., Card, D. (Eds.), Handbook of labor Economics, Vol. 3B, Amsterdam: North Holland, 2567-627.

Narendranathan, W., Nickell, S., Stern, J. (1985). Unemployment Benefits Revisited, in: Economic Journal, 95(378): 307-29.

Newell, A., Syrnons, J. S. V. (1985). Wages and Unemployment in OECD Countries, London School of Economics, Centre for Labour Economics, Working Paper No. 219.

Newell, A., Symons, J. (1993). Macroeconomic Consequences of Taxation in the '80s, CEP Discussion Paper No. 121.

Nickell, S. J. (1979). Unemployment and the Structure of Labour Costs, in: Carnegie-Rochester Conference Series on Public Policy, 11(1): 187-222.

Nickell, S. J. (1982). The Determinants of Equilibrium Unemployment in Britain, in: Economic Journal, 92(367): 555-75.

Nickell, S. J. (1987). Why is Wage Inflation in Britain so High?, in: Oxford Bulletin of Economics and Statistics, 49(1): 103-28.

Nickell, S. J. (1995a). The Performance of Companies, Oxford: Blackwell.

Nickell, S. J. (1995b). The Distribution of Wages and Unemployment across Skill Groups, Oxford: Institute of Statistics.

Nickell, S. J. (1997). Unemployment and Labour Market Rigidities: Europe versus North America, in: Journal of Economic Perspectives, 11(3): 55-74.

Nickell, S. J. (1998). Unemployment: Questions and Some Answers, in: Economic Journal, 108(448): 802-16.

References

Nickell, S. J. (2003). Employment and Taxes, London School of Economics. Presented at the CESifo conference on Tax Policy and Employment in Venice, July 2003.

Nickell, S. J., Andrews, M. (1983). Trade Unions, Real Wages, and Employment in Britain 1951-79, in: Oxford Economic Papers, 35(Supplement: The Causes of Unemployment): 183-206.

Nickell, S. J., Bell, B. (1995). The Collapse in Demand for the Unskilled and Unemployment across the OECD, in: Oxford Review of Economic Policy Spring, 40-62.

Nickell, S. J., Bell, B. (1996). Changes in the Distribution of Wages and Unemployment in OECD Countries, in American Economic Review, 86(2): 302-08.

Nickell, S. J., Denny, K. (1992). Unions and Investment in British Industry, in: Economic Journal, 102(413): 874-87.

Nickell, S. J., Kong, P. (1988). An Investigation into the Power of Insiders in Wage Determination, University of Oxford Institute of Economics and Statistics, Applied Economics, Discussion Paper No. 49.

Nickell, S., Layard, R. (1999). Labor Market Institutions and Economic Performance, in: Ashenfelter, O. C., Card, D. (Eds.), Handbook of Labor Economics, Vol. 3C, Amsterdam: Elsevier, 3029-84. [Chapter 4 in this volume]

Nickell, S., Nunziata, L., Ochel, W., Quintini, G (2002). The Beveridge Curve, Unemployment and the Wages in the OECD from the 1960s to the 1990s, Centre for Economic Performance, London School of Economics, Working Paper No. 502.

Nickell, S. J., Wadhwani, S. (1988). Insider Forces and Wage Determination, London School of Economics, Centre for Labour Economics, Mimeo.

Nickell, S. J., Wadhwani, S. (1991). Employment Determination in British Industry: Investigations Using Micro-Data, in: Review of Economic Studies, 58(5): 955-69.

Nickell, S. J., Wadhwani, S., Wall, M. (1992). Productivity Growth in UK Companies, 1975-86, European Economic Review, 36(5): 1055-1085.

Nickell, S. J., Vainiomaki, J., Wadhwani, S. (1994). Wages and Product Market Power, in: Economica, 61(244): 457-73.

Nicoletti, G., Scarpetta, S., Boylaud, O. (2000). Summary Indicators of Product Market Regulation with an Extension to Employment Protection Legislation, OECD Economics Department Working Paper No. 226.

Nissim, J. (1984). The Price Responsiveness of the Demand for Labour by Skill: British Mechanical Engineering: 1963-78, in: Economic Journal, 94(376): 812-25.

Ochel, W. (2000). Collective Bargaining (Centralization and Co-ordination), Munich: Ifo Institute.

Ochel, W. (2001). Collective Bargaining Coverage, Munich: Ifo Institute.

OECD (various years). Employment Outlook, Paris: OECD.

OECD (1991). Labour Market Policies and the Public Employment Service, Paris: OECD.

OECD (1994a). The OECD Jobs Study, Evidence and Explanations, Vols. I and II, Paris: OECD.

OECD (1999). Implementing the OECD Jobs Strategy: Assessing Performance and Policy, Paris: OECD.

Oswald, A. (1987). Efficient Contracts are on the Labour Demand Curve: Theory and Facts, London School of Economics, Centre for Labour Economics, Working Paper No. 284.

Oswald, A. (1996). A Conjecture on the Explanation for High Unemployment in the Industrialised Nation, University of Warwick, Mimeo.

Oswald, A. (1997). The Missing Piece of the Unemployment Puzzle, Inaugural Lecture, University of Warwick.

Oswald, A., Turnbull, P. (1985). Pay and Employment Determination in Britain: What are Labour Contracts Really Like?, in: Oxford Review of Economic Policy, 1(2): 80-97.

Padoa-Schioppa, F. (1992). A Cross-Country Analysis of the Tax Push Hypothesis, IMF Working Paper No. 92/11.

Pencavel, J. (1972). Wages, Specific Training, and Labor Turnover in U.S. Manufacturing Industries, in: International Economic Review, 13(1): 53-64.

Phelps, E. S. (1994). A Program of Low Wage Employment Tax Credits, Russell Sage Foundation Working Paper No. 55.

References

Phelps, E. S. (1994). Structural Slumps, the Modern Equilibrium Theory of Unemployment, Interest and Assets, Cambridge, MA: Harvard University Press.

Pilat, D. (1996). Labour Productivity Levels in OECD Countries, OECD Department of Economics Working Paper No. 169.

Pissarides, C. A. (1978). The Role of Relative Wages and Excess Demand in the Sectoral Flow of Labour, in: Review of Economic Studies, 45(3): 453-67.

Pissarides, C. A. (1984). Regional Migration, Wages, and Unemployment: Empirical Evidence and Implications for Policy, London School of Economics, Centre for Labour Economics, Working Paper No. 204.

Pissarides, C. A. (1986). Unemployment and Vacancies in Britain, in: Economic Policy, 1(3): 499-541.

Pissarides, C. A. (1998). The Impact of Employment Tax Cuts on Unemployment and Wages: the Role of Unemployment Benefits and Tax Structure, in: European Economic Review, 47(1):155-83.

Pissarides, C. A. (1990). Equilibrium Unemployment Theory, Oxford: Basil Blackwell.

Pissarides, C. A. (1996). Are Employment Tax Cuts the Answer to Europe's Unemployment Problem, London School of Economics, CEP, Mimeo.

Pissarides, C. A., (2000). Equilibrium Unemployment Theory, Cambridge, MA: MIT Press.

Pissarides, C. A., McMaster, I. (1984). Sector-Specific and Economy-Wide Influences on Industrial Wages in Britain, London School of Economics, Centre for Labour Economics, Working Paper No. 571 (2nd Revision).

Puhani, P. A. (2003). Transatlantic Differences in Labour Markets, University of St Gallen, Mimeo.

Prais, S. J. (1981). Vocational Qualifications of the Labour Force in Britain and Germany, in: National Institute Economic Review, 98(1): 47-59.

Ruhm, C. J. (1996). The Economic Consequences of Parental Leave Mandates, NBER Working Paper No. 5688.

Saint-Paul, G. (1991). Productivity Growth and Unemployment in OECD Countries, DELTA Working Paper No. 91-09.

Saint-Paul, G. (1997). Employment Protection, International Specialization and Innovation, DELTA, Paris, Mimeo.

Scarpetta, S. (1996). Assessing the Role of Labour Market Policies and Institutional Settings on Unemployment: a Cross-Country Study, in: OECD Economic Studies, 26: 43-98.

Schwanse, P. (1995). The Effectiveness of Active Labour Market Policies: Some Lessons from the Experience of OECD Countries, paper presented to the OECD technical workshop, Vienna, November 1995.

Shapiro, C., Stiglitz, J. E. (1984). Equilibrium Unemployment as a Worker Discipline Device, in: American Economic Review, 74(3): 433-44.

Soskice, D. (1990). Wage Determination: The Changing Role of Institutions in Advanced Industrialised Countries, in: Oxford Review of Economic Policy, 6(4): 36-61.

Spulber, D. F. (1989). Regulation and Markets, Cambridge, MA: MIT Press.

Stewart, M. B. (1983). Relative Earnings and Individual Union Membership in the UK, in: Economica, 50(198): 111-25.

Stewart, M. B. (1985). Collective Bargaining Arrangements, Closed Shop and Relative Pay, University of Warwick, Mimeo.

Stewart, M. B. (1990). Union Wage Differentials, Product Market Influences and the Division of Rents, in: Economic Journal, 100(403): 1122-37.

Stewart, M. B., Greenhalgh, C. A. (1984). Work History Patterns and the Occupational Attainment of Women, in: Economic Journal, 94(375): 493-519.

Tyrväinen, T. (1994). Real Wage Resistance and Unemployment: Multivariate Analysis of Cointegrating Relations in 10 OECD Economies, OECD Jobs Study Working Papers No. 10.

Van Reenen, J. (1986). The Creation and Capture of Rents: Wages and Innovation in a Panel of UK Companies, in: Quarterly Journal of Economics, 111(1): 195-226.

Wadhwani, S. (1985). Wage Inflation in the United Kingdom, in: Economica, 52(206):

195-208.

Wadhwani, S., Wall, M. (1991). A Direct Test of the Efficiency Wage Model Using UK Micro-Data, in: Oxford Economic Papers, 43(4): 529-48.

Warr, P., Jackson, P. (1985). Factors Influencing the Psychological Impact of Prolonged Unemployment and of Re-Employment, in: Psychological Medicine, 15(4): 795-807.

Wells, W. (1983). The Relative Pay and Employment of Young People, UK Department of Employment Research Paper No. 42.

Westergaard-Nielsen, N. (2002). The European Labour Market Now and in the Future, Paper presented at EU Employment Committee EMCO, July 18, Elsinore.

Widmalm, F. (1996). Tax Structure and Growth: Are Some Taxes Better than Others?, Department of Economics, Uppsala University, Discussion Paper No. 21.

Winkelmann, L., Winkelmann, R. (1998). Why Are the Unemployed so Unhappy? Evidence from Panel Data, in: Economica, 65(257): 1-15.

Zabalza, A., Arrufat, J. (1983). Wage Differentials between Married Men and Women in Great Britain: The Depreciation Effect of Non-Participation, London School of Economics, Centre for Labour Economics, Working Paper No. 151.

Index

Index

About the Authors...

 ***Richard Layard*** is Co-Director of the Centre for Economic Performance at the London School of Economics. Since 2000 he has been a member of the House of Lords. He has written widely on unemployment, inflation, education, inequality, and post-Communist reform. He was an early advocate of the welfare-to-work approach to unemployment. From 1997–2001 he helped implement these policies as a consultant to the Labour government. His current research focus is on happiness, aiming to achieve a unified understanding of the insights of economics, psychology, neuroscience, and philosophy. He also has a strong interest in unemployment and educational policy.

 ***Stephen J. Nickell*** has been Warden of Nuffield College, Oxford, since 2006. He was previously a School Professor of Economics at the London School of Economics and a member of the Bank of England Monetary Policy Committee. His research interests include unemployment, wage determination, productivity, and labor supply. He is past President of the Royal Economic Society. He was elected to a Fellowship of the Econometric Society in 1980 and of the British Academy in 1993. He has been an Honorary Member of the American Economic Association since 1997.

Richard Layard and ***Stephen J. Nickell*** received the IZA Prize in Labor Economics in 2008.

...and the Editors

Werner Eichhorst studied sociology, political science, psychology, and public policy and administration at the universities of Tuebingen and Konstanz, where he graduated in 1995. From 1996 to 1999 he was doctoral and post-doctoral fellow at the Max Planck Institute for the Study of Societies in Cologne. In fall 1998 he received his doctorate from the University of Konstanz. He joined IZA as Research Associate in July 2005, became Senior Research Associate in February 2006 and Deputy Director of Labor Policy in April 2007. At IZA he takes care of international and European policy-oriented research activities.

Klaus F. Zimmermann has been Full Professor of Economics at the University of Bonn and Director of the Institute for the Study of Labor (IZA Bonn) since 1998. From 2000 until 2011 he was President of the German Institute for Economic Research (DIW Berlin). Zimmermann is Honorary Professor of Economics at the Free University of Berlin (since 2001) and Honorary Professor at the Renmin University of China (since 2006). He is also Chairman of the Society of the German Economic Research Institutes (ARGE) (since 2005), and a member of the German Academy of Sciences Leopoldina (since 2001), the World Economic Forum's Global Agenda Council on Migration (since 2009) and the Academia Europaea (since 2010).